Interviewing in Action
PROCESS AND PRACTICE

Bianca Cody Murphy, Ed.D., is chairperson of the Psychology Department at Wheaton College and a licensed psychologist practicing with Newton Psychotherapy Associates. Two of her primary areas of interest and research are reflected in her numerous publications on clinical issues with gay and lesbian clients and on families coping with exposure to nuclear and environmental toxins. A noted speaker and writer, she is former chairperson of the Committee on Women in Psychology of the American Psychological Association, cofounder of the Institute for Ecopsychology and Psychotherapy, and current president of Psychologists for Social Responsibility.

Carolyn Dillon, LICSW, BCD, is Clinical Professor and chairperson, Practice with Individuals and Families, Boston University School of Social Work. She has received teaching awards from Boston University and from the Massachusetts Chapter of the National Association of Social Workers (NASW) and has served on the state boards of NASW, the Massachusetts Academy of Clinical Social Work, and the Social Work Assistance Network. Carolyn has 30 years of practice experience with adults coping with mental illness, family breakdown, and health challenges. She has written and lectured widely on managing stress in the professions and on improving clinical services to lesbian and gay people. She refreshes herself with loved ones (including cats), music, outdoor work, movies, and travel.

Interviewing in Action
PROCESS AND PRACTICE

Bianca Cody Murphy

Wheaton College

Carolyn Dillon

Boston University School of Social Work

Brooks/Cole Publishing Company

I(T)P® An International Thomson Publishing Company

Pacific Grove ◆ Albany ◆ Belmont ◆ Bonn ◆ Boston ◆ Cincinnati ◆ Detroit ◆ Johannesburg
London ◆ Madrid ◆ Melbourne ◆ Mexico City ◆ New York ◆ Paris ◆ Singapore
Tokyo ◆ Toronto ◆ Washington

Sponsoring Editor: *Lisa Gebo*
Marketing Team: *Margaret Parks, Jean Thompson*
Marketing Representative: *John Moroney*
Editorial Assistant: *Lisa Blanton, Susan Carlson*
Production Editor: *Nancy L. Shammas*
Manuscript Editor: *Barbara Kimmel*
Permissions Editor: *May Clark*

Design Editor: *E. Kelly Shoemaker*
Interior and Cover Design: *Lisa Mirski Devenish*
Cover Art: *Judith Larzelere*
Art Editor: *Lisa Torri*
Indexer: *James Minkin*
Typesetting: *Graphic World*
Printing and Binding: *Malloy Lithographing, Inc.*

For more information, contact:

BROOKS/COLE PUBLISHING
COMPANY
511 Forest Lodge Road
Pacific Grove, CA 93950
USA

International Thomson Publishing Europe
Berkshire House 168-173
High Holborn
London WC1V 7AA
England

Thomas Nelson Australia
102 Dodds Street
South Melbourne, 3205
Victoria, Australia

Nelson Canada
1120 Birchmount Road
Scarborough, Ontario
Canada M1K 5G4

International Thomson Editores
Seneca 53
Col. Polanco
11560 México, D. F., México

International Thomson Publishing GmbH
Königswinterer Strasse 418
53227 Bonn
Germany

International Thomson Publishing Asia
221 Henderson Road
#05-10 Henderson Building
Singapore 0315

International Thomson Publishing Japan
Hirakawacho Kyowa Building, 3F
2-2-1 Hirakawacho
Chiyoda-ku, Tokyo 102
Japan

Printed in the United States of America

10   9   8   7   6   5

Library of Congress Cataloging-in-Publication Data
Murphy, Bianca Cody.
    Clinical interviewing in action : process and practice / Bianca Cody Murphy, Carolyn Dillon.
        p.   cm.
    Includes bibliographical references and index.
    ISBN 0-534-34125-X
    1. Interviewing in psychiatry. I. Dillon, Carolyn, [date].
II. Title.
    [DNLM: 1. Psychology, Clinical--methods. 2. Interviews--methods.
3. Professional-Patient Relations. 4. Cultural Diversity--United
States. WM 105 M978c 1997]
RC480.7.M87 1997
616.89--dc21
DNLM/DLC
for Library of Congress   97-17140
                                                                              CIP

To our students
who taught us how to teach

To our clients
who taught us how to practice

To our teachers
who taught us to learn from
our students and our clients

CONTENTS

CHAPTER 2

Getting Started 21

CHAPTER 3

Attending and Listening 55

C H A P T E R   4

Support and Empathy: A Sustaining Presence   77

CHAPTER 7

**Gaining New Perspectives:
Helping Clients See Things Differently**　　　　　**155**

CHAPTER 8

Changing Behaviors:
Helping Clients Do Things Differently   179

Endings and Transitions   251

CHAPTER 12

Professional Issues: Ongoing Education and Self-Care   277

PREFACE

Both of us have been teaching social work, counseling, and psychology courses for many years. We are also both clinicians who love our work with clients. This work has kept us in touch with issues in practice and with the many complexities in clients' lives today. Meanwhile, as academics, we have a special fondness for teaching the fundamentals of practice to students, whose good values, eagerness to help, and great hearts never fail to touch and reinvigorate us.

We have developed a book/video learning package to support what we have come to call the *re-view practice method* of clinical skills development, in which students:

Read about the skill
Explore the skill in class through discussion with the professor and colleagues
View experienced clinicians employing the skill
Implement the skill in videotaped role-play interviews
Evaluate their performance together
Watch the videotape with others, giving and receiving feedback

This method consistently conveys the message that purposeful use of self and goal-focused work with clients gets better with practice and more practice.

But interviewing is more than just learning specific skills. Successful interviewing is embedded in a relationship between two or more people. We believe that clinical education must attend to the professional's self as well as the professional's skills. It is precisely this self and its values, attitudes, and beliefs that will mediate the development of helping relationships and the application of specific skills. We believe that the essence of our teaching role is to develop a comfortable and safe ambiance for reflection and exchange and, within this sustaining environment, to attend to the step-by-step evolution of the learner's professional self and skills.

Just as good interviewing requires a trusting relationship with a helpful other, learning how to be that helpful other also requires a trusting relationship with a helpful teacher and colleagues. We believe that practice learning is not a self-instructional process. Skills cannot be learned in isolation simply by watching a video, by reading a book, by typing responses to a computerized interview format, or through esoteric discussions of principles. We believe that skills are best learned in relationship with skilled and thoughtful mentors and instructors, who can help students master skills while simultaneously developing professional attitudes and knowledge from many sources. It is through the relationship and interaction with instructors and fellow students that the self as well as the professional skills are honed. Our book and video are based on these principles.

Interviewing in Action: Process and Practice is a clinical skills text coordinated with an accompanying keyed video that shows diverse clinicians employing a range of skills with clients. Thus, after students read the text at home, they can then watch short clips in which real working clinicians demonstrate the specific clinical skills discussed in the text. The students will get to know five clinician-client pairs as client stories and the clinical relationships unfold in the video. Moreover, because the students have the opportunity to read the text and watch the demonstration clips before coming to class, more class time is available to elaborate, question, or role-play skills already observed in action at home. Instructors will no longer have to devote large portions of class time to the passive watching of videos that only marginally illustrate the content they wish to develop. Instructors can now use specific clips from the accompanying video to raise issues or to make different or additional teaching points.

We are very excited about what we have developed, and we believe that readers and viewers will also like it. Students who have used these materials tell us that the materials speak to their own experiences and issues and fulfills a longing of theirs to see how different clinicians apply the principles and skills of clinical interviewing.

Special Features of this Package

The text and video for *Interviewing in Action: Process and Practice* have the following special features.

◆ *Realistic for today's practice:* The text and video address the complexity of issues clinicians confront while recognizing the limited time and few resources they often have.

◆ *Integrates multicultural issues:* Cross-cultural issues are integrated throughout the text and video, and both address how cultural issues affect the interview process. The clients and clinicians in the video represent both men and women of different ages and sexual orientations, as well as from different ethnic and racial backgrounds.

◆ *Concrete examples:* The text is filled with examples of dialogues demonstrating how a skill is implemented. The accompanying video shows actual clinicians using these skills in clinical situations. Clinicians comment on the selective use of their skills, and some comparisons are made between useful and less useful skill applications.

◆ *Multiple models, multiple voices:* Both the book and video provide students with many opportunities to benefit from the knowledge and experience of different clinicians. The book contains relevant, quite moving stories from the field in which seasoned clinicians share personal accounts of their real-life experiences. The video shows five different clinicians in the process of interviewing five different clients as narratives and problem-solving work unfold. Students see that the implementation of skills is neither uniform nor always on target.

◆ *Comprehensive:* The book and video encourage the development of both the skills of the professional and the self of the professional, addressing knowledge base, values, attitudes, and purposeful use of self, as well as a range of skills commonly used in practice.

◆ *Applicable to many disciplines:* Although we have used the generic term *clinician* in the text, we have given practical examples from a variety of clinical settings and professional roles, including those of drug counselor, social worker, group home worker, rehab counselor, school psychologist, human service worker, milieu therapist, and psychiatric nurse. We believe that, in the future, much more practice will occur in interdisciplinary teams and groups and that we need to move toward a shared practice language that can facilitate dialogue and collaboration. We are not entirely satisfied with the use of the words *clinician* and *clinical* because of their medical connotations, nor with the word *helper* because of its implication of one-way process. We would prefer a language that better expresses the mutuality and shared humanness of the interview process, but as yet that language does not exist.

◆ *Flexible package:* We strongly recommend that students purchase both the book and the video. The video, though produced so that it can stand alone, is composed of clips keyed to demonstrate specific skills discussed in the book. An icon appears in the text indicating that there is a corresponding clip on the video. We suggest that students read the book and watch the appropriate video clips at home, leaving much more time for in-depth exploration and role-play practice in class with the input of an experienced teacher. Students may later want to review sections of the video at home or in the media lab, when their internship or practicum work presents them with interviewing challenges that require further reflection on and refinement of skills. Faculty can also purchase the video for use in class sessions or for distance education; or the book and video can be used separately or combined with other materials.

◆ *Practice based:* The book is filled with exercises for students to do both at home and in class. There are role-play and group exercises for use in class or use in distance learning and discussion.

◆ *Journal assignments:* We encourage students to keep a journal in which they can reflect on their experiences. Many of the exercises in the book require students to discuss in their journals what they have learned from various in-class exercises and discussions.

◆ *Utilizing today's technology:* We not only provide a book and video package, we suggest that students videotape themselves as they practice—a key component of what we have called the *re-view practice method* of clinical education.

Our Ultimate Goal

This book / video project is designed to help students become knowledgeable and comfortable in the purposeful use of skills with clients. It is our hope that they will also learn how to give and receive feedback as a way of developing their skills and professional selves throughout their careers, as they "re-view" their practice. As continuing students of clinical interviewing ourselves, we too are constantly reviewing our work and enlarging our understanding through collegial exchange and feedback. We welcome and value your comments and suggestions as you review our concepts and materials and use them to facilitate growth of students' clinical interviewing skills in action.

About the Book

Although the book is an effective tool on its own and follows the principle of learning through action and review, we encourage use of the book and video together, as we believe the components to be sensibly sequenced together and mutually reinforcing.

The first three chapters serve as an overview of the process of helping, detailing the unique features of clinical relationships and practice and underscoring the impact on practice of values, ethics, theory, the zeitgeist of the times, and the nature of surrounding systems of power and influence. Using exercises and discussions, we ask students to explore their own culture and its relationship to their guiding beliefs and values. In Chapter 1 we also present the ecological and systems perspectives that undergird our view of clinical work.

Chapters 2 through 4 approach interviewing as a unique kind of talking, with roles, rules, mutual expectations, boundaries, layers, and the require-ment of intentional or purposeful behaviors on the part of the clinician. Chapter 2 explores planning and preparation for work with clients who come with varying backgrounds, experience, communication skills, and service needs. In addition, we discuss special issues related to a variety of interview environments (home, shelter, hospital, street, agency office), including issues of confidentiality and safety, and we suggest ways of adapting self and strategies to the needs of a host of diverse populations and settings. In Chapters 3 and 4 students learn and practice basic attending and listening skills, learning to appreciate and provide support and empathy and to develop a sustaining presence that will serve as a holding environment for all ensuing clinical work.

However, supportive ambiance and empathy alone are not sufficient to help clients better understand their situations and bring about the changes they desire. Because clients need to be able to explore and articulate their stories and develop reasonably attainable goals, Chapter 5 addresses skills of elaboration and exploration, including questioning, prompting, reflecting, and other techniques for helping clients to expand on their stories. Chapter 6 moves to the issues and skills of setting goals appropriate to time constraints and participants' needs and resources. Students are guided in developing, carrying out, evaluating, and altering working agreements or contracts.

Chapters 7 through 9 focus on the skills of helping clients change and the use of the clinical relationship in that process. Many clients seek help from clinicians because they feel stuck and unable to see things differently. In Chapter 7 we focus on those skills that clinicians use to help clients gain new perspectives and work toward altering mood, behaviors, circumstances, and relationships. The importance of behavioral models, alternatives, encouragements, and reinforcements to help clients change their behaviors is stressed in Chapter 8. Important aspects of working on and within the clinical relationship are detailed in Chapter 9, with emphasis on purposeful and ethical use of self.

Chapter 10 takes up the thorny topics of self-disclosure and other professional boundary issues, with discussion and numerous dialogues suggesting potential clinician responses to complex boundary problems arising in an era when so many boundaries and standards are becoming increasingly relaxed and ambiguous.

In Chapter 11 we elaborate on the issues, tasks, and skills related to transitions and endings in clinical work, and we discuss positive and problematic developments within the ending phase of work. Exercises allow students to practice conversations related to ending so they can develop increased comfort in viewing endings from a broad perspective.

Because of our concern for the well-being and sustainment of clinicians themselves, Chapter 12 addresses issues of professional supervision, consultation, continuing education, mutual aid, activism, and self-care. We believe clinicians, from the outset, should be aware of the stresses and challenges that await them in working situations of increasing complexity and demandingness.

Through numerous examples using clinical dialogue, as well as from clinicians' first-person accounts from the field, students have many opportunities to "see" how clinicians employ a skill and "hear" a variety of approaches to clinical issues. Dialogue examples and clinician narratives are wide-ranging, multicultural, and directly related to the complex and difficult realities clinicians face in practice arenas today. The book contains a number of exercises that call for both personal reflection and the rehearsal of skills in role plays. Through these exercises, students can gain comfort in observing and being observed, and in exchanging feedback with their colleagues. Wherever possible, students are encouraged to videotape themselves in dialogue with others so that they can learn through self-observation and peer supervision. Where appropriate, the chapters include samples of professional forms or assessment tools. Each chapter concludes with "Suggested Readings," which provide the reader with opportunities to explore in more detail topics raised in each chapter.

About the Videotape

The 120-minute videotape is keyed sequentially to the book chapters. The videotape package includes a program guide that indicates the skill demonstrated in each segment and its location on the tape (using minute counter numbers) so that it is easily located by the viewer. Each segment has an introduction to skill issues followed by brief clips from interviews with actual clinicians illustrating either a problematic or an effective use of a technique. All the interviewers are seasoned clinicians who demonstrate a variety of different styles in skill use, and all the participants reflect the diversity of clinicians and clients. Students will be able to see clinicians and clients from different racial and ethnic groups, of both genders, and of different ages.

As students read each chapter, they are encouraged to watch the corresponding segments of the tape at home, which are indicated by an icon in the text. Chapters 2 through 11 each have approximately 10 minutes of illustrative video clips. The video helps students see that there is more than one "right way" to respond to a client. Seeing a variety of professionals use the same skill with the same or different clients will help students recognize that they have to find their own voice while learning with many different people.

Ancillaries

The instructor's manual is filled with ideas for teaching clinical interviewing that we have found to be particularly useful. We suggest exercises for use in class and assignments for homework. For instructors new to clinical practice education, we suggest ways to structure time and to use oneself as a model in order to bring a spirit of collegiality to work with students in class. We also provide a 10-minute demo video demonstrating how students and instructors can use the book/video package in class, in distance education, and in professional settings as well. You will get to "meet" us and some of our students as we work from the package in class, at home, and in other domains.

Acknowledgments

This book has been an enormous undertaking and we would like to express our appreciation to a number of people. Lisa Gebo, our editor, has been our prime mover and inspiration for this project. We deeply appreciate her never-ending enthusiasm, insightful feedback, encouragement, and laughter.

We are deeply grateful to our friend and video producer, Nick Kaufman, for the art, humor, and balance he brought to the development of our video. He helped us concretize our thinking and push our imagination. Many thanks as well to Peggy and Sashi Kaufman and to the talented video crew. Our very patient and skilled video editor, Roberta Sensenhauser, lent style and a great eye for flow to the video project. The video couldn't exist without the talented clinicians who so generously shared of themselves: Brenda Clarke, Joel Hencken, Terry McCandies, Jon Reusser, and Lourdes Rodríguez-Nogués.

Many friends and colleagues have read the manuscript and given us useful feedback: Grace Baron, Lauren Berman, Rita Messing, and Paulina Watson. We are also grateful to all the people who gave us permission to use their stories and first person accounts. We thank Leah Fygetakis, Rich Rasi, Lourdes Rodríguez-Nogués, and Liz Roebuck for providing us with sample forms. We appreciate the help of two student research assistants in obtaining and checking references: Sarah Witham from Wheaton College and Patricia Lynn Gray from Boston University. We also thank Nancy Shepardson, faculty secretary, and Marcia Grimes, reference librarian, colleagues at Wheaton College, for their generous assistance.

The creative team at Brooks/Cole-ITP has been all we could ask for in terms of skill and support, and we extend thanks for artistic and production support to Nancy Shammas, Kelly Shoemaker, and Faith Stoddard. Special thanks to our copy editor Barbara Kimmel and to John Moroney for his initial encouragement to develop the project.

Finally we wish to express our continuing gratitude to our faithful outside reviewers, several of whom have followed our project for two years, providing guidance and feedback which changed and improved our work at many points along the way: Ann A. Abbott, Rutgers University; John A. Casey, Sonoma State University; Alan Davis, Montana State University—Billings; Andrew Fussner, Rutgers University and Bryn Mawr College; Patricia Kerstner, University of Phoenix; Marva Larrabee, University of South Carolina; Rob Lawson, Western Washington University; Beverly Palmer, California State University, Dominguez Hills; and Cathy Pike, University of South Carolina.

From Bianca Cody Murphy. I will always be indebted to three special teachers at Northeastern University: Kathy Pigott Newman, Barbara Okun, and Al Zalinger. By their way of being, they showed me how to make a difference in the lives of clients and students. Almost 20 years ago, Walter

Abrams and I started using homemade video vignettes to teach Counseling Practice at UMASS/Boston. The creativity of our clinician friends who played roles in those original videos—Nick Browning, Rita Messing, Jon Reusser, Liz Roebuck, and Alan Slobnick— laid the groundwork for the video that accompanies this book. Three outstanding clinicians, my partners at Newton Psychotherapy Associates—Priscilla Ellis, Sarah Greenberg, and Joan Berlin—have greatly shaped the way I think and practice. More than partners, we are a team, and our 20 years of peer supervision, love, and laughter have nurtured me both as a clinician and as a person. I am also blessed with a family of women friends: Sandy Albright, Anne Davidson, Harriet Gordon, Susan Kent, Ann Maguire, Rita Messing, Lin Reicher, Lourdes Rodríquez-Nogués, and Liz Roebuck. Their love and encouragement are sustaining.

From Carolyn Dillon. I am deeply indebted to Wilma Peebles-Wilkins, Dean of the School of Social Work at Boston University, for her generosity and encouragement throughout this project. Two other colleagues at the School have made all the difference: Larry Shulman, an admired colleague who, a decade ago, showed me how to use a video camera and how to set up a video lab to advance student interviewing skills; and Gail Steketee, a valued guide and mentor for practice and writing issues. I have never forgotten the wisdom, kindness, and patience of great teachers who influenced my professional self and practice: Esther Clemence, Mary C. Farr, and Bob Eisendrath. Many thanks to Cassandra, Joanne, Jane, and Trudy for the Vision Thing, and to Jim and Paulina, faithful encouragers and friends.

Bianca Cody Murphy
Carolyn Dillon

CHAPTER 1

A Different Kind of Talking

Introduction

There have always been people who have helped others cope with difficulties or emotional distress. At different times and in different cultures, these helpful people may have been called shamans, elders, curanderos, healers, wise women, or pastors (Stone, 1997). These people were perceived to have special gifts or talents, or they received specialized education or training, resulting in their being viewed as skilled in helping people deal with problems in their lives (Torrey, 1972).

While these helpers still exist, a new group of helpers has evolved in the Western world—professional clinicians. This group includes, among others, counselors, social workers, psychologists, milieu therapists, psychiatric nurses, psychiatrists, and human service workers. Although each of these disciplines has its own philosophy and emphasis, each requires highly specialized education to teach clinicians how to become more effective helpers. As knowledge of human behavior and the social environment has advanced over the last 150 years, this education has become more organized, scientific, and theory-based.

Heavily influenced by advances in medicine, neurology, psychology, and sociology, helping professionals created scientific procedures for data collection, intervention planning, and evaluation. Clinical education emphasized objectivity, detachment, and neutrality. Although Freud analyzed his friends (Roazen, 1992) and Jane Addams lived in the settlement house among the immigrants with whom she worked (Addams, 1910), an emerging emphasis on detachment and "scientific objectivity" contributed to clinicians removing themselves more and more from daily interactions with their clients.

A major purpose of clinical education has been to develop expertise in helping. As a result, clinicians began to be seen (and to see themselves) as "experts." For many, expert status conferred power and prestige, and led to a privileging of the clinician's knowledge over that of clients. The media, which both reflect and help create social realities, often portrayed the muddled client seeking help from the well-dressed, respected authority, creating a dichotomy between the person needing help and the "wise helper." The licensing of clinicians further reinforced an aura of special wisdom and capability, as it required years of formal preparation. It became easy for people to think of clients as empty vessels into which clinicians poured their special knowledge. Ironically, the use of arcane language and complex theory often made this knowledge less accessible to the very people with whom clinicians were trying to talk.

Clinicians have also become both geographically and economically less accessible. As helping has become organized and professionalized, it often has moved out of homes, neighborhoods, and street corners and into offices and agencies where help is shaped by time constraints, bureaucratic procedures, and the income requirements of agencies and clinicians (Iglehart & Becerra, 1995; Pruger, 1973). Indeed, as helping has become a source of income for clinicians, they may find their clinical decisions increasingly affected by their own financial concerns. Furthermore, a focus on finances has contributed to an atmosphere of entrepreneurial competition among the various disciplines for power, authority, and clientele. Finally, the ability to pay for services affects basic access to clinical help, as well as the type and amount of help that clients receive (Gorden & Kline, 1997). These financial issues can have a particularly negative effect on ethnic minorities and people from lower socioeconomic classes (Snowden, 1993).

Western medicine has a long history of explaining and treating emotional distress in physical or medical terms (Weick, 1983). Clinicians are often trained to diagnose pathology—to find what is wrong or broken and needs to be fixed. In mental health, the mandatory use of the *Diagnostic and Statistical Manual* (DSM) (American Psychiatric Association, 1994), with its classifications of symptoms and disorders, exemplifies this emphasis on pathology. Both clinicians and clients may accustom themselves to focusing on problems and difficulties in the client's story and history to the near exclusion of strengths and successes, eliciting what family therapists Michael White and David Epston (1990) have called "the problem-saturated narrative" (p. 19). The word *clinical* itself reflects a medical orientation, as it is derived from the Greek *klinike*, referring to the work of the physician at the sickbed.

This focus on the "sick individual" has sometimes separated people from their families and other natural helping networks. Clinical work has often focused on issues of individual autonomy and achievement, rather than on connection and collective action for social change. Furthermore, most models of helping, counseling, and psychotherapy were developed by and for white, middle-class, able-bodied, heterosexual males and may not be appropriate for most clients (Dworkin & Gutierrez, 1992; Ellis & Murphy, 1994; Lum, 1996; Stiver, 1991; Sue & Sue, 1990).

As a result of all of these complex forces, what could be a special conversation between two or more people all too frequently becomes a ritualized and rather formal interview. At times the voice and strength of the client may seem less important than the voice and strength of the professional. The clinician has become distanced and less accessible, and it sometimes may seem more important to diagnose than to relate.

In contrast, when we speak of clinical interviewing, we mean a conversation characterized by equality and mutuality, by immediacy and warm presence, and by emphasis on strengths and potential. Since clinical interviewing is essentially relational, it requires ongoing attention to *how* things are said and done, as well as to *what* is said and done. This emphasis on the relationship is at the heart of the "different kind of talking" that is the clinical interview.

E X E R C I S E 1.1 *Characteristics of Helpful People*

Think about someone who has helped you in the past—a friend, teacher, colleague, supervisor, therapist. Make a list of some of that person's characteristics that you found particularly helpful in talking with that person. Compare your list with those of your colleagues. Of all the helpful characteristics on everyone's list, which ones do you find in yourself and which ones do you want to acquire? In your journal, record specific ways in which you need to change in order to be a more helpful person.

After an extensive review of the literature (Carkhuff & Berenson, 1967; Combs, 1989; Egan, 1990; Rogers, 1958; Sue & Sue, 1990), Barbara Okun (1997) summarizes what she considers to be the "qualities, behaviors, and knowledge of helpers [that] are most influential in affecting the behaviors, attitudes, and feelings of helpees" (p. 37): these are self-awareness, gender and cultural awareness, honesty, congruence, ability to communicate, knowledge, and ethical integrity.

A Different Kind of Talking

Every day we have lots of conversations with people. Some of these conversations may be helpful to us as we struggle in our daily lives. Talking with a friend may help us get out of a bad mood or cope with a discouraging loss. A colleague or teacher may help us feel less anxious. We may feel less depressed after a conversation with a loved and loving family member. Yet a clinical interview involves a different kind of talking from other types of conversations and other types of interviews.

Purpose

Clinical interviewing is *purposeful*. It requires an intentional focus on the client's story, needs, and goals. This focus distinguishes it from friendly or casual conversation, in which people can talk randomly about whatever they wish. Clinicians need to stay very clear about the purpose of interviewing to avoid drifting from subject to subject in nonproductive ways. Specific purposes for clinical interviewing vary from client to client and from setting to setting. For example, the purpose may be to help a client cope with debilitating anxiety, to determine a client's eligibility for public assistance, or to help a child adjust to her parents' divorce.

Although there is a general purpose for the overall work together, there may be a number of specific *goals* for each session. Even if these goals are not explicitly stated, the clinician keeps them in mind. For example, the overall purpose of the work may be to help the client develop stable relationships; but within a particular session, the goal may be to move into the history of how others in the family handle anger or to discuss why the client has canceled the last three sessions.

Although clinicians have additional reasons for clinical interviewing—it's part of their job, to earn money, to feel good about themselves—-the guiding purpose is to help clients. Interviewers agree *to hold primary their service obligations to clients* over all other interests. This commitment to put clients' needs first is abrogated only when clinicians are concerned about the safety of clients or others.

Theory

Unlike casual conversation, clinical interviewing is informed by theory. *Theory* refers to a systematic set of principles used to understand and explain observable phenomena. There are numerous clinical theories, each of which provides a framework for understanding and interpreting the client's story. Theory also shapes the content and process of clinical interviews. The interviewer's theoretical stance affects the purpose and goals of the interview, as does the way the interviewer listens and responds to the client's story.

A confused or unclear theoretical stance will often manifest itself in scattered focus or abrupt shifts in style, which are jarring for the client and can derail purposeful work. At the same time, it is important not to confuse having a theoretical base with orthodoxy. An adherence that is too rigid to theory may impede the flexibility necessary to work with clients and their stories and may limit the imagination out of which new theories may evolve.

Structure

Clinical interviews are not only purposeful and informed; they are also *structured*. Both the specific interview and the overall process have a beginning, a middle, and an end, and each phase of the process has its own tasks and emphases. The first and continuing task is to make and sustain a warm, trustful, and collaborative relationship in which clients feel comfortable sharing and elaborating their stories. In the middle phase, clinicians and clients work together to develop new perspectives, skills, and resources from which change can evolve. In the last stage, review and evaluation of the work and relationship occur, and plans for the future, including follow-up, are discussed.

A second kind of structure is the organization the clinician brings to the clinical interview. At times, clinicians may guide the conversation by the questions we ask, by the issues we respond to, by introducing new subjects, or by limiting the focus. In addition, we establish rules and norms for behaviors, as well as boundaries around the relationship itself.

Time constraints also impose structure. Clinical interviewing is usually limited to a specified amount of time. The length of any individual meeting, as well as the number of meetings, is usually fixed. The time set aside for the clinical interview is usually regarded as inviolable except in extreme circumstances.

Contract

The participants in a clinical interview enter into a contract. The *contract* is a working agreement that includes such things as who will participate and the purpose, goals, roles, expectations, techniques, time, structure, and fees. Contracts should be mutually arrived at so participants are clear about their responsibilities and commitments, and agreements should be tailored to the client's style, needs, and language. The specific goals should be realistic and attainable, taking into account the stresses, strengths, and resources in the client's network. The more explicit the contract, the better; the clearer the map, the more likely the participants will arrive at the desired destination. Due to the shifting realities and resources in people's lives, contracts need to be flexible and subject to renegotiation.

Roles

Clinical interviews usually have two major prescribed *roles:* that of client, and that of clinician. The clinician brings special knowledge of human behavior, psychological theory, and communication skills. The client brings special knowledge of his or her own history and traditions, resources for growth and development, and particular strengths and coping skills.

The behavioral components of these roles are complex and varied, and they often overlap. People frequently think of the client as narrating the story and the clinician as listening, sustaining, and guiding. However, in most interviews there is flexibility in behaviors: either participant can be speaking or listening, guiding or following. Although the client is expected to do more of the talking, at times the clinician will say more, as when sharing hunches, confronting client behaviors, educating about resources, or detailing necessary procedures. Regardless of participants' behaviors at any given moment, the interviewer is always cognizant of his or her responsibilities as clinician: to remain focused on the purpose of the interview and on the client's needs. This principle applies whether we are trying to engage gang members on a street corner, are listening to a new mother grieve the sudden loss of her baby, or are taking an intake phone call from a lonely elderly man threatening to kill himself.

Neither the clinician nor the client role comes naturally to people; both clinicians and clients have to be educated about the expectations, responsibilities, and behaviors required within each role. Clinicians learn about the requirements of their roles from their teachers, supervisors, and work settings. Because clients may have no experience with clinical interviewing, it is incumbent on the clinician to orient clients to roles, procedures, and expectations, inviting feedback to minimize confusion or misunderstandings.

Whenever I begin to work with a new client, I spend part of the first interview talking about the nature of the clinical relationship. I have always liked the feminist therapy analogy that compares the clinician to a midwife. Therapy is explained as a process in which the client gives birth to new parts of herself. Like birth, the process is often painful but very exciting. I see myself as someone who has skills and training to assist her with the birthing process. I stress that I will work with her, sometimes comforting, sometimes supporting, sometimes encouraging as she gives birth.[1]

Labels

Labels and titles are other features that distinguish clinical conversation from other forms of talking. A variety of labels may be used to describe the participants in a clinical interview. At times the labels for clinicians designate a discipline—mental health counselor, psychologist, social worker, clinical psychiatric nurse, human service worker, psychiatrist. At other times these labels are used to try to capture the roles and tasks of particular groups of clinicians—group facilitator, intake worker, case manager. And sometimes the label designates a specialization within a discipline—school counselor, neuropsychologist, geriatric social worker, forensic psychologist.

---

[1] Numerous first-person accounts from clinicians in the field are included in this text.

EXERCISE 1.2 *By Any Other Name*

Below is a list of terms used to describe the role of a clinical interviewer. Each may have different meanings or nuances for different people. Apply each term to yourself, and as you do so, notice any change in your feelings about or perception of yourself. Record these feelings in your journal. If you were a client, how would you feel seeing a professional with each of these labels?

interviewer	case manager
provider	shrink
therapist	helper
clinician	change agent
counselor	personal consultant
crisis worker	advocate
milieu therapist	analyst

There are also a number of labels used to designate people with whom clinicians work—client, patient, member, resident, student, consumer, helpee. At times these labels connote the setting; persons in a hospital may be called patients, those in a halfway house may be referred to as residents. At other times the labels reflect the customs of specific disciplines, agencies, or individuals.

> *I remember when many social workers in the fifties and sixties called their clients "patients," wishing to achieve a professional standing or recognition similar to that of psychiatrists and psychologists. A woman would come to the family service agency seeking housing and financial aid, but in case conference, she would be described as "the patient." During the activist period of the seventies there was a shift to calling people "clients" in order to be more egalitarian. With the advent of managed care and its medical model, I've noticed a resurgence in the use of the term* patients.

> *I've worked in a couple of day treatment programs for mentally retarded adults. In one we called the participants "patients"; in another, "clients"; in another, "club members."*

> *I have lots of discussions with colleagues who object to my using the term* patients. *They say it reflects a medical model that focuses on illness. They accuse me of being into power dynamics and suggest I call them "clients" instead. I like the word* patient *because for me it implies a caring for the other.*

Labels can be helpful in directing people toward specific disciplines, functions, or specialties. They can also be confusing: people with differing labels can all be performing the same roles or functions. The social worker, psychologist, and counselor may all provide counseling or psychotherapy.

The client, the patient, and the resident may all exhibit the same behaviors or share similar problems.

Labels can obfuscate the fact that clinicians can have problems at the same time and of the same type as clients do. A clinician may see a client during one hour and then the next hour go see a clinician her- or himself. The distance between labels can appear great, whereas the actual distance between people and their narratives is less so.

Labels may be used to express power, prestige, and status; they can be used to distance, demean, and stereotype. The way we connote ourselves and others impacts on our relationship and interactions with others.

Unique Relationship

Clinical interviewing engenders an *intimacy between strangers*. Even though the client and clinician have different roles, the relationship is like a fishbowl in which both regularly observe and experience nuances of each other's behaviors and feelings. Just as we observe clients, clients observe us and note our subtle reactions. They observe when we seem focused and present and when we seem distracted and preoccupied. They notice what we attend to and emphasize and what we overlook and ignore. And, just as clinicians may sit around and discuss clients in a team conference, clients may sit around and discuss clinicians' mannerisms and idiosyncrasies in great detail. Both clinicians and clients become known to each other in ways that are truly intimate, special, and rare.

> *I have a client who has noticed that when I sneeze it's usually in a series of three sneezes. I can't believe how attentive he is to my behavior.*

Clinical interviewing occurs within a relationship that involves a peculiar kind of mutuality. *Mutuality* refers to the fact that, although the interview focus is on the client's needs, the clinician is also affected by the give and take of the relationship. Both people inevitably grow and change through the authentic and genuine relationship with each other (Jordan, 1991a). The peculiar part of the mutuality is that while it is mutual, it is not equal. It is chiefly the client who will be regularly expected to reveal personal information in exquisite detail, and the clinician who discloses personal information only on a very selective basis.

> *I often talk with clients about this "weird" relationship of therapy. Although clients may not know much about the facts of my personal life, and I usually know a lot about theirs, I still feel as though they know me in a very real and intimate way.*

Whereas both the clinician and the client share responsibility for process and progress, the clinician, because of his or her training and experience, is held accountable for the effectiveness of the work and assumes greater responsibility for the safety of the relationship. Furthermore, there is frequently a power imbalance in the relationship due to the authority vested in the clinician by virtue of professional role, training, education, and experience. Finally, it is the client who may literally pay for the relationship, and the clinician is the one being paid.

> *I have had clients say, "I can't believe I have to pay someone to listen to me" or "I can't believe I have to pay to have a friend." I remind them that they're paying for my skills, not my friendship.*

Use of Self

Clinicians pay careful attention to their *use of self* in the interview process. One of the paradoxes of clinical work is that clinicians are asked to be genuine while at the same time asked to be self-aware and deliberate (Rogers, 1980).

> *When I'm supervising students, they always ask how to decide when it's okay to be spontaneous and "real" and when it's not. It's one of the hardest things to teach and learn in clinical work. Even after I share my opinions and the theories behind them, students will often act spontaneously, doing and saying things without much thought beforehand. They confuse being deliberate with being artificial. It takes a while to learn that one can be both genuine and deliberate.*

Insofar as possible, clinicians behave in considered ways. At times, we may intentionally alter our behaviors to promote client growth.

> *I am usually a very quiet, laid-back kind of counselor. I convey my attentiveness through eye contact, facial expression, and head nods. This usually works well with the clients I see at the clinic. When I was seeing Juan, I realized I had to change my style. He was legally blind and needed more verbal feedback and responsiveness from me.*

Clinicians also make very deliberate decisions about what they share about themselves with their clients. Personal sharing should occur only if the clinician believes that it forwards the goals of the work, and only after careful consideration of its effect on the client. Later, in Chapter 10, we will examine in greater depth the issues surrounding personal sharing and disclosure.

Throughout the interview process, clinicians also attend to their own actions and reactions. This *attending to the self* is important for several reasons. First, clinicians need to be aware of what their reactions may convey to clients, either intentionally or unintentionally. Second, the reactions that the client's story evokes in the clinician may provide important information about responses the client may engender in others. Third, introspection increases self-knowledge, which is essential to appropriate use of self in clinical interviewing. In addition, reactions within the clinician may stir up old, unfinished business that needs further attention. One of the most complex tasks that clinicians have to master is that of attending to many things simultaneously.

Listening Intently

All conversation is about communication, and in any conversation there are many levels and forms of communication. There is verbal and nonverbal communication, overt and covert communication, content and process communication, and metacommunication—the messages about the message. In clinical interviewing, the clinician *listens intently* to all of these types and levels of communication. We listen to what our clients say as well as to how they say it. We listen to our own inner process and the relationship process. And we listen to what is happening in the work and what is happening in the surrounding world.

Values and Ethics

Clinical interviewing is also informed by a set of *values* expressed in *codes of ethics.* (See the Appendix for a listing of where to obtain the ethical codes of psychologists, counselors, social workers, and marriage and family therapists.) These ethical codes stress the primacy of the service obligation to the client, confidentiality, integrity, and follow-through. They enjoin clinicians from practicing beyond their level of competence and prohibit dual relationships between clinicians and clients.

Clinical interviews should reflect that clinicians value the dignity and worth of all people. Clinicians should convey a nonjudgmental acceptance without necessarily approving of specific behaviors. Clinicians should actively work toward eliminating ways of thinking, speaking, and acting that reflect racism, sexism, ableism, ageism, homophobia, religious discrimination, and other oppressive ideologies.

We believe that clinicians should do more than just think or behave ethically with clients. Our ethical codes encourage us to take stands against those social forces and institutions that impinge on our clients' rights, health, and welfare.

Multiculturalism

In previous decades, people who were different from the dominant cultural groups in the United States were referred to as ethnic minorities. As Lum (1996) notes,

> ethnic affiliation was seen as an important factor in individual and group identity . . . [and the descriptor minority] highlighted the limited political, economic, and social opportunities of African Americans, Latino Americans, Asian Americans and Native Americans. Minority status denoted a numerically smaller or politically powerless group in relation to a larger, controlling, and dominant majority. Whites were cast as the majority, while nonwhites were the minorities. (p. 1)

However, Victor De La Cancela, Yvonne Jenkins, and Jean Lau Chin (1993) state that the term *minority* used as a label to refer to populations of color ignores the reality that Caucasians are the numerical minority globally. They go on to say that the use of the term *minority* has "oppressive connotations of disempowerment and poverty that are inappropriate and offensive in the context of African, Latino, indigenous, and Asian ethnic groups who are becoming economically strong and sociopolitically organized" (p. 7).

The changing demographics of the United States make it clear that the "majority" will soon also be the minority in the United States. According to Lillian Comas-Diaz (personal communication, 1996) and Beverly Greene (1994), "By the year 2056, the United States will be a demographic mosaic and the typical resident will trace his or her descent to Africa, Asia, the Latin American world, the Pacific Islands, Arabia—almost anywhere but White Europe" (p. 3).

Thus, today instead of *ethnic minority*, we more commonly hear the terms *multiculturalism* and *diversity*. Lum (1996) points out that multiculturalism implies that cultural groups will preserve their distinctive identities—their language, beliefs, customs, religions, and so on—and that "these distinctive practices represent enormous cultural wealth and are a source of enrichment for society as a whole" (p. 1).

Multiculturalism includes attention to more than ethnicity or color; it includes class, religion, sexual orientation, and disability. Paul Pedersen (1991) suggests that by defining multiculturalism broadly, "the construct 'multicultural' becomes generic to all counseling relationships" (p. 7). We believe that only if we are knowledgeable about and sensitive to cultural values, norms, and nuances can we hope to devise clinical interventions that will be both appropriate and effective (Atkinson & Hackett, 1995; Boyd-Franklin, 1989; Devore & Schlesinger, 1996; Sue & Sue, 1990).

EXERCISE 1.3 *Matching*

In your journal, discuss the pros and cons of matching clients and clinicians in terms of gender, ethnicity, or language. Does matching people along those lines ensure that they are from the same culture? Share your responses in class.

Our society is pluralistic and multicultural, and clearly our practice must be as well. But what does that mean? The American Counseling Association (ACA), the National Association of Social Workers (NASW), the American Psychological Association (APA), and the American Association for Marriage and Family Therapy (AAMFT), among other professional mental health organizations, have recognized the importance of training clinicians in issues of multiculturalism. Most clinicians who have written about *competencies and standards in multicultural counseling* suggest that the following three dimensions be addressed in training: attitudes and beliefs, knowledge, and skills (Sue, Arredondo, & McDavis, 1992).

1. As clinicians, we need to be aware of our own ethnic, gender, and cultural heritage. We need to be aware of our negative and positive reactions to the values and traditions of other groups and of how our own cultural values affect our worldview. We can only truly enhance our awareness when we live, work, and make friendships with people different from ourselves—people with whom we can discuss our feelings and reactions, and with whom we can exchange honest questions and feedback. These kinds of experiences are still too limited in the lives of many people, and must be assiduously developed and nurtured. However, it is important to recognize that we are responsible for our own learning and should not always depend on others who are different from ourselves to teach us what we should know about them.

2. Clinicians need to acquire knowledge about the cultures and customs of the clients with whom we work. We need to know information about the specific history and background of the cultural group; about family structures, communication patterns, gender roles, traditions, and values; about the impact of immigration; the role of spirituality, and so on. We need to explore how culture and ethnicity affect help-seeking behaviors. We must attend to the effects that racism, stigmatization, and discrimination have on our clients' daily lives.

3. Finally, as clinicians we need to use this self-awareness and knowledge to devise flexible strategies for intervention that are effective and congruent with our clients' values. We must be aware of bias in research and assessment instruments, and we must design interventions and strategies that are appropriate and linguistically suitable.

EXERCISE 1.4 *Cultural Awareness*

Listed below are certain personal and cultural characteristics that have profound influences on how people understand the world and interact with others. In your journal, record your answers to the following statements. Begin by describing yourself, then record how each characteristic affects your understanding of yourself and how you relate to others. In class, discuss this exercise with your colleagues. Learning how they have answered the items and contrasting those answers with your own can be extremely enlightening.

1. My gender is _____ .

2. My age is _____ .

3. My physical appearance includes the following qualities (describe these as accurately as you can and try to avoid oversimplifying or using racial terms):
Skin:
Hair:
Facial features:
Build:
Other features:

4. The nationality and cultural background of my parents and grandparents are:
   My father's mother
   My father's father
   My mother's mother
   My mother's father
   My father
   My mother

5. With regard to economic resources, the family I was raised in was _____ .

6. The religious orientation of my mother is _____ .

   The religious orientation of my father is _____ .

7. My mother's educational background is _____ .

   My father's educational background is _____ .

8. My own educational background is _____ .

9. My physical and health abilities are _____ .

10. My sexual orientation is _____ .

11. Other characteristics that have influenced my experiences and understandings of others:

Source: Adapted from *The Internship, Practicum and Field Placement Handbook,* by Baird, Brian N., pp. 81–82, © 1996. Adapted by permission of Prentice-Hall, Inc., Upper Saddle River, NJ.

Evaluation

Unlike most conversations, clinical interviewing involves *evaluation*. Clinicians examine their work, session by session, to assess the effectiveness of specific focus, techniques, or uses of self. Progress and process notes, audiocassettes, and videotapes are all helpful in this process. We review our work on a regular basis with supervisors and, on occasion, with outside consultants with particular expertise. It is also important that clinicians engage clients in an ongoing evaluation of how things are going. Finally, there is a process of evaluation at the end of the working relationship. Clinician and client may use formal outcome measures, or may simply review the relationship and what has been accomplished.

Our Perspective

All clinical interviewing is embedded in a worldview—a system of values and beliefs—that shapes the clinical work we do. This worldview usually has both explicit and implicit elements, both conscious and unconscious influences. We believe it is very important for clinicians to be aware of the assumptions that guide their professional practice and to be able to articulate them clearly.

EXERCISE 1.5 *Your Values and Beliefs*

In your journal, record some of the guiding assumptions and values that underlie your approach to clinical helping. Discuss your assumptions and values in class.

Our own worldview is both *ecological* and *systemic*. Like all ecological and systemic practitioners, we recognize and appreciate the interactivity and interdependence of all living and nonliving things and believe that there are biological, psychological, sociocultural, political, economic, spiritual, and environmental influences in what appear to be "individual" human behavior or isolated family interactions (Bateson, 1972; Bronfenbrenner, 1979; von Bertalanffy, 1968). We believe that people can best be understood within the context of the relationships and resources in their lives. Furthermore, like many ecopsychologists, we believe human beings are affected not only by their relationships with others but also by their relationships with both the animate and inanimate environments (Roszak, Gomes, & Kanner, 1995). Therefore, we pay as much attention to the circumstances and the relationships of our clients, and to the effects the larger world has on them, as we do to their internal processes.

Example

Mickey, a drug-abusing teenager, is arrested carrying a gun. In the subsequent court evaluation, it is learned that his mother is a prostitute doing prison time for heroin addiction and shoplifting. His father was killed a few years earlier in a drug raid. The boy lives with an aunt who works two jobs to support many extended kin; however, he often sleeps at friends' apartments, doing and selling drugs, and watching MTV. One could speculate that underlying Mickey's behavior may be his negative perceptions of self, which he has internalized because of the neglect and abandonment he has experienced from his adult caretakers. In addition, Mickey suffers from attention deficit disorder related to ingesting lead paint and being exposed to other environmental toxins dumped in his community, and he could be using drugs to calm his symptoms. Several local companies have moved their factories and supermarkets out of the community, leaving few jobs or career prospects in the town other than drug dealing. Furthermore, expanded military expenditures at a time of balanced budgets resulted in the closing of teen programs in his area, so that his main opportunity for friendship is gang membership. The clinician working with Mickey needs to recognize all the factors that impact on him, including family, friendships, economic trends, corporate policies, political decisions, and environmental pollution.

In clinical interviews, we always listen for *reciprocal influences*—the ways in which every member of an interaction influences the others. Because of our belief in reciprocal influence, we do not believe that clinicians are "detached," "neutral," or "objective observers." Therefore, we pay special attention to the ways in which clients and clinicians influence and affect each other's behaviors.

Our work is also influenced by the family systems concept of *circular causality* (Bateson, 1979). Events in complex systems often exist as both causes and effects of the others. Clinicians frequently see couples in which each partner blames the other for the troubles in their relationship. For example, one partner showers the other with affection, wishing to become more intimate. The other partner, feeling smothered and invaded, becomes unresponsive and withdrawn. The first partner, alarmed at this distancing, redoubles his or her attentions. This dance often goes on indefinitely, ending all too frequently in acrimonious debates about who is doing what to whom. In this example, the first partner may describe the interaction thus: "My partner pulls away so I have to chase after him to get close." The second partner may say, "My partner invades me, so I retreat." In trying to make sense out of complex related behaviors, people tend to see behaviors as having starting points (causes) and stopping points (effects). However, the choice of a specific event as a starting or stopping point is an arbitrary one.

Furthermore, we recognize that systems are in *constant flux*, that life is not homeostatic and that we are only seeing the client at one point in time. It is important to note that if we entered the relationship with a client at another point, we might see a different person. Clients often make contact with clinicians at a time of crisis, when they are stressed and burdened. What we see is but one snapshot of that person at that difficult moment in time. If we were to see that person at other times, in more supportive circumstances or in more empowered interaction with others, we might describe and respond to the person very differently.

Leslie was a very quiet, shy girl in my office. She was often quite teary and self-effacing. She had almost no self-confidence and was very soft-spoken. When I went to see her on the soccer field, I couldn't believe it was the same girl. She was so sure of herself: she gave orders to the other kids on her team, she laughed and yelled.

Furthermore, clients may show different aspects of themselves even within the same session. A client may talk about a parent in a regressed, childlike manner, then speak with authoritative confidence when discussing something at work.

We believe that there are *multiple realities,* or differing views about the way things are, how they got that way, and the way things ought to be. As clinicians we need to be careful not to assume that our "reality" or point of view is necessarily more correct or more helpful than the client's. We believe that all people's ideas are worthy of consideration and that silencing or excluding individuals or groups is the surest road to misunderstanding large pieces of human experience. Moreover, clients are sometimes more attuned to both the hard realities and the natural supports of complex environments than clinicians are. Clinicians can often learn a great deal from client knowledge, experience, and perspective.

Experienced clinicians have long observed that no matter how "irrational" things may seem to us as outside observers of others' lives, to the people living those lives, that irrationality may represent their best adaptation at the moment or a sensible way of negotiating daily life under oppressive circumstances. As clinicians we must make continuing efforts to *immerse ourselves in the client's perspective,* rather than dragging the client over into our own constructions of reality .

Clients often seek clinical help when they are stuck because they have a limited perspective. One of the major goals of therapy is to help clients broaden their perspectives, to see things using different lenses, to construct new realities, or to *reframe* their situation. Indeed, we wish to foster in ourselves and in our clients a growing capacity to appreciate different and even competing perspectives.

> *I often tell clients that we don't have to agree and twin with each other, but we both need to listen with open minds. What appears off-target one week may resonate clearly three weeks later.*

Our perspective is characterized by a deep and abiding belief in the capacity of human beings to grow and change within positive relationships and contexts that activate potentials and provide for the meeting of basic human needs.

A *strengths perspective* undergirds all effective clinical intervention. Working within a strengths perspective, we try as often as possible to elicit and underscore the often undervalued or unnoticed strengths with which clients have successfully addressed problems (Saleebey, 1997; Weick, Rapp, Sullivan, & Kisthardt, 1989). Clients report that they have so often been asked by professionals to recite what is *not* working that they forget to mention or to value what *has* worked. Our valuing of these unsung acts of valor or achievement, no matter how small, can often fan a spark of hope. Noticing and validating strengths can bring new meaning to clients who have seen themselves (or been seen by others) as hopeless, incompetent, or of no importance.

In addition to helping clients gain new perspectives on their circumstances, clinicians may also work with clients to modify their circumstances. We may do this through *direct advocacy* for a particular client, such as helping a client get welfare benefits, find day care, or get access to a training program. We may also advocate for particular populations, as when we work on getting legislation passed that will fund school lunch programs, support funding of community day programs for people with Alzheimer's disease, or testify regarding the need for programs for the homeless (Rappaport, 1987).

Finally, we believe that clinicians must *work for social change.* An old public health adage maintains that, instead of retrieving individual drowning victims one after the other from the river, we must go upriver to determine and eliminate the causes of the drownings. Part of our professional responsibility is to work for the health and mental health of our clients and to prevent those conditions that contribute to disease and distress.

Our professional ethic of care extends to a social responsibility to work for a healthy world that promotes the mental health of all people. We must nourish structures and processes that encourage growth and development and oppose all forms of oppression and environmental degradation.

Our activism may be a part of our professional role, as when we join with other clinicians to work for social change through organizations such as Psychologists for Social Responsibility, Social Workers for Peace and Disarmament, and The Public Interest Directorate of the American Psychological Association. At times we may use our professional skills as volunteers in community agencies, or in responding to national disasters.

> *Following the bombing of the Federal Building in Oklahoma, I was part of a team of clinicians who volunteered to work with child survivors and their families. As an expert on trauma in children, I was glad to offer my services.*
>
> *I always feel that it is important to do volunteer work using my clinical skills. A couple of years ago, a group of friends and I began a series of support groups for people newly diagnosed with AIDS. Now we are using the same skills to help train peer leaders for a breast cancer support group. I can't tell you how much both experiences have enriched my life, and my clinical work.*

Our sense of social responsibility also involves personal activism, which leads us to organize, disseminate leaflets, and march. It takes us to state and national capitols to lobby, picket, and become leaders in political bodies that wield real power to effect large-scale change. It stimulates us to speak and write in the media and not only for scholarly meetings and journals.

OO **CLIP** **1.1**
Introduction to the
Video

> *I was part of a team that conducted research with families about the psychological effects of exposure to nuclear radiation. We interviewed atomic veterans who were exposed during the above-ground atomic testing in the United States. A couple of years later, I went with a group of mental health clinicians to the nuclear test site in Nevada to protest continued underground nuclear testing. We were subsequently arrested with hundreds of other protesters for trespassing on federal property.*

Conclusion

Our worldview, with its emphasis on systemic and ecological principles and attention to multicultural issues, shapes our practice, informs our teaching, influences our lives, and, of course, permeates this book. As you proceed with your learning and practice, we encourage you to develop and refine a socially responsible worldview that will guide your professional development as a clinician.

Suggested Readings

We highly recommend the following books to complement your readings on skill development.

Baird, Brian N. (1996). *The internship, practicum, and field placement handbook: A guide for helping professionals.* Upper Saddle River, NJ: Prentice-Hall.

Ram Dass, & Gorman, Paul. (1985). *How can I help?* New York: Knopf.

Ryan, William. (1976). *Blaming the victim.* New York: Vintage Press.

There are a number of excellent books on culturally responsive practice, including practice with women; with gay men, lesbian women, and bisexual men and women; and with people of color.

Comas-Diaz, Lillian, & Greene, Beverly (Eds.). (1994). *Women of color: Integrating ethnic and gender identities in psychotherapy.* New York: Guilford.

Dworkin, Sari, & Gutierrez, Fernando, J. (Eds.). (1992). *Counseling gay men and lesbians: Journey to the end of the rainbow.* Alexandria, VA: AACD Press.

Lum, Doman. (1996). *Social work practice and people of color: A process-stage approach.* Pacific Grove, CA: Brooks/Cole.

Jordan, Judith V., Kaplan, Alexandra G., Miller, Jean Baker, Stiver, Irene P., & Surrey, Janet L. (1991). *Women's growth in connection: Writings from the Stone Center.* New York: Guilford.

Mirkin, Marsha. (Ed.). (1994). *Women in context: Toward a feminist reconstruction of psychotherapy with women.* New York: Guilford.

Pinderhughes, Elaine. (1989). *Understanding race, ethnicity, and power: The key to efficacy in clinical practice.* New York: Free Press.

Sue, Derald W. & Sue, D. (1990). *Counseling the culturally different: Theory and practice.* New York: Wiley.

In addition, we believe everyone should read:

McIntosh, Peggy. (1989, July/August). White privilege: Unpacking the invisible knapsack. *Peace and Freedom*, pp. 10–12.

The following texts provide good overviews of the major schools of clinical practice and counseling theory.

Corey, Gerald. (1996). *Theory and practice of counseling and psychotherapy.* Pacific Grove, CA: Brooks/Cole.

Corsini, Raymond J., & Wedding, Danny. (1996). *Current psychotherapies.* Itasca, IL: Peacock.

Dorfman, Rachelle. (Ed.). (1988). *Paradigms of clinical social work*. New York: Brunner/Mazel.

Patterson, Cecil H., & Watkins, C. Edward. (1996). *Theories of psychotherapy*. New York: HarperCollins.

For those interested in an overview of ecological and environmental issues in practice we recommend the following.

Germain, Carol, B. (1979). *Social work practice, people and environments*. New York: Columbia University Press.

Parks, Katherine M. (1996). The personal is ecological: Environmentalism of social work. *Social Work, 41*, 320–322.

Roszak, Theodore, Gomes, Mary E., & Kanner, Allen D. (Eds.). (1995). *Ecopsychology: Restoring the earth, healing the mind*. San Francisco: Sierra Club Books.

CHAPTER 2

Getting Started

The Interview Environment

 **CLIP 2.1**
Variety of
Settings

Today, more and more clinicians interview in a variety of settings. Since the location of the meeting and the physical surroundings affect the aura and process of an interview, it is incumbent on clinicians to be thoughtful in setting up their interview environments. Here we refer not simply to arranging an office but to making every interview space as amenable to confidential conversation as possible.

The Professional Office

Most people think interviews take place in an office, and clinicians may do a lot of thinking about office size, location, comfort, and accessibility. Much has been written about the effects on the interview process of office arrangement and decor, including the presence or absence of the clinician's personal belongings (Kadushin, 1997).

E X E R C I S E 2.1   *Your Ideal Office*

You have an 8 × 12 office with one window. Draw a rectangle on the sheet of paper in your journal. Imagine how you would like to set up your office. What furniture would you have? How would you arrange it? Would you have pictures on the wall? Would your furniture be movable? Where would you imagine sitting in relationship to your clients? Would you have snapshots of your family on your desk? Would you

21

hang your degree on the wall? Draw it all out. What factors influenced your thinking about arrangements?

Office Setup

Few clinicians have the opportunity to create their own offices. Interns and clinicians pressed for space in community agencies may share office space with others and so have little control over the physical environment in which they work. Whether clinicians have control over their own office setting, as they might if they were in private practice, or work in an agency where they share space with others, it is important that they take responsibility for the space in which they work.

> *I had been hired for a new clinic that admitted patients before the physical space was ready. I did counseling sessions in a hallway between two metal file cabinets for four weeks. Nervous about confidentiality, I hung a big cardboard sign on one of the drawers: "Counseling in progress. Keep a wide berth."*

Whenever possible, clinicians should attempt to use the following guidelines in arranging office setup.

Offices should be private, soundproof, and as free of interruptions as possible. Unfortunately, even these basic requirements for privacy can be hard to meet.

> *When I was an intern, I was seeing a client at the community mental health center. Our offices were very small with no windows and it really felt like a rabbit warren. One major problem was that at times you could hear clients in other rooms. I remember sitting with a 20-year-old woman who had trouble expressing her feelings. We had been talking about her abusive mother when suddenly through the walls we heard the client next door screaming "I hate her, I hate her." We both looked at each other, and my client said, "I guess she is mad at her mother . . . . " We both laughed. Later I talked at staff meeting about the problem and eventually we bought lots of those little sound machines to mask noise. That worked—for the most part.*

Although interns often feel powerless to affect the systems in which they are trained, perceptive interns have often brought about needed change by pointing out problems and working with clients and fellow professionals to resolve them.

Offices should be accessible to persons with disabilities. There should be ramps and accessible bathrooms. Ideally, there should be phones with TTY so that those who are deaf or hard of hearing can easily communicate. Offices should be able to accommodate walkers, wheelchairs, and Seeing Eye dogs. While accessibility in public settings is mandated by federal law, professionals may have to work hard to ensure that private practice offices and smaller settings adhere to these guidelines.

Accessibility issues also include such things as being located near the population served, having office hours that are convenient to clients' schedules, being on or near public transportation, providing child care, providing language interpreters, and providing affordable services scaled to income.

Offices need to be flexible enough to allow both client and therapist a comfortable personal space. Most people have an invisible area around them that serves as a protective barrier. Intrusion into this *personal space* creates discomfort. Personal space varies from person to person, culture to culture, and situation to situation. People probably have less need for personal space with a friend than with a stranger. Gender also plays a role; in Western cultures, men tend to leave more interpersonal space between themselves and male strangers than do women with women strangers (Harper, Wiens, & Matarazzo, 1978). Cultural norms also dictate personal space. Allen Ivey (1994) notes that most North Americans seem to prefer a conversational space of about an arm's length, whereas the British prefer greater distance: "Hispanic people often prefer half the distance, and those from the Middle East may talk practically eyeball to eyeball" (p. 29). Personal space is often influenced by power dynamics. Those in positions of relatively less power may have their personal space invaded by those with greater power.

E X E R C I S E 2.2 *Observing Personal Space*

The next time you are in a social situation, be aware of people's personal space. Notice what happens when you move very close to a person. Record reactions in your journal.

Having movable chairs or furniture helps create a comfortable environment for both client and clinician. When there is a difference in comfort level about personal space, clinicians should respect the clients' needs. However, there are exceptions: if the clinician feels that the client's needs will interfere with the ability to attend or to get work done, the clinician may have to ask the client to move away a little. We will talk about other issues relating to physical contact and closeness in Chapter 10.

> *In my private practice office, I have two chairs set up with about 2 1/2 feet between them. One time I saw a client who pulled her chair up so close that our knees were touching. I pulled my chair back a little and she moved closer. I felt very uncomfortable with that much closeness. I wondered what it meant but did not feel like making a "big deal" about it yet. I had only just met her. I said that I noticed that she felt comfortable sitting very close*

and I said that made it hard for me to see her. I said I feel more comfortable with a little more distance between us. I stored the information away for future use.

Furniture arrangement should reflect equality and respect.   Seating should be comfortable for anyone to sit for long periods of time, yet not so comfortable that one is likely to fall asleep. The relative height and style of the seats as well as their position in relationship to each other should reflect the equality and respect of the client-clinician relationship. Clinicians should have a flexible office arrangement that can accommodate people in wheelchairs and other assistive devices. While it is important to pay attention to the seating arrangements, remember that it is the sitter, not the seat, who communicates professionalism and respect.

> *I have a colleague who has one of those huge Lazy-Boy recliners for himself and a small folding chair for his clients. I've always wondered how the clients feel about that.*

> *I was working with Karlene, a woman who was somewhat overweight. One day, my usual office was not available. We used another office that had comfortable chairs, but no couch, love seat, or chairs without arms. I didn't notice anything was wrong until she leaned back in her chair and the chair began to tip sideways. I commented on this and suggested that we move to an office with more comfortable seating. I only realized how tight the chair was when she struggled to get out of it. Even though she had been fairly open with me in the past, she said she would not have raised the issue of the chair if I had not brought it up. She cried as she talked about how bad it felt to live in a world where usual things (stores with turnstiles, movie theaters, and airplanes) were not accessible. She later shared that she had interviewed several therapists before deciding to see me. One of the factors that clinched her decision was the sturdy love seat in my office. The experience opened my eyes to the covert discrimination people experience when the world is not designed to be accessible to them.*

> *The first time I worked with a woman in a wheelchair, I quickly removed the chair that normally is placed opposite mine in the office, assuming that she would place her wheelchair in that spot. I thought I was being sensitive. I didn't realize that she might prefer transferring out of her wheelchair to sit in an office chair until she told me. It also reminded me that I should be careful that the furniture in my office be solid and stable enough to support a transfer.*

Many interviewers sit beside their desks, rather than behind them, so that the desk does not create a symbolic barrier. If the desk is placed against the wall and a chair is placed beside the desk, the client seated there can be invited to fill out information on the desktop or work side by side with the clinician on genograms, ecomaps, lifecharts, letters, or artwork. Some clinicians prefer a desk out of the way in a corner, with comfortable chairs placed in the main space of the office. Clinicians concerned about safety may want to place their desks or chairs near the door so that they can exit quickly to summon help in the event of an emergency. If the interviewer has a preferred seat, it should be pointed out to clients while encouraging them to take any other seat they wish.

Examples

" Mrs. Lindahl, have a seat wherever you would like."

"Lawrence, feel free to sit on the sofa or any of the chairs."

"Janelle, I'll be sitting here; take any of the other seats you would like."

Many offices can include sofas and couches. Clinicians seldom sit on a couch with a client, because doing so may suggest a familiarity or informality that may be uncomfortable. In a home visit, however, sitting on a couch may be necessary and appropriate.

After being forced to work behind a desk in a regulation office setting, I devised a living room milieu for my private practice office. I associated the environment with a place for private intimate talk and hoped my clients would, too. I've set up my office with a large window behind me so clients can take a break from looking at me. It also gives a feeling of openness and airiness to the room.

With children, some teens, and some adults, casual seating on the floor may be used as long as clients manifest comfort with this arrangement and there is a clinical reason for it. Children especially appreciate the clinician's willingness to "come down to size" rather than loom over the process. Family therapists, psychodramatists, relaxation trainers, and process group facilitators may all use floor seating from time to time.

Interviewing offices should be able to accommodate unexpected others who may accompany clients to the meeting. The clinician should anticipate where extra chairs could be found if needed and where others may wait comfortably for the client if they are not to be part of the meeting. It goes without saying that attending to the needs of these others is also a way of demonstrating caring to the client.

As in all clinical work, the interviewer considers possible symbolic meanings of seating arrangements and behaviors. The clinician takes note of where the client, group, or family customarily choose to sit in relation to each other and to the clinician. These choices may signal alliances, degree of comfort with closeness and distance, and subtle shifts in relationships.

I can often tell what's happening in the midpoint of therapy by the chair the client takes. When we've gotten to the most psychologically affecting material, clients sometimes switch seats. Those needing more intimacy move closer to me; others needing more distance sit farther away.

No matter how the office is arranged, it is important to make sure that the client feels that there is some flexibility in the office seating. The clinician can indicate flexibility in a number of ways. One is by directly asking after the client sits: "Is that okay?" Another is by moving a chair in some small way.

> *I had brought a client into my office, which has two chairs and a couch in one area and a desk and chair in another. I told her to have a seat wherever she would like and she took a seat on the couch. I took a seat in one of the chairs and angled it a little to face the couch. I asked her my usual pro forma question: "Is that all right?" She responded by jumping off the couch and saying that she felt that the couch was much softer than it looked and that she felt like she sank into it. She said she was glad I had asked because she really didn't want to sit on the couch and felt uncomfortable about moving. She took the other chair and I turned my chair to face her more directly.*

Office decor should not be distracting.   Office decor should be soothing. Warm colors and soft lighting can help create a sense of caring, privacy, and intimacy. Remember, however, that we are not creating a romantic setting: the office is a professional environment. Lighting should be bright enough for people to see clearly. If possible, it is nice to have some pictures on the walls, but they should not be distracting.

Two relatively common pieces of office decor are a box of tissues and a clock. Some clinicians place the clock so that it is over the client's shoulder and they can unobtrusively note the time without distracting the client. We have found it useful to have the clock positioned in such a way that both the client and the clinician can easily see it. Sometimes it's helpful to have two clocks. Some clients will feel more in control of the session if they know how much time is left; they will feel able to pace themselves. Others might prefer not to see the clock because it reminds them of the arbitrary time limits of the clinical relationship.

Some clinicians like to have a few personal belongings in their office and may have pictures of pets and loved ones on their desks. Others feel it is more appropriate to have a personally neutral office. Each clinician has the right to establish his or her own environment as long as it isn't overly stimulating, distracting, or offensive. Clinicians should always think about the possible effects of displaying personal belongings and be prepared to respond should questions arise about the objects displayed.

Some clinicians, frequently those who work with children or who do art therapy, may display their clients' artwork in the office. Other clinicians may place presents that clients have given them in the office. We will discuss the implications of client gifts to clinicians in Chapter 10. For now, let us just say that there are a number of important considerations concerning things clients give us. What will other clients think about these items? Will clients feel compelled to give the clinician similar presents? If the clinician is hanging some client drawings, should all drawings be hung? Would this be distracting to others?

It is important, however, to make sure that the space isn't overly cluttered. Avoiding clutter applies to clinicians' desks as well. Having a desk that is relatively cleared lets the client know that you have made room to see him or her. However, it has been suggested that having a messy desk might humanize the clinician in the client's eyes.

Office decor should be appropriate to the types of clients we see and should reflect the cultures of the people with whom we work. For example, if we are seeing families and children, our offices should have toys and playthings. If we work with Mexican immigrants, we may want to have some pictures or posters with Mexican themes. Clinicians must be careful about superficial or cosmetic fixes—displaying things just to make an impression.

Clinicians should experience what the office is like from the client's perspective. Sitting in all the available places in the office enables the clinician to consider whether sunlight shines in the client's eyes; what is in the client's line of vision; and whether the chair is comfortable.

Clinicians should consider other client needs. Is a bathroom available to clients? Is it wheelchair accessible? What about drinking water? Is there a play area for children while their parents are being seen? Is there a place where clients can hang their coats? Is there a phone available for client use? Are clients routinely asked at intake whether they need any special arrangements or accommodations to facilitate the interview process (for example, child care, translator services, ramp entrance)?

E X E R C I S E 2.3 *Field Visit*

Visit an agency where clinical interviews take place. Briefly sit in the waiting area and note what you would observe as a client. Go to one of the offices and sit in all the chairs. In your journal, make notes on what you see and learn. Be aware of privacy, lighting, furniture arrangement, decor, and so on. Are there ways that the agency reflects the cultures of the diverse populations it serves? Does the staff reflect the cultures that the agency serves?

Out of the Office and into the Streets

Many clinicians do not see clients primarily in office settings, and many clients may not find an office setting comfortable or safe. To engage the client, clinicians may do a lot of interviewing in kitchens, hospital rooms, on benches outside shelters, over coffee at fast-food restaurants, or in classrooms.

*I got a call on intake at the mental health center from a family whose
17-year-old daughter had started to hear voices. My supervisor approved an
in-home crisis evaluation to determine whether the girl could be sustained at
home. I would be in touch with my supervisor by phone to determine next
steps once in the home. When I arrived, the daughter, dressed in a long wool
coat, was fully immersed in a bathtub full of warm water, laughing and
singing. She knew I was coming and invited me in "to see I'm just fine."
Since she wouldn't leave the tub, I perched on the closed toilet and
interviewed her there long enough to get a sense of her need for protection.
Thus began a relationship that, following her 30-day hospitalization,
continued for 2 1/2 years.*

Home Visits

There is a lot to learn about clients by meeting with them in their homes.
People may behave very differently in their homes than they do in the office;
they may be more comfortable, more outgoing—literally more at home. The
clinician may be able to observe things about the client and his or her
situation that are not readily visible in the office, thus expanding the
clinician's perspective.

*As a counseling intern at a suburban mental health clinic, I decided to do a
home visit with the family of a 14-year-old adolescent I was seeing. When
I arrived at the house, I noticed the striking contrast between the fortresslike
outside (gate locked, curtains drawn, double locks on the door) and the
absence of doors in any of the rooms inside the house. I began to wonder
about family secrets and family boundaries. Later, my client revealed that she
was sexually abused by her father.*

The home visitor often has greater opportunity to meet the client's
friends and family; see family pictures; note relationships with cherished
pets and neighbors that the client may not think to mention in the office;
and experience the way the client puts together, develops, and protects
living space. Just as we attend carefully to the messages conveyed by our
own office arrangements, we also note the client's environment and the
messages it conveys about the client and his or her situation. Culture, income
levels, and personal taste all need to be taken into account before making
inferences.

Home visits present a number of challenges to the clinician.

1. Clients may live in circumstances different from those of the interviewer.
   A variety of factors, such as poverty, exploitation, mental illness, and
   addiction, can cause clients to live in inadequate or dilapidated housing
   lacking basic amenities. Large numbers of extended kin may have to live
   in two or three rooms. At the other extreme, clinicians may visit the
   homes of wealthy clients living in opulence. Interviewers may thus work
   in alien and unfamiliar environments, at times feeling uncomfortable or
   intimidated.

2. The home is not a controlled environment, nor is it set up to ensure privacy, flexibility, and comfort for interviews the way offices may be. Phone calls, kids waking from naps, elders calling out for help, visitors dropping by—all may seem like intrusions on the interview. We must remember that, as important as our work may seem to us, it is but a small part of many clients' hectic lives and may at times seem to them to be the least important thing they have to worry about.

3. From the client's perspective, the clinician may feel like the intruder, the outsider. The clinician is the guest and may feel less in control of the environment or the agenda. In some situations, clients may not welcome the clinician and may want the clinician to leave their homes. This may contribute to the unfortunate reluctance of many professionals to make home visits.

   Tshanga, a 14-year-old isolated and depressed teen, was referred to family services by her mother "to see if you can find out why she is so sad." Since she would not come to see me, I made several home visits to try to engage her, but she would never let me inside the apartment. My supervisor made me go back for four weeks running and interview her standing outside, talking through the door and feeling ridiculous as neighbors passed in the hallway and stared at me as I talked to an invisible other. I did process recording on each of these visits, and my supervisor treated them like office visits, helping me focus on feelings, use humor, ask about school, boyfriends, and so on. At about the fifth week, Tshanga suddenly said she would let me come in today, but only if she were allowed to stand on the opposite side of the room. I was very receptive, and this is how our visits went the rest of the year.

4. Home visits may begin with greetings, social conversation, and sharing coffee or food. Some clinicians may experience discomfort over the thought that in home visits they are not "doing the work" and are "just socializing." We believe that all these rituals are an integral part of the interview process, and may contribute to the development of the positive working alliance as well. In many cultures, sharing food and informal conversation are an important part of the interview itself.

   Mrs. Lanzarone was not able to meet with me in the office because she had custody of her four grandchildren while her daughter was in prison for selling drugs. So I met with her weekly in the kitchen of her apartment, and I often held one of the kids in my lap while Mrs. L. cooked me Italian food for lunch. At first I would come away from these sessions exhausted, which helped me understand what Mrs. L. was up against every day. Once I got used to it, I looked forward to our meetings and so did Mrs. L. She called this "Gramma's time."

5. Home visits may present the clinician with special safety challenges. There can be weapons or drugs in the home which, when coupled with simmering resentments, can present serious danger. (We will discuss safety issues further in a later section.)

Other Settings

In addition to home visits, interviews may occur in a variety of non-office settings. The workplace, the school cafeteria or playground, the shelter, the restaurant, the street corner, the locked facility—all are frequent sites of clinical interventions. Today's practitioners learn to move flexibly and comfortably between locales, tailoring their interviewing strategies to the exigencies and advantages of nontraditional sites.

Major challenges confronting the clinician in the *"borrowed environment"* include the maintenance of confidentiality and focus, the intrusion of others with different roles and needs, and the pressure of time in an environment whose purposes can shift from moment to moment.

> *It was amazing how much we were able to do at the diner. Russell didn't want anyone in his small town to know that he had AIDS. He was afraid to come to the clinic so we met at the Busy Bee diner in the next town. We could get a lot done as long as we found a corner table in the back, kept our voices low, and screened out all the hubbub around us by focusing intensely on our work.*

We think it is crucial to remember that what the clinician sees in meetings with a client is only part of the larger picture—snapshots of a person's life at a particular time. To see clients in situations where they are interacting with others may broaden the clinician's perspective in unanticipated ways. The quiet teenager in the office may be very outgoing and funny in the playground. The woman suffering from major depression, tearful and seemingly paralyzed during therapy sessions, may still be functioning in superhuman ways in her leadership position at work. Whenever feasible, wise clinicians attempt to see clients in a variety of contexts to get a fuller picture of client strengths and issues. School counselors may observe students in classroom settings. Day treatment staff may observe their clients in community meetings. Workers in an adolescent residential treatment center often make home visits to observe the teens interacting with their families. Carel Germain and Alex Gitterman (1996) use the term *lifespace interviews* to describe these informative in vivo transactions.

The Portable Office: A Quiet Conducive Presence

Part of preparing for the interview is creating an atmosphere quiet and circumscribed enough to be conducive to reflecting and talking together. Creating a safe, quiet space for talking reflects an appreciation of the fact that people often share their stories more easily in an atmosphere of privacy and relative calm. Such an environment can often be established more easily in office settings in which there is some degree of control over noise and intrusions. Whatever the environment, the clinician should try to take into each unique situation an invisible bubble of calm and focused attention.

The interview ambiance is portable and almost palpable, arising from the professional's respectful, caring, and attuned presence. It can be experienced on a bus en route to a court hearing, in a kitchen with children and neighbors coming in and out, and on a park bench outside a homeless shelter. With few exceptions, the clinician's steadiness and thoughtfulness regarding clients' needs and style will act as a containing and soothing environment, no matter the setting in which the interview occurs. Clients often experience the relationship as respite and may describe to their clinicians how much they look forward to their time together, or what a "breather from the usual" this encounter is, or how safe and peaceful they feel with the clinician—a unique experience for many. Janet Surrey (1991) also views this unique good feeling of safety and support as a source of enhanced client agency, since relatedness stimulates confidence and initiative.

Safety

Physical Safety

Few things concern both clients and clinicians today more than physical safety. Many clients come from situations characterized by past or present violence, abuse, or neglect. Neighborhoods can be unsafe for travel at the very times busy families are free to come for interviews. Clinicians, too, can worry about physical safety. The violence of home and neighborhood can spill unpredictably into practice settings, and clinicians need to be prepared for the unexpected (Griffin, 1995).

> *I'll never forget the first time I heard about a clinician who was murdered. I was working at a community center when we received a call that a former colleague of ours had been shot by a client who had come to the clinic with a gun. He killed one psychologist and wounded another.*

> *At my agency people would be yelling all the time. We became somewhat oblivious to the sound of loud voices. We noted that if a clinician was in trouble and was calling out, no one would pay attention. We realized that we needed a code word that would alert us. We decided to use the word* emergency.

> *I made a visit to a client recovering from an overdose in a hospital in a high-crime neighborhood. She had been a tough client, challenging me constantly, dismissing me as unable to understand her because of our differing backgrounds. When I walked into her hospital room, she was shocked to see me. "You're so little and you come all this way to see me?" she said. We visited for a while and as I got up to leave she said, "Now on your way to the subway, walk tall and put your hand in your pocket so they think you have a gun." I laughed, but believe me, I followed her advice. The next time I saw her, the hostility was gone.*

As more and more clinicians conduct interviews in the community, they find themselves in situations in which they fear for their own safety.

> *When I was a counseling intern at an alternative high school, two of my students got into a fight and one, Doreen, had her arm slashed with a knife.*

After taking her to the hospital and dealing with the police who had been called, I brought Doreen home to her family. Her older sister ran into the bedroom and came out with a gun saying, "We have to kill that bitch who cut you." I was terrified.

Clinicians need to feel relatively safe in order to be effective. It is hard if not impossible to attend to clients and their needs when feeling personally at risk. A clinician who is too anxious to concentrate won't be able to help others. It is extremely important that clinicians turn to supervisors, colleagues, or consultants when alarm bells go off about physical safety. Don't be embarrassed to ask for help before, during, or after critical incidents. In fact, many agencies have formalized critical-incident review processes, whereby staff review incidents together and determine future strategies based on learning from each situation.

I was seeing a young woman who was a police officer in my private practice in my home. She always had to carry her service revolver with her—even when off duty. I was constantly distracted by it. I didn't worry that she would get angry and use it—I just felt uncomfortable having a gun in my home where my children are. I talked about it with my group practice and they suggested that I ask her if she would leave her gun locked in the glove compartment or trunk of her car when we met. That was fine with her.

The following cautions should be kept in mind.

1. Clinicians should avoid working alone in a building or isolated location, especially after dark. Lighted offices in otherwise darkened buildings can target both clinicians and clients as vulnerable.

2. At times clinicians may have to discuss with supervisors or consultants whether someone should accompany them on a family visit.

3. Clinicians should let someone at the agency know where they are headed when they leave for visits in the field.

4. As a general rule, clinicians should not see people who are intoxicated or who might have weapons with them.

5. Where possible, clinicians should carry a pocket cell phone programmed to instantly access emergency help.

6. If feeling seriously endangered, the clinician should leave immediately and get help. Bradford Sheafor and Charles and Gloria Horejsi (1997) advise clinicians not to touch or turn their backs on people whose escalating rage or fear might lead to an attack.

I didn't tell you what happened before I brought Doreen home and her sister pulled out the gun. I was the counselor in the classroom when another student, Yvette, pulled a knife on Doreen. I remember thinking, "I am the counselor—I should do something about this." I actually stood in between the students, and tried to talk Yvette into putting her knife away. All the while Doreen was egging her on. I was lucky Yvette didn't use the knife on me to get to Doreen.

No one can be completely safe. Clinicians and agencies may have to decide what risks they are willing to assume. These are important practice issues to be addressed with colleagues and supervisors.

Other Safety Concerns

Clinicians also need to be concerned about other kinds of safety not related to the physical environment. Clients may be threatened with harm if they elect to share their stories with a professional. Undocumented immigrants may worry about deportation if they are identified through service provision. Battered wives may fear reprisals from spouses if they disclose their abuse. Mothers may fear losing custody of their children if they reveal their lesbianism. It makes little difference to people in crisis whether we are called psychologists, counselors, or social workers if what we provide seems to hazard more risk than gain. Even clients without these impinging concerns may worry about confidentiality of the interview process.

Some clients worry that they will be harmed by clinicians themselves. Unfortunately, these concerns are sometimes justified. There has been a steady increase in the number of complaints against clinicians about sexual abuse, physical abuse, and financial exploitation (Pope, Sonne, & Holroyd, 1993; Reamer, 1995). These issues will be discussed in Chapter 10.

◯◯ **CLIP 2.1**
A variety of settings

Even Before We Meet

Great Expectations

It's human nature to anticipate what people and events will be like before engaging with them. Thinking about things in advance may reduce anxiety about the unknown and may prepare us to cope with contingencies that may arise from contact with the unfamiliar. Clinicians and clients also develop a set of expectations about each other and about the relationship even before meeting.

Clinician Expectations

The following exercise will help you identify some clinician expectations you may have about clients even before you meet them.

EXERCISE 2.4 *Anticipation*

Write down in your journal the immediate ideas that come to your mind about these clients.

Terry Mahoney is referred to the mental health clinic because of drug abuse.

Domingo, a high school sophomore, is referred by his teacher because he is failing math.

A young couple comes to you wanting to talk about the process of artificial insemination.

Mrs. Giorgio is a 67-year-old woman whose husband has just died.

Chang Yang is a 33-year-old Chinese immigrant accused of spouse abuse.

It is important to explore the sources of clinician expectations. Some expectations come from information about the client: for example, the client's gender, age, ethnicity, or presenting problem. We refer to these factors as *client information variables.* In Exercise 2.5, see whether your expectations about each client change as information is added or altered.

EXERCISE 2.5 *Changing Expectations*

Terry Mahoney is referred to the clinic because of drug abuse. She is a 54-year-old social worker.

Domingo, a high school sophomore, is referred by his teacher because he is failing math. He is 22 years old and is mentally retarded.

A young couple comes to you wanting to talk about the process of artificial insemination. They are lesbians who have been in a committed relationship for seven years.

Mrs. Giorgio is a 67-year-old woman whose husband has just died. They were married one year ago.

Chang Yang is a 33-year-old Chinese immigrant accused of spouse abuse. Chang Yang is a woman.

What other variables might shape what you think about these clients? Note the similarities and differences in your reactions with the added information.

In answering the last question in Exercise 2.5, you may have focused on other attributes of the client, such as sexual orientation, class, race, ethnicity, family background, diagnosis, or appearance. Much of this client information may precede the client into the office.

Very seldom do I see a client without having some information about him or her. Often it comes from a phone call with the client in which I learn a little about the reason for the meeting. Sometimes I receive information about the client from the referral source. I am frequently given a case file before I meet the client. I must admit that when I see a very thick case file, I worry that I've been given "a chronic client." I haven't even read any information, but I already have my pre-formed ideas.

Clinician preconceptions about clients based on client information variables are mediated by what we like to think of as the *clinician gestalt.* As you may have already noted, it is not just the information about clients that shapes how clinicians respond to them: it is the information interacting with the clinician's values, beliefs, and past experiences. In turn, values, beliefs, and experiences are mediated by familial and cultural background, including one's own gender, class, ethnicity, age, sexual orientation, and physical ability.

> *I remember my first week of internship at the community mental health center. I was assigned a "young divorced woman with two children coming to the clinic because she was depressed." My picture was of a woman who was 23, with kids about 2 and 4. I was so shocked when I went to the waiting room and found a 39-year-old woman! I was 27 at the time. I realized my supervisor, who is in her fifties, thought of the client as a young woman; but here she was older than I was. Before meeting her I had pictured myself as older and wiser, even though I didn't have any children and was just starting out. Now here she was, and I was closer in age to her 20-year-old daughter than to her. Suddenly I felt so nervous.*

Furthermore, characteristics of individuals and groups obtain meaning within larger social contexts. These larger social contexts include geography, historical period, and prevailing cultural norms. For example, the behavior of a woman who hears voices and talks back to them might have different meaning in different contexts. In 16th-century Europe, she may have been defined as a witch; in 20th-century United States, she may be seen as having schizophrenia or as being "perfectly normal," depending on whether her behavior occurs on the subway in New York City or in a Pentecostal church. Finally, we must always remember that the larger social context for most "minorities" in the United States is a prevailing climate of color prejudice, gender bias, homophobia, and ethnic discrimination.

E X E R C I S E 2.6 *Clinician Gestalt*

In your journal, identify those aspects of your own clinician gestalt that mediate your reaction to or preconceived ideas about the clients described in Exercises 2.4 and 2.5. These can include your beliefs, cultural heritage, past experiences, gender, class, race, ethnicity, age, orientation, and ability in the particular larger social context in which you find yourself.

Another piece of information that may precede a client into the office is the *diagnosis*. A diagnosis is not a description of a person; rather, it is a shorthand way of referring to a complex set of dysfunctional behaviors and characteristics. At times diagnoses can be useful in facilitating communication between clinicians, which is essential for research and treatment planning. However, when clinicians reduce the rich complexity of a person to a few behaviors, the diagnosis becomes a label. Labeling is particularly pernicious because labels can predispose us to categorize people and react to them in formulaic ways. Sometimes labels cause us to see things, like symptoms, that aren't there, and sometimes labels cause us not to see things, like strengths, that are there (Szasz, 1960). In the now-famous study conducted by David Rosenhan (1973), eight associates of the researcher acted as if they had a mental illness (schizophrenia) to get admitted to various hospital psychiatric wards. Once admitted to the hospital, each of the mock patients behaved normally. The hospital staff, however, continued to see them as mentally ill, despite their protestations and even though they were no longer manifesting symptoms. Once they had been given a diagnosis—a label—their protestations were defined as further evidence of their mental illness. (Interestingly, the "real patients" on the units could tell that the researchers were not actually mentally ill and did not belong in the hospital.)

Certain diagnoses are particularly stigmatizing. *Stigma* refers to the negative assumptions and biases attached to people because of their membership in particular groups (Goffman, 1963). Judgments about people with particular diagnoses are culturally determined and can be reflective of the zeitgeist of the times, of the community, or of the agency. These diagnoses may frighten clinicians, constricting their openness and negatively impacting the interview process.

> *An elderly woman called the clinic asking for someone to come out and talk her schizophrenic son into coming out of a closet where he had been holed up for two days. I was on intake and went out with the on-call psychiatrist. I didn't want the doctor to see how anxious I was. I had seen* Psycho *and thought we might be heading into a situation like that one. The man turned out to be a quiet, sad person who began to cry with relief when the doctor said he had come out to help him.*

> *The three supervisors in day treatment told us that most of the women in the Daily Living Group were "borderlines" who would try to manipulate us because we were interns and didn't know any better. They explained the importance of setting firm limits on client behaviors and not giving "these people" extra attention if they did dramatic things. We were very anxious about starting the group and felt irritated with "these women" before we got to know them.*

Diagnoses are usually determined after an extensive process of assessment, which may include observing, testing, interviewing, collecting historical data and life records, and conducting medical exams. While some of the people we see may not have been through an assessment process, some clients come to us with an already established diagnosis.

E X E R C I S E 2.7 *Diagnosis*

In your journal, discuss how knowing the diagnosis of a client before you meet can be helpful and how knowing the diagnosis can be problematic.

Client Expectations

Clients, too, come in with a set of expectations about clinicians and the therapeutic environment. These expectations may come from the media, from previous experiences with mental health workers, from the reputation of the agency or setting, or from the information the clients have about the clinician.

The media often show exaggerated or stereotypic representations of "shrinks" and social workers. These images are almost exclusively of white, able-bodied, middle-class individuals. Clients may expect the clinician to be like Bob Hartley, Frasier Crane, or Dr. Joyce Brothers. They may expect the clinician to be helpful, but they may also be aware of sensational stories in the press that report clinicians' sexual and financial exploitation of clients.

Some clients will have had previous interactions with the mental health system. The man with schizophrenia who has seen nine other counselors at the day treatment program may come to see you with the expectation that you, just like the others before you, will be leaving soon. The woman who has received a psychiatric evaluation resulting in the loss of custody of her children may feel hostile and wary before meeting a new clinician. The Mexican American family may be reluctant to seek help from the school counselor because, in previous encounters with other mental health clinicians, family members felt that the Anglo professionals were condescending and showed no respect for their strong family and community bonds.

Other clients may be reacting to information about the agency's reputation. For example, the factory worker seeking assistance about his troubled adolescent daughter may come to the Employee Assistance Program because his friends have told him that the people there are very helpful. A single mother may resist bringing her children to a homeless shelter because she has heard that it is dangerous there.

Clients may also respond to clinician information variables that they know in advance. The knowledge that the clinician is a man, Latino, a social worker, or an intern may influence clients' preconceptions. Remember that just as clinician reactions to client variables are mediated by the clinician's values, beliefs, and personal background, so, too, are client reactions to information about the clinician mediated by the client's values, beliefs, and personal background in the larger social context—the *client gestalt.*

> *When I was an intern, I was assigned to a white, middle-class woman in her forties who was a survivor of serious physical and sexual abuse. After we had worked together for five years and were in the process of terminating, she told me that when I walked into the waiting room on the first day, she almost walked out. She couldn't imagine how a young black woman from what she guessed to be a working-class background (she was right) could be helpful to her. She said that she was glad she had stayed.*

Preconceived Ideas and Clinical Intuition

Seasoned practitioners may refer to their preconceived ideas as *clinical intuition*. Clinical intuition is of course much more than just preconceived ideas. The working hypotheses of the skilled practitioner are developed over time by comparing preconceived ideas and feelings with subsequent experience and learning. However, clinicians must always recognize that, at times, preconceived ideas and clinical intuition may interfere with the ability to be genuinely open to the client's story. In Chapter 7, we will discuss the use of clinical intuition and hypothesis building in ongoing work with clients.

Getting Ready

Students have often wondered about the reasoning behind the "50-minute hour"—why the clinical hour is often reduced to 45 or 50 minutes. Although many clinicians do not see clients for an hour, they still try to reserve a space between clients or engagements for a number of reasons: to jot down notes from the last meeting, to return phone calls, to consult with colleagues, to provide an intellectual and emotional space between the last experience and the one to come, to refresh themselves between visits, and to prepare for meeting with the next client. When clinicians are meeting with clients outside of agency settings, they may use travel time for many of these purposes.

Attending to Self

Before the actual meeting with the client, experienced clinicians prepare for the meeting in a number of helpful ways. They try to relax. Some clinicians take a short walk, some get a breath of fresh air, some stretch, and others meditate to get into a *quiet state of readiness*. Clinicians also try to clear away any impinging thoughts or take care of any personal needs that may affect their ability to attend to the incoming client.

> *I had received a message from the clinic secretary that my son had called. He seldom called me at work and I knew that if I didn't call him back I would be sitting with my next Adult Children of Alcoholics (ACOA) group wondering what he wanted. I also knew that if I called I might be a minute or two late, and I had to decide whether I should keep my group waiting for two extra minutes or be distracted for the entire 90-minute group meeting. I returned his call.*

> *It took me a long time to realize that all the cups of coffee I was drinking to help me stay awake briefly stimulated me but then caused me to feel sleepy 15–20 minutes later. I had to learn to avoid caffeine, chocolate, and heavy meals before working with clients.*

> *I realized after much trial and error that I could competently do five sessions in a row with 15-minute breaks in between. But I found at the end of*

the day I couldn't calm down fast enough to get to sleep. Now I do no more than three in a row at one time.

Thinking about the Client

In preparation for meeting with the client for the first time, clinicians should review the information that is available to them. This information may be in the form of client records; test results; referral forms; intake forms; comments from family, friends, or professionals; symptom checklists; and so on. Box 2.1 shows a sample intake form.

Some clinicians prefer not to have any information before meeting with the client for the first time. They prefer to see the client with fresh eyes so that they are not contaminated by colleagues' judgments. Others feel it is essential to read all available material and develop hunches about where to go in the interview.

We believe that, whenever possible, the clinician should review all available material before meeting the client. The client needs to know that the clinician has done his or her homework. If the client has been asked questions, filled out complicated forms, or talked at length with an intake worker, he or she needs to know that the clinician cares enough to become informed about the information the client has provided. We regard this as indispensable preparation for a respectful encounter. At the same time, it is important that the clinician understand that these materials may contain omissions and distortions and that they are only snapshots of the client's life.

It is essential that the clinician not rely solely on such material. Clinicians need to have an *informed openness.* They attempt to sustain this openness by not making judgments too quickly and by recognizing that clients may present themselves very differently in the interview situation, from moment to moment, from interview to interview, and from clinician to clinician. It is especially important to note that people may reveal themselves more deeply

---

B O X 2.1 *Sample Brief Intake Form*

1. Client Name:
2. Address and telephone:
3. Who referred (self, others) and why:
4. Presenting problem(s):
5. Brief description of client and current situation:
6. Previous history with service agency:
7. Any immediate crises or action needing to be taken:
8. Insurance/payment information:
9. Recommendations:

within an unfolding relationship of trust and helpfulness than they do at the beginning of the relationship. Furthermore, people usually react very differently to a person than to a questionnaire.

> *I was about to see a client whom the intake worker described as hostile, suspicious, and guarded. When I met with her she seemed open, comfortable, and self-disclosing. Only later did I learn that she felt very uncomfortable talking with men. The intake worker was a man.*

In addition to reading the available materials, the clinician may need to do some additional reading and preparation. For example, before seeing a client who has just surrendered a child for adoption, the interviewer may want to read some material about birth mothers and the psychological sequelae of surrendering a child. Before meeting with a young woman struggling with her lesbianism, the clinician may need to read about issues of sexual orientation, lesbian identity development, and the effects of sexism and homophobia. Before assessing the needs of a newly arrived Pakistani family, the clinician might want to learn about Pakistan's long civil war and the plight of its refugees.

In addition to preparing for the topic of the interview, clinicians may also need to gather resources to share with the client as appropriate. It is often helpful to create a resource file that can be shared by others. These resource files may include lists of contacts in specific areas, community services for particular populations, or copies of articles from the periodical literature. To help a woman deal with her child's adoption, for example, the clinician may want to know about any groups for birth mothers and get the address of Concerned United Birthparents (CUB). When preparing to work with a lesbian woman, the clinician should find out about lesbian support groups in the community, discover if there is a gay/lesbian health center or women's bookstore, and have a list of books on lesbianism that the client or her family can read.

The available information is used to help the clinician develop *anticipatory empathy*. *Empathy* is the ability to immerse oneself in another's experience and to imagine the feelings that might arise for that person in that situation. (We will have a more thorough discussion of the concept of empathy in Chapter 4.) Shulman (1992) emphasizes a similar process, *preparatory empathy*, involving "tuning in" efforts to "get in touch with the feelings and concerns that the client may bring to the helping encounter" (p. 56).

EXERCISE 2.8 *Anticipatory Empathy*

Client 1: Helena

Helena is a 39-year-old woman who is an active crack cocaine addict. Her 6-month-old baby has just died of pneumonia. To support her habit, she has been working as a prostitute. She has two other children, ages 2 and 3. You are the protective services worker who has been asked to assess whether the two children should be left in her care. Imagine Helena's experience and the feelings that might arise for her in this situation.

> What different things might Helena be feeling about the death of her baby?
>
> What are some of the feelings Helena might have about her other children?
>
> What kind of feelings might Helena have about this upcoming meeting with the protective services worker?

Client 2: Jorge

Jorge is a 45-year-old man who has just lost his job in the defense industry. He has a wife with leukemia and two children—a boy, age 7, and a girl, age 9. He has worked for the plant as a bomb assembly expert for 15 years. He is seeing an employment counselor for help in getting a new job. Imagine Jorge's experience and the feelings that might arise for him in this situation.

> What pressures might Jorge experience at this time in his life?
>
> What are some of the feelings Jorge might have about his wife's leukemia?
>
> What feelings and anxieties might Jorge have about losing his job?
>
> What expectations might Jorge have of the interview or the interviewer?

Thinking about the Interview

Because of the many different reasons for interviewing and the different types of interviews, the following *interview parameters* can help organize thinking in preparation for meeting clients for the first time.

1. What is the purpose of the interview? Why am I meeting with this client? Why do I think the client is meeting with me? How might the client's ideas about this meeting be different from mine? How much of the purpose is governed by the agency, by the insurance company or funding source, and by the client's or interviewer's own agenda?

2. What are the time constraints on this interview? How long do we have to meet today?

3. How long do we have to work together? Is this a time-limited or an open-ended contract?

4. What resources are available to the clinician and the client? What other supports does the agency have? Does the client have extended family, friends, or others available to help?

5. Are there any procedural requirements, such as forms to fill out, fees to negotiate, discussion of confidentiality, permission releases?

6. What would be desired outcomes of today's meeting? What do we hope to get done?

Each of these questions is important in helping focus the interview. For example, a clinician meeting with a client for a brief 10-minute session may spend little time exploring the details of the client's developmental history. In an agency that requires that an intake form be completed at the end of the interview, a clinician will want to be sure to gather all information necessary to complete that task. If the purpose of the meeting is to evaluate a third-grader's readiness for special education classes, a clinician may focus on the child's competencies and areas that need remediation.

In addition to thinking about the tasks of the interview, each clinician will develop a sort of mantra of reminders, or *watchwords,* that are particularly important to keep in mind during the interview. These may be simple things, such as reminders about attending behaviors like "Keep good eye contact," "Relax," or "Be honest when you don't know something."

As an interviewer seasons with experience, education, and supervision, these beginning reminders will become second nature, replaced by watchwords about specific relational dynamics or complexities of interview techniques. For example, a clinician who has been working with a family for a while may have to remind herself before the next interview: "You know how anxious you get when this family argues. Remember to stay out of the fray." Another clinician, approaching an interview with a client who is slow to speak, may say to himself, "Her mother puts words in her mouth, so leave some pauses for her to initiate talking."

Usually watchwords develop out of supervision, from reading the professional literature, or from direct observation of colleagues at work. Watchwords are used to promote careful attentiveness and responsiveness, rather than to admonish or punish.

> As a new interviewer, I always felt that I needed to talk or do something when pauses or uncertainties arose in the interview. I still remember a piece of advice a supervisor gave me way back in 1969: "When in doubt, butt out."

But sometimes words aren't necessary. An image can replace words as a mantra.

> Sometimes as I prepare to see a client for the first time, I imagine that as I'm sitting in the room with the client, my team is sitting behind me with their hands on my shoulder. That helps me remember that I'm not alone in the work that I'm doing.

Although we have been talking about how clinicians prepare for the first meeting with a client, we feel that this process of getting ready—attending to yourself, to the client, and to the interview—should occur before *all* interviews.

Preparation for subsequent interviews differs little from preparing for the first interview: the goals are to create a calm state of mind, screen out intrusions, and prepare for the client by attuning to his or her particular style, circumstances, and focal content of prior sessions. Notes about previous meetings are reviewed, attending to themes, emphases, or notable interview

CLIP 2.2
Getting Ready

exchanges that may need revisiting in the next or subsequent sessions. Careful attention is given to the ongoing process and the clinician-client relationship (see Chapter 9).

Greeting and Welcoming

The interview begins when the clinician greets the client. Clients may have some preconceived ideas before meeting the clinician. Later they may say that they began to have strong positive or negative feelings about the clinician based on the clinician's manner of speaking when he or she called to set a meeting, or on the promptness with which the clinician responded to an urgent walk-in request to be seen, or even on their accumulated feelings about helping professionals in general.

The Agency as Representative

It is often the agency that first greets the client. Clinicians should spend time conferring with colleagues about how to create a warm and welcoming entry area appropriate for the cultures the agency serves. Where possible, reading materials, pictures, and background music should reflect the local diversity of tastes and interests. While waiting, clients may have the opportunity to observe clinicians as they interact with agency personnel and with other clients, and these observations may color the client's feelings about the agency and the staff. Thus, it is important that staff members be aware of their demeanor and behavior at all times. Time spent in waiting areas also allows clients a first impression of the degree to which the staff and setting are or are not representative of their own ethnicity, culture, and language group.

Public Areas

Agency personnel, forms, and public waiting areas can be intimidating. In addition, public areas present unique problems for the interviewer in maintaining professionalism and confidentiality. While most clinicians enter the waiting area and call out the client's name, clinicians should be aware that this may compromise confidentiality. An alternative might be for the clinician to announce his or her own name, rather than the client's. For example, a clinician would announce, "I'm Kalana Johnson."

What's in a Name?

Styles of address differ from culture to culture, locale to locale, and person to person. In some agencies, informality dictates that clients and staff alike are called by first names; in others, more formality and hierarchy are observed. It is important that, at the outset of contact, clients and clinicians discuss the names by which each prefers to be addressed.

> *In my internship at an outpatient unit, we were taught to call our clients by their last names, like Mrs. Huggins or Mr. Ward, as a sign of respect. So I was shocked when I transferred to another outpatient unit and heard my supervisor call her adult client "Billy." She explained that this was the way they did things there. She said it reflected a more laid-back, intimate style. Now I notice that I sometimes call people by their first names, and sometimes by their last. It depends on the situation and what the client and I work out together.*

> *As a geriatric social worker, I have heard many complaints from older women patients who resent being called by their first names by people who don't know them. One woman told me: "It felt disrespectful when, the first time we met, this young boy half my age asked, 'How are you, Bernice?' He didn't ask me what I wanted to be called. I got him back. I said, 'Not bad, Tom.' I read his name from his name badge. He was surprised that I called him by his first name. He was the doctor and wasn't used to this."*

Some clients may anglicize their first or family names because they feel that their names may be too difficult for others to pronounce, to avoid discrimination based on ethnicity, or to "fit in" with the mainstream culture. Clinicians should always take the time to learn the pronunciation of clients' names. The whole idea of first and family names has different meanings in different cultures.

> (I)n most Asian countries, women keep their own family surname when they marry, even though they may often be referred to as the "mother of X" or the "wife of X" in their mother tongue. Do not assume, therefore, that the wife of Mr. "X" will be Mrs. "X." You will also find that some women have encountered so much confusion on the part of U.S. government agencies or other social agencies that they have started using their husbands' last names. And even if an Asian woman does use her husband's name, the therapist should find out if it is a true choice or just a way of avoiding lengthy explanations to agency personnel. For example, you could say, "I know you use Mrs.'X' with your son's teachers but your own name is Mrs. 'Y.' Which would you prefer me to use?"(Chao, 1992, p. 167)

Christine Chao goes on to state, "Refugees . . . have given up everything they once knew; unless it is their choice, they should not be made to give up their names" (1992, p. 168). No one should be made to give up his or her name. Regardless of the formality or informality of the culture or setting, it is important for the clinician to be respectful of clients' wishes. Clients' preferences should dictate how they are addressed.

⊙⊙ CLIP 2.3
Greeting and
Welcoming

EXERCISE 2.9 *Names*

Remember a time when someone called you by your first name and it felt strange to you. In what circumstances do you like to be called by your first name? When do you prefer to be called Mr.? Ms.? What other appellations may be appropriate (for example, Señor, Madam, Reverend)? Do you have a nickname? Who calls you by that name? In what circumstances do you like to be called by your nickname? When would it feel odd?

Think about the professionals with whom you interact. Notice what they call you and what you call them. What did you learn from your observations? In the future, when would you call clients by their first names and when would you call them by their last names? Would you ever call clients by their nicknames?

Opening Lines

Wherever the interview takes place—in the office, at home, on the street—there are a number of helpful ways to begin. Factors that influence the opening style include the meeting location, people present, motivation of all participants, purpose of the meeting, and time available. Cultural styles are also important to take into account, as some clients may need a more informal period of social exchange at the beginning of the interview to assess the clinician's skill and authenticity, whereas others may prefer a more formal expert-consultee approach (Pinderhughes, 1989).

EXERCISE 2.10 *Opening Lines*

You're a counseling intern at a community mental health center. You're about to meet Rich Navic, a 44-year-old depressed man about whom you have no other information. In your journal, write four or five opening lines you might use with him.

Participants, Roles, Tasks, and Time

After a friendly greeting, the interviewer usually begins by acknowledging the names and roles of all present and reviewing either the initial request for help or the reason for the interview. The clinician should use clear language, avoiding professional jargon, and should clarify his or her role by giving examples of the types of help he or she can provide. Many clients may not know that, in addition to counseling, clinicians can also provide testing and evaluation. They may serve as teachers and trainers, advocates for services, links to other staff, conflict mediators, and so on.

The clinician makes sure to clarify the amount of time available for the initial meeting, as well as the total number of sessions available to the client, so that participants can ready themselves psychologically for time-sensitive conversation. Usually these issues are all briefly addressed in the first moments of the interview. How the clinician begins the interview may reflect a number of factors, including values, personal style, intent, or goals.

Examples

"I'm the social work intern on the team, Ngo Diap. I meet with all patients' families to find out how the transplant process has affected everyone. We know how hard and complicated it can be. I also want to talk with you about how to manage when Tim comes home. We have 40 minutes to meet today, and we can meet for an additional two sessions before Tim's discharge. I can also help arrange for VNA and home PT when Tim comes home. You might also be interested in our Wednesday night family group . . . I could tell you about that later, if you like."

"I understand you wanted to speak to someone about your divorce. I'm a counseling intern here at the center, and I'd be happy to meet with you to see whether I could be of assistance. We have 50 minutes to meet today."

"Thank you for letting me come out to see you, Señora Ramirez. As I said over the phone, I'm the psychologist at Centro Hispano Well-Baby Clinic and I wanted to talk with you about getting Carmelita ready to go to preschool. If it's okay with you, I can stay for about 45 minutes."

Confidentiality and Its Limits

In the opening lines, it is important for the clinician to share with clients how the information they provide will be used. The clinician must also discuss confidentiality and its limits, lest the client reveal information before understanding its possible consequences. Many agencies have specific handouts that directly address confidentiality and its limits. Box 2.2 contains a sample confidentiality statement.

Clinicians are mandated to break confidentiality if they determine that potential for harm of the following types exists: (1) the client is at risk for harming self or others, (2) there is possible abuse or neglect of children, or (3) there is possible abuse of the elderly or disabled. Clinicians may also be forced to testify in certain legal proceedings, such as at a custody hearing or if the clinician is conducting a court-ordered evaluation before a possible criminal trial. If the client sues a clinician, the clinician may use client materials in his or her defense. Furthermore, insurance companies or quality-assurance reviewers may require information in order to pay claims. However, in such cases, the clinician is careful to limit the amount of information that is disclosed, often disclosing only the diagnosis and dates

Massachusetts law requires that I provide you with the following information concerning confidentiality at the initiation of our professional contract. It is important that you understand these issues as we begin our work together. Please review this material carefully so we may discuss any questions or concerns.

In general, the confidentiality of all communications between a client and a clinician is protected by law, and I can only release information about our work to others with your written permission. There are a number of exceptions.

I will ask you to sign this as an indication that you have read and understood the following points, and that we have had an opportunity to discuss any confusion you have about them.

Situations in Which There Is Potential Harm to You or Others

There are some situations in which I am legally required to take action to protect others from harm, even though that requires revealing some information about a client. These situations have rarely arisen. Should such a situation occur, I will make every effort to fully discuss the situation with the client before taking any action.

If I believe that a child, an older person, or a person with a disability is being abused, I must file a report with the appropriate state agency. If a client reveals information that constitutes physician misconduct, I am required to report the physician to the state medical board; however, I will not reveal the client's name or give any information that would allow the client to be identified unless she/he agrees to it.

If I believe that a client is threatening serious bodily harm to another person, I am required to take protective actions, which may include notifying the potential victim, notifying the police, or seeking the client's hospitalization. If a client threatens to harm self, I may be required to seek hospitalization or to contact family members or others who can help provide protection.

Professional Records

I am required to keep appropriate records. Because these records may contain information which can be misinterpreted by a nonclinician, it is my general policy to allow a desirous client to review them only in my presence after the matter has been fully discussed and where both agree that such a review would not interfere with the service. If I decide that reviewing the records would be emotionally damaging, I will be happy to forward a summary to the client's designee.

Professional Consultations

I may occasionally find it helpful to consult with professional colleagues to enhance the services that I am able to provide my clients. In these consultations, I make every effort to avoid revealing the identity of my client. The consultant is also legally bound to keep the information confidential.

Unless there is a specific clinical reason to do so, I will not inform you that these consultations are taking place.

Insurance Reimbursement

If you expect to receive insurance (third party) reimbursement, be aware that I am required to provide certain information. This information includes clinical diagnosis and in some cases a plan/summary. Clients are entitled to receive a summary of these records, unless I believe that the information would be emotionally damaging. In those cases, the summary can be given to the client's designee. If clients are concerned about the policies of their insurance company, they should check with the appropriate resource before any insurance forms are submitted. The client has the option of not using insurance and paying directly, thereby not creating a record outside this office.

Collection of Overdue Accounts

If a client's account is overdue, and suitable arrangements for payment have not been agreed to, I have the option of using legal means to secure payment. Unless questions are raised about the quality of services I have provided, the only information which will be released will be the client's name, the nature of the services, dates of service, and other relevant financial data.

Legal Proceedings

In most judicial proceedings, clients have the right to prevent me from providing any information about them. However, in child custody proceedings, adoption proceedings, and proceedings in which the client's emotional condition is an important element, a judge may require my testimony if he/she determines that resolution of the issues before him/her require it. Testimony may also be ordered in (1) a legal proceeding relating to psychiatric hospitalization; (2) in malpractice and disciplinary proceedings brought against me; (3) court-ordered psychological evaluations; and (4) certain legal cases where the client has died.

I have read this statement about confidentiality and have had an opportunity to discuss any confusion I have about it with my clinician. I understand that I may discuss any concerns about it with my clinician at any time.

_____   _____
Client Signature   Client Name (Please print)

_____   _____
Clinician Signature   Clinician Name (Please print)

_____
Date

Source: Contributed by R. Rasi.

of service. When clinicians receive supervision or consultation from other professionals, they may discuss their clients, but they are careful to avoid disclosing any information that would reveal the client's identity. Some agencies have specific limits on confidentiality—a school may require that clinicians report all drug usage, for example. Since most clients believe that whatever they tell a clinician is strictly confidential (Miller & Thelen, 1986), the clinician must inform the client in advance of the limits of confidentiality.

Examples

"Mrs. Franz, our conversation today is private except that counselors are mandated to disclose information if they feel that the client is a danger to herself or others. I also know that your insurance company is going to want to know your diagnosis and the number and length of visits."

"Most people think that what they tell a social worker is totally confidential. However, we are evaluating your family to decide if your son should live with you or your husband after the divorce. Since we have been asked to do this evaluation for the court, you should know that whatever you tell me can be shared with the judge and with the other lawyers involved in the case."

"Julie, an exception to the confidentiality of our meeting is that, as an intern, I review with my supervisor my conversations with clients to make sure I'm giving you the very best service. Do you have any questions about what I've said about confidentiality?"

Client Rights and Responsibilities

Many agencies and clinicians have developed a list of clients' rights and responsibilities: for example, the right to see one's record upon request; the right to receive information about the range of available treatments; the right to be treated with respect. Frequently, information regarding confidentiality and clients' rights is posted in waiting areas or is available as handouts. However, the clinician should review these issues directly with clients to be sure they are understood. Box 2.3 contains a sample client agreement that spells out client rights.

Focal Opening Lines

Focal opening lines offer an initial framework or guidelines that are especially helpful when clients are new to talking with a professional or when they are feeling confused, overwhelmed, or scattered. Theses guidelines lend structure to the process without foreclosing client contributions to the direction of the interview. Structure and guidance are also crucial when time is limited and focus and roles need to be developed without delay. For the case

BOX 2.3 *Principles of Care*

Part of our obligation to our clients is to inform them of the Principles of Care under which we operate:

1. As the person(s) served by _____ , you have the right to a high standard of care.

2. You have the right to be treated with courtesy, respect, and dignity.

3. You should be informed about various services offered and the process by which the decision is reached as to which of these services is/are most helpful to you.

4. You may request at any time to know who is responsible for the program that is providing you service and how he/she may be contacted.

5. You have the right to ask about the relevant qualifications of the people who are helping you.

6. You have the right to review your record. You may exercise this right providing a written request to review your record, together with your reasons, to the director of the program which is providing you with services.

7. You and your clinician should review your treatment plan periodically. You have the right to ask your clinician or the program director for a reevaluation or consultation by another clinician. This may be at your own expense.

8. If a medication is prescribed by a physician, you should be informed as to what the medication is, why it is being prescribed, what it is expected to change, and common side effects.

9. If research is being conducted or any experimental procedure is being recommended, you will be informed before being involved in any such study-procedure. You have the right to refuse to participate in any research without jeopardizing your care here. Your written consent must be given before you would be included in any research or experimental procedure.

10. If you wish to be referred to another agency or to a private practitioner, we will make every effort to refer you to the most appropriate resources.

11. You have the right to receive an explanation of the basis by which your fee is set and to ask for a reevaluation of your fee. You have a right to a copy of the bills or statement of charges submitted to any third party.

12. You have the right to receive care in a place free of architectural barriers if you have a limiting physical condition.

_____   _____
Client's Signature   Date   Witness's Signature   Date

_____ Client given copy but did not sign.

_____ Rights explained but client not given copy because _____

_____

examples given on page 46, after routine introductions stating (1) names and roles, (2) reason for meeting, and (3) time available, the clinician may use focal opening lines like the following.

Examples

"Let's review the plans for Tim's return home."

"Tell me about the circumstances that led to the divorce."

"Let's talk about how Carmelita feels about starting preschool."

Still, professionals remain flexible and ready to respond to the unexpected. The clinician is always open to the clients' needs and to making culturally appropriate accommodations.

Example

Clinician: Are you Larry Kwan?

Client: Yes.

Clinician: I'm Gaylord Dunes, the social worker from the New Horizons work training program. I've come to the hospital to meet with you today to discuss what our program could offer you after you leave here. If you want, we can meet down the hall where it's quiet. Then you could tell me what you think and ask any questions about the program.

Client: My brother and uncle are coming to pick me up for my weekend pass at home. Can they listen, too? They are out of work also and our family is suffering from this.

Clinician (recognizing the importance of family in the Asian culture) Of course we can all meet together. I have from 9:00–10:00 free to talk with you and them. Let me just tell the nurse where we'll be so that your family can join us. Maybe there's more I could help with besides employment.

Nondirective Opening Lines

Nondirective opening lines provide less information in order to leave the client greater opportunity to set agenda, pace, focus, and tone. Using nondirective opening lines, the clinician would begin with introductions including names and roles, the reason for meeting, and the time available and then provide only minimal prompting to get things started.

Examples

"I believe you asked to see one of the social workers this morning."

"Where should we start?"

"What would be most helpful to talk about?"

These nondirective openings provide the professional an immediate opportunity to assess client skills in organizing, communicating, and relating to both interviewer and tasks. However, if the interviewer finds that the client is unable to respond to nondirective openings, he or she may need to provide more focus and structure.

◙◙ C L I P **2.4**
Opening Lines

Opening Lines Help Set the Tone

In addition to communicating information, opening lines convey a tone that can have lasting effects on the relationship. Opening lines can communicate warmth, indifference, welcome, aversion, hierarchy, disorganization, comfort, or fear. In Chapter 3 we will discuss how tone is conveyed by means other than just words; in Chapter 9 we will talk about the clinical relationship and its important elements and dynamics.

E X E R C I S E 2.11 *Noting Tone*

Go back to Exercise 2.10 at the beginning of this section. Review the opening lines you wrote in your journal for Rich Navic. Were they focal or nondirective? What tone do you think you conveyed? Record your observations about your style in these opening lines. What would you change about them at this point and why? What complicates openings for you?

Conclusion

Clinical interviewing can occur in a variety of settings. No matter where the interview happens, clinicians carefully prepare for the meeting, getting both the environment and themselves ready for the encounter. The way the clinician greets the client and begins the interview can set the tone for future work. Once the client and clinician have made initial contact, the clinician uses a number of basic skills to establish an empathic relationship to help the client tell his or her story and begin the process of problem solving. In the next chapter we will focus on the basic skills of attending and accurate listening, skills that are essential to all good clinical interviewing.

Suggested Readings

The following readings address home visits.

Hancock, Betsy L., & Pelton, Leroy H. (1989). Home visits: History and functions. *Social Casework, 70,* 21–27.

Hodges, Vanessa G., & Blythe, Betty J. (May, 1992). Improving service delivery to high-risk families: Home-based practice. *Families in Society: Journal of Contemporary Human Services,* pp. 259–265.

Clinician safety is addressed in:

Griffin, William. (1995). Social worker and agency safety. In Richard L. Edwards (Ed.), *Encyclopedia of social work,* (pp. 2293–2305). Washington, DC: National Association of Social Workers.

There are numerous articles on confidentiality. We suggest that you carefully review your professional ethics code and the laws of your state. The following articles may be helpful.

Gustafson, Kathryn, & McNamara, J. Regis. (1987). Confidentiality with minor clients: Issues and guidelines for therapists. *Professional Psychology: Research and Practice, 18,* 503–508.

Miller, David, & Thelen, Mark. (1986). Knowledge and beliefs about confidentiality in psychotherapy. *Professional Psychology: Research and Practice, 17,* 15–19.

Sheeley, V. L., & Herlihy, B. (1986). The ethics of confidentiality and privileged communication. *Journal of Counseling and Human Service Professions, 1,* 141–148.

Critiques of the use of labels and diagnoses can be found in the following sources.

Caplan, Paula. (1996). *And they say you're crazy.* New York: Houghton Mifflin.

Goffman, Erving. (1963). *Stigma: Notes on the management of spoiled identity.* Englewood Cliffs, NJ: Prentice-Hall.

Szasz, Thomas. (1960). The myth of mental illness. *American Psychologist, 15,* 113–118.

Szasz, Thomas. (1993). Curing, coercing, and claims-making: A reply to critics. *British Journal of Psychiatry, 162,* 797–800.

CHAPTER 3

Attending and Listening

Interviews

Interviews are a specific form of conversation, and like all conversations, interviews are mutual—both parties have a stake in the outcome of the conversation. Indeed, dictionary definitions of *interview* include "sight shared by two people" and "a mutual view."

There are many layers of meaning and influence in interviews, only some of them apparent to participant-observers. If we have learned anything from clinical experience, it is that there are multiple realities. Individuals speak, listen, and make meaning from their own unique perspective. Two people may share the same experience and yet each perceive it uniquely. Individual experience and meaning are mediated by such things as age, class, gender, ethnicity, and individual and societal ideologies. However, two people may share similar backgrounds, values, or belief systems but experience and interpret things differently. Therefore, as clinicians go about the task of attending and listening, we need to remember that there is no fixed truth or reality. Clinicians must consider and value multiple perspectives, even though they make our task of attending and listening more complex.

In this chapter we will focus on attending to the verbal and nonverbal content, to the affect that they may signify, and to emergent themes and patterns. In later chapters we will discuss how participants in an interview mutually affect each other.

Focused Attending

It is important for clinicians to create an ambiance of focused attention in which meaningful communication can occur. Clinicians attend in order to listen; they listen in order to understand. Understanding contributes to empathy, and empathy engenders a readiness to respond. Thus, *focused attending* is an essential component of the therapeutic process. Focused attending consists of physical attending and psychological attending.

Psychological Attending

We spoke earlier of the bubble of calm attentiveness the clinician brings to each interview. Much of this calm is the result of (1) psychological readiness and openness to the client; and (2) the clinician's commitment to creating an environment in which other people feel as welcome, appreciated, and heard as possible. *Psychological attending* involves putting aside personal distractions, worries, and self-concerns to give center stage to the client's story. We think of psychological attending as setting up radar to receive the signals the client is sending.

Psychological attending requires both discipline and flexibility. The client's story and demeanor inevitably arouse responses in the clinician that can distract attention from the client's experience. These "blips" on the radar screen need to be noted. As we will discuss in Chapter 9, the clinician's reactions to the client's story will provide important information and should not simply be dismissed as "interference."

Physical Attending

The *posture of attention* is the physical manifestation—literally, the embodiment—of the clinician's interest and openness to the client, to the story, to the relationship, and to the work to be done together. It readies the interviewer to listen.

Egan (1994) describes the components of physical attending using the acronym SOLER:

S—sit squarely

O—open posture

L—lean forward

E—eye contact

R—relax

EXERCISE 3.1 *Physical Attending*

These beginning in-class exercises are designed to not only help you practice basic clinical skills but also to allow you to get to know your fellow students and to begin to develop a relationship with each other. Therefore you are asked to talk about yourself.

In class, divide into groups of four, with each student assigned role A, B, C, or D. Student A talks to Student B about his or her day, why he or she is in the class, or why he or she wants to be a clinician. Student B is to practice attending behaviors, while Students C and D observe and make notes about Student B's attending behaviors. If possible, videotape the interaction and, after getting feedback from Students C and D, watch the video together. Rotate roles until each student has had the opportunity to be both the speaker and the attending listener. Don't worry about what you say; just focus on your physical behaviors.

Record your own thoughts about the exercise in your journal. What did you discover about yourself in the exercise? Note how comfortable or uncomfortable you felt when you both gave and received attention, as well as when you were an observer.

The clinician adopts a posture of attention to communicate presence, interest, and following. In a society characterized by rushing and preoccupation, this type of attention can be a unique experience. For many clients, such attending will feel reassuring, caring, and desirable. For others, however, this close attention between strangers may feel inappropriate, invasive, or threatening.

> *My first job was at a family agency where I was taught the importance of eye contact. When I moved on to work with clients with persistent mental illness, my supervisor told me my gaze was too direct and "hot" for clients with low tolerance for contact, and that I needed to learn to look away and down briefly, without seeming to drift from the subject. I found this one of the hardest things I ever had to learn.*

Furthermore, attending behaviors are *culture-bound*. What is considered attentive in one culture might be offensive in another. We cannot emphasize enough the importance of getting to know the expressive nuances of the cultures and people with whom we work.

> *I was conducting an in-service training for teachers in the local grammar school. One of the Irish Catholic teachers was talking about how disrespectful and stubborn the Vietnamese students were. I asked her to give me an example, and she said: "They never look at me when I talk to them. Even when I tell them to pay attention, they sullenly look away." The Vietnamese translator, who was part of the training, came to see me and told me that for a Vietnamese child to look an adult in the eyes is "like an American child sticking his tongue out at an adult."*

Egan's SOLER description of attending may seem easy to do in an office. But because clinical interviewing may happen in a variety of nonoffice contexts, it is important to think about how to adapt a posture of attending for nonoffice settings. A clinician accompanying a client in a car, bus, or taxi is usually sitting side by side with the client. In such circumstances, a useful way to attend is to look where the client is looking so as to join the client's perspective or position, heightening a sense of connection. In such crowded, side-by-side situations, there may be jostling together and body contact which may feel uncomfortable. It is crucial to remember the *R* in SOLER—to relax and not let the unanticipated create anxiety that distracts from focused attending. We will talk more about issues concerning physical contact in Chapter 10.

In a home visit, the client may move around, carrying out tasks while sharing information and feelings. For example, in visiting with a young mother with kids at home, we may interview in the kitchen while the mother makes formula, folds laundry, or attends to a child's needs. In such situations, the clinician's comfortable repose acts as a pivot for the client's moving about and often has a calming or settling effect. In those situations in which a client feels more comfortable pacing about, entering and leaving the room, or attending to the needs of young children, the clinician's stable presence remains a constant in good attending.

> *I used to interview Janice, a young woman with schizophrenia, in a tiny office on the inpatient unit. She was often not comfortable in close proximity, but I didn't want to talk with her in the dayroom, where others could overhear. I would see her in that little office, but in a different way than I was used to. I would just remain comfortably seated while she paced, walking in and out of the room. Eventually she would relax some and sit down with me briefly. I was surprised by how much she was able to share with me in this sporadic way.*

In group work, family, or team meetings, the interviewer faces the additional challenge of attending to more than one person at the same time. In interview situations where there are multiple participants, the key is *flexible attentiveness*. On occasion the clinician may pan the group, not making extensive or specific eye contact with any one individual. At other times the clinician may make sequential eye contact with each individual, or focus on specific members. It is important to make periodic eye contact with each interview participant, even if eye contact is not returned, conveying our continuous interest in each person.

Clients also have a posture of attention. Their attending or nonattending behaviors affect clinicians in much the same way that clinicians' behaviors affect clients. In our experience, clinicians are more likely to attend to clients who attend to them in an open and welcoming way. Clinicians may become more anxious, stiff, or self-conscious in the presence of clients who the clinician feels are demonstrating hostility, indifference, or nonattending behaviors. Again, the clinician needs to be careful about misinterpreting client behaviors.

E X E R C I S E 3.2 *Nonattending*

Ask a friend to have a conversation with you. Videotape it if you can. After a minute or two of talking, purposefully withdraw your attention—you might look away, look at your watch, cross your arms, or tap your foot. Notice what happens to the conversation. Watch the video together, and ask your friend what it felt like when you stopping attending.

There's no one "right way" to attend. Over time, clinicians learn to communicate attentiveness without rigidly adhering to behavioral guidelines. For example, we can cross our legs, look away, close our eyes, or lean back and still be conveying attentiveness. Moreover, as we get to know our clients better, we adapt our physical attending to their nuances and changing needs.

> *A few years ago I was working with Oscar, a man who had difficulty talking in therapy. He suffered abuse as a child and was unable to share feelings, fearing that if he expressed them, they would not be validated by the clinician. We talked about this and brainstormed how he could feel more comfortable talking with me. In one session, he shared that he thought he might be able to talk to me if I didn't look at him. We tried different ways of arranging things. When I turned my chair around, Oscar could talk more freely, but he missed my facial expressions, and I had a hard time hearing exactly what he was saying. Through trial and error, we discovered that if I just closed my eyes, he was able to open up and share feelings he had never shared before. I think it was the act of letting myself be vulnerable that made it safe enough for him to take a chance. With my eyes closed I felt less secure and found that I had to trust him in a new and challenging way. Emotionally, I joined him in the process of taking a risk, while never leaving my essential role as the therapist. I also discovered that without visual distraction I could tune in to his words in a more deliberate and focused way.*

Some clinicians believe that clearing the mind is a prerequisite for physical attending. Others believe that assuming a posture of physical attending helps clear the mind. In our view, physical and psychological attending are exquisitely intertwined and continuously resonate with one another: the psychological attending enhances the physical attending, which enhances the psychological attending, and so on.

⊙⊙ C L I P 3.1
Attending

Clinical Listening

A major task in any interview situation is to listen. *Clinical listening* is more complicated that just hearing the words the client says. Clinical listening requires focused attention and alertness to everything that is going on in the interview and in the relationship. Clinical listening means that clinicians attend to both verbal and nonverbal communication, listening to what clients say, how they say it, and how they feel about what they say. Clinicians also listen to what clients don't say. We listen for themes and patterns that emerge both during an individual interview and over time. In addition, we listen to the relationship that develops with the client. Equally as important, we listen to our own inner process.

What we listen to—and are able to hear—is shaped by our own experiences, our family, our culture, the media, and the zeitgeist of the times. That's why when a group observes an interview and discusses what happened, each person will have a slightly different take on it. Supervision, process recording, and videotaping are so important to clinical learning because they often pick up what we didn't hear or notice.

> *I remember talking with my supervisor about a client. She asked how the client handled her abortion. I had no idea where this came from. I didn't hear the client say she had an abortion. Then we listened to the tape together and my supervisor pointed out that the client had said she "had a termination."*

What the clinician hears may not be what the client intended. It is possible that the client has unintentionally revealed something. It is also possible that the clinician may have misinterpreted the client's meaning. The factors that may contribute to inaccuracies or distortions in listening include lack of knowledge, lack of experience, cultural bias, defensive filters, and counter-transference. These factors will be discussed in Chapter 4.

Listening to Verbal and Nonverbal Comunication

Nonverbal Communication

People often think of an interview as the words that are spoken between two or more people. It has been suggested, however, that as much as 65% of what is communicated is communicated nonverbally (Birdwhistell, 1970). Nonverbal communication includes physical appearance, body posture, gestures, movements, and facial expressions. Because nonverbal communication can be easily misinterpreted, clinicians need to be extremely careful that they do not misperceive the client's nonverbal communication. It is often helpful for the clinician to observe the nonverbal communication and later check in with the client about its meaning.

EXERCISE 3.3 *Noting Nonverbal Information*

Break up into groups of four. Focus on Person A (who remains silent throughout), and record what information you have about Person A that is communicated nonverbally. Compare your lists. What did you observe? What was the person communicating to you? What were the similarities and differences in what you each observed? Note that you are making assumptions that have to be confirmed or corrected by Person A.

EXERCISE 3.4 *Videotaping a Conversation*

Make a 5-minute videotape in which you have a conversation with a colleague. You can talk about yourselves, about your work, or about experiences of the day. After making the videotape, watch it once with your colleague with the sound on. Note your nonverbal behavior. Watch the tape a second time, without the sound, and again note your nonverbal communication. Did you notice different things? Record in your journal what you have learned.

Appearance. When we meet someone for the first time, we often make assumptions about their gender, race, ethnicity, and class based solely on their physical appearance. However, these assumptions may or may not be accurate. Race and ethnicity are not absolute characteristics, and people are often multiracial and multiethnic (Root, 1990; Spickard, Fong, & Ewalt, 1995). Clinicians also use physical appearance, style of dress, and hygiene as indicators of clients' functioning and their ability to care for themselves at the most basic level. Many intake forms include dress, manner, and bearing as important diagnostic information. Of course, it is always important to take into account personal taste, cultural styles, and the realities of clients' lives. A client who enters the agency without a coat on during a midwinter snowstorm may be demonstrating disorganization and poor judgment—or the client may be poor or was simply unprepared for an unexpected storm.

Body posture. The body often reveals a lot about mental and emotional states. When people are depressed, they may slouch or walk with their shoulders hunched. When people are happy, they may stand erect and have a "spring in their step." The connection between body and feeling states has received increased attention from both the psychological and medical fields (Benson & Klipper, 1976; Borysenko, 1988; Lowen, 1975). Will Schutz (1967) notes that the connection between body and feelings is captured in North American colloquialisms such as "lump in the throat," "butterflies in the stomach," "hair-raising," "green with envy," "pain in the neck," and "heartsick." Other cultures also note the connection between mind and body through their choice of words. Carla Bradshaw (1994) notes that Asians and Asian Americans have a strong tendency to somatize emotional distress. Therefore, the clinician must carefully attend to physical complaints, according them their "rightful" place in the clinical encounter.

> *I was working with a Vietnamese woman who came to see me complaining of headaches and wanting to know how to get rid of them. Being Vietnamese American myself, I knew that her headaches were a way of her telling me about the emotional pain she felt. I told her that I often got headaches when I was worried about my family, and she began to talk about*

what kinds of things were going on in her head that may have been causing her pain.

One of the things we pay attention to in clients is the range and fluidity of their body motion. As we get to know our clients, we can observe from the way they use their bodies how they may be feeling. If the presence of disease or disability limits the client's range of motion or use of the body, the clinician will of course be sensitive to other nuances of expression.

Gestures. Many people gesture when they communicate. People may tap their feet, flail their arms, shrug their shoulders, clench their fists, or wring their hands. Each person has a unique style of gesturing, and the clinician needs to become familiar with each client's style and learn what each client's particular gestures express.

> *Whenever Shanika was nervous, she would jiggle her hands by her chair. Toni would play with the top button of her blouse, whereas Rob would rub his left wrist with his right thumb, and Concetta would stare up at the clock as though wishing the time to hurry by.*

Facial expression. Participants in conversations tend to pay a lot of attention to the face and facial expressions. People may smile, frown, wrinkle their foreheads, raise their eyebrows, or purse their lips at particular moments in the conversation. Again, it is imperative to be careful that we do not overgeneralize or make culturally inappropriate interpretations. Clinicians should also take note of sudden changes in facial coloration or the stress-induced development of hives or facial tics.

> *I was working with a co-therapist, seeing a heterosexual couple. At the end of the interview, my colleague expressed concern about the wife's emotional state. I hadn't noticed anything particular, so I asked why he was concerned. He said that her arm broke out in hives when we were talking about how they handled anger in the family. Because of where I was seated, I had missed the blotches, which he spotted.*

It has been said that the eyes are "the windows to the soul." Eyes may tear with sadness, widen with surprise, or narrow with suspicion. Eyes can also reflect organic problems; for example, pupil dilation may signal a tumor or drug use. People convey a lot with their eyes, which may be one reason that they sometimes close their eyes or look down and away in order not to reveal their inner experiences. Clinicians often put a lot of significance on eye contact, noting when eye contact is made or broken. As always, clinicians must be sensitive to cultural and idiosyncratic differences in making and interpreting eye contact. For example, Teresa La Fromboise, Joan Saks Berman, and Balvindar Sohi (1994) recount the Navajo myth about a monster called He-Who-Kills-With-His-Eyes, which they believe "teaches Navajo children to avert their eyes to avoid bringing harm to others" (p. 32).

Clinician nonverbal communication.   It goes without saying that clinicians also communicate nonverbally through dress, manner, bearing, facial expression, eye contact, gestures, and so on. Clinicians always need to be self-aware in interviews with clients. Because of early abuse or trauma and because of the perceived power inherent in the clinician's role, many clients may be highly sensitized to nonverbal changes in demeanor. They will be scanning us all the time. A continuing task of clinical learning is to increase awareness of what we might be conveying at any given moment. We should think about what we want to communicate nonverbally and, whenever we can, have ourselves videotaped in clinical interactions so as to increase awareness of our styles and mannerisms.

> *I remember the first time I ever watched myself on videotape. I was shocked to discover that throughout the entire interview I kept nodding my head. I looked like one of those dolls you see in the back of a car, whose head keeps bobbing up and down in a spring. I still have to work on only nodding occasionally.*

Our facial expressions are often a focus of client attention. While we may be paying attention to our gross body movements—posture, gestures, and head nods—it may be harder to be aware of the subtleties of our facial expression.

EXERCISE 3.5   *Mirror, Mirror, on the Wall*

Spend 5 minutes in front a video camera acquainting yourself with the subtleties of your facial expression. If you do not have access to a video camera, use a mirror. Relax your face completely, noting what your face looks and feels like when you are completely at rest. See how it looks and feels when you are happy, when you are unhappy, when you want to look inquisitive, or show disapproval. Record in your journal what you learned by observing your facial expressions.

When looking at your facial expressions in Exercise 3.5, you were trying to become aware of one facial expression at a time. However, when interacting with others, facial expressions are constantly changing. In the previous exercise, you may have smiled to convey happiness; however, you may be unaware that you also smile when you are nervous. It is helpful to have an opportunity to look at your facial expressions in videotaped conversations. We are not always conscious of shifts in expression or of the meaning that other people may attribute to our facial expressions. Clients are particularly attuned to the facial expressions of the clinician. That's why in Exercise 3.6 you are asked to both observe your own facial expressions during a conversation and get feedback from others.

CLIP 3.2
Nonverbal
Communication

E X E R C I S E 3.6 *Facing the Camera*

Break up into pairs and have a 10-minute conversation. For the first 5 minutes, Person A is the "face" and the camera is focused in a close-up of Person A's face. For the second 5 minutes, the camera focuses on Person B's face. You may talk about any topic that you wish. After making the video, watch it with two other colleagues and get feedback about your facial expression. What did you learn about yourself and about others?

Verbal Communication

Much of what happens in the interview consists of what the client says and what the clinician says. The clinician listens to both the words the client says and the ways in which she or he says them. It is amazing how difficult it can be to recall exactly what another person has said.

E X E R C I S E 3.7 *Repeat After Me*

Break up into groups of four and assign roles A, B, C, and D. Person A is the speaker and Person B is the "parroter." Persons C and D attempt to record verbatim what Person A says so that they can correct Person B's accuracy. Videotaping the conversation will give you much more accuracy.

Person A begins by saying one sentence. Person B repeats the sentence exactly, using the formula "You said '_____.' " Persons C and D report on the accuracy and then watch the video to check it. Since clients seldom talk in single sentences, Person A then says two additional sentences, which Person B parrots. Finally, Person A says three additional sentences that Person B attempts to parrot. This is harder than it seems. By watching the video, you can see how much you miss when someone talks to you. Discuss what factors may get in the way of your ability to remember.

Of course, clinicians do not often parrot back to clients their exact words. It is important, however, to pay careful attention to the specific words that clients use, as these words may have particular and crucial meanings to explore further.

I remember working with a female client who told me about a disagreement she had had with her husband. I said, "So you and Jacques had an argument about money." She said, "No, we had a fight." When I asked her to clarify, she explained that they had come to physical blows. For her, argument *implied disagreement, while* fight *implied physical contact. I learned to listen carefully for when she used the word* argument *and when she used the word* fight.

Just as words can be a vehicle of communication, they can also be a barrier. Clients (and clinicians) can use a barrage of words to distract from topics they wish to avoid. They can also use specialized language or in-group jargon to distance or demean. Beginning clinicians often feel as though they have to pretend that they understand what the client has said, even when they don't. (This can also happen in supervision or team meetings, when others are using jargon or affecting superior knowledge.) Beginners often hope that if they just wait and listen, they'll catch on. By doing so, they may make faulty assumptions. Even when clinicians honestly think they understand the words clients are using, they may be wrong.

> *In a supervision class, a student from Romania reported a conversation she had with a British patient from a nearby state hospital. The patient told the student that he got "really pissed" the night before. Because she was unfamiliar with American colloquialisms, she asked him what he meant by "pissed." Since I'd read the student's journal and knew what the patient had answered, I asked the other members of the class what they thought he meant. They all assumed he meant he was angry. I then asked the student; she reported that the patient said it meant he had gotten very drunk. In this instance, the student's unfamiliarity with American jargon gave her the permission to ask what the client meant. If she'd understood jargon better, she might not have asked and thus might have misunderstood the client's words.*

Paralinguistic Cues

How clients (and clinicians) say things is as important as what they say. The tone and pitch of voice, rate of speech, emphasis, stuttering, sighing, and other vocalizations are a crucial part of verbal conversation (Hall, 1959; Pope, 1979). There are cultural differences in paralinguistic communications. For example, Terry Tafoya (1989) discusses the sociolinguistic concept of "pause time" and notes that Native Americans often leave a longer space between the ending of one person's statement and the beginning of another's.

EXERCISE 3.8 *Paralinguistic Cues*

Practice saying the following sentences with different tones, speed, emphasis, and other paralinguistic cues. Demonstrate how the same words can convey different meanings.

Are there any other solutions to this problem?

Tomorrow is Christmas.

Mrs. Jorgensen wants me to come to school tomorrow morning at 7 A.M.

Exercise 3.5 helped you see how you look to clients. Allen Ivey (1994) offers a similar exercise in getting feedback about how you sound.

EXERCISE 3.9 *Vocal Qualities*

In class, divide into groups of four. Use a videotape or audiotape for the exercise, if possible. One person becomes the speaker, who tells the others a story in a normal tone of voice while the others listen for vocal qualities. Observers will note their reactions to the speaker's volume, speech rate, and regional or ethnic accent and will provide feedback. Rotate roles until everyone has been the speaker and received feedback. In your journals, record what you have learned.

Source: Adapted from Ivey, 1994, p. 30.

Silence

Silence is a form of communication, not just a blank space between communications. Clinicians attend to silence, noting when it occurs, its frequency or patterning, and any affective coloration that may accompany it. For example, a client may fall silent after talking about the death of his mother. Another client may be silent because she doesn't know how to proceed. A third client may sit silently because of lack of trust. Often, clues about the meaning of silence may be gleaned from the content immediately preceding the silence and the nonverbal communication that may occur during the silence.

Metacommunication

Metacommunication refers to messages about the message, as well as messages about the relationship between the communicators (Bateson, Jackson, & Weakland, 1963). Clinicians attend to the relationship between the verbal and the nonverbal cues and to changes in the client's style of communication. Sometimes verbal, nonverbal, and paralinguistic cues are concordant, as when an angry person says "I'm mad!" in a loud voice while hitting the table with his or her fist. Sometimes they are discordant, as when a client timidly says in a low voice while looking away, "I know I can get that job." Clinicians look for the ways in which the verbal and nonverbal cues do or do not match, paying careful attention to discrepancies, as these may signal ambivalence or important areas for further exploration. Some clinicians think that the nonverbal aspect is more important—that nonverbal communications reveal the client's "true feelings." We think it is important that clinicians take note of any discrepancies, whatever form they take, without making too facile an interpretation.

It is also important to note any changes in style or manner of communication; for example, when a usually animated speaker becomes quiet and soft-spoken or when a client who is usually very attentive looks away. Taking careful note of nuances and alterations of style applies to the clinician's communications also.

EXERCISE 3.10 *Communication Discrepancies*

Two people go to the center of the room to talk about what it is like to try to make friends when they are all newcomers to a training program. Half the class should take notes on Person A and the other half on Person B. Record their verbal and nonverbal behaviors and whether they are concordant or discordant. Share your observations with each other. Note the variations in what observers report.

Listening to Clients' Stories

Clinicians listen to verbal and nonverbal communications. But what are we listening for? We listen for the behaviors, feelings, thoughts, context, and meanings that constitute the client's story.

Behaviors

Behaviors refer to the actions people take in their lives in response to other people, ideas, impulses, feelings, events, or outside stimuli. Clinicians listen for those behaviors that are effective and that promote connection with others, as well as for behaviors that appear to be self-defeating. We listen for the extent to which behaviors are impulsive or well thought out, and the degree to which they are elective or driven by inner compulsions, organic factors, external demands, or other people. We also listen for how flexible or rigid behaviors are, and how rational or irrational they appear to be within each client's particular situation. We note the effect that people's behaviors have on each other.

Clinicians need to make sure that they accurately understand the meaning of the client's behavior. The clinician may make faulty interpretations of the client's behavior, particularly when the clinician's cultural background is different from the client's. For example, a clinician might regard a client's tearing at her clothes and falling to the floor upon news of a death in her family as out of control behavior, rather than as a form of culturally appropriate grieving.

Feelings or Affect

We listen for the variety and range of feelings (such as sadness, surprise, anger, happiness, anxiety). We note the frequency of each feeling state and which feelings seem to predominate. We listen for the behaviors clients use to express their feelings (for example, whether anger is expressed through sulking, silence, withdrawing, hitting, threatening, self-harming, throwing objects, or direct angry statements). We listen to learn whether clients believe they can modulate their feelings or whether they feel overwhelmed by them.

Thoughts and Cognitive Style

Clinicians listen for clients' thoughts and cognitive style. We listen to what our clients think about—people, things, events, feelings. We listen for the degree to which clients seem to think about their inner lives, external events, or their connections with others. We listen for the degree to which their thoughts are positive and hopeful, or negative and pessimistic. We also listen to how they think. We listen for how clients handle new thoughts or conflicting ideas. Is their thinking flexible? Do they think in an organized and rational way? Do their thoughts jump from one topic to another? Do they feel obsessed by particular thoughts? Do they think concretely or abstractly? Can they express their thoughts openly and directly?

Context

Clinicians listen for the context in which their clients' stories take place. The *immediate context* refers to the client's personal circumstances: things that may be happening in regard to current living arrangements, family and social relationships, economic status, personal history, health, and the particulars of the client's daily life. For example, it would be important for the clinician to know that a woman's mother was just diagnosed with Alzheimer's disease, which might contribute to the client's feeling of depression. In another instance, it would help if a white clinician appreciated that racial discrimination and being passed over for a promotion might contribute significantly to the suspiciousness and distrust shown by an African American client.

The immediate context is always embedded in a *larger systems context*, including economic, social, political, and religious forces and institutions and even global relationships and developments. For example, a woman may be sad and anxious because she has lost her job (immediate context). She lost her job because she couldn't get reliable day care and often had to leave work to take care of her 2-year-old daughter (immediate context). One of the reasons she couldn't find reliable day care was that, as a result of increased defense spending, Congress had cut federal subsidies to day care providers so there are now fewer providers in her neighborhood (larger systems context).

> *A number of years ago, I was working with a family in which the parents reported that their daughter was having nightmares about nuclear war. Although my first instinct was to wonder about what "wars" were happening in her "nuclear" family, I also had to consider the fact that she had just seen the movie* The Day After, *a dramatic representation of the consequences of nuclear war.*

Similarly, the immediate context can affect larger systems. In the preceding example of the woman who lost her job, the woman could organize her neighbors and colleagues (immediate context) to write Congress to get federal funding for day care programs reinstated (larger systems context). The clinician listens to how the immediate and larger systems contexts of our clients' lives resonate with and mutually influence each other.

EXERCISE 3.11 *Immediate and Larger Systems Contexts*

In your journal, identify some of the larger systems contexts that currently affect your feelings, thoughts, and behaviors. Identify some of the more immediate contexts affecting you. Notice any interrelationships between immediate and larger systems contexts in your life. It is probably easier to see the ways in which larger systems contexts affect your personal circumstances, but remember to think about how your personal situation and actions may also affect larger systems contexts.

Meaning

It is imperative that we listen for the ways clients interpret or make sense of their situations, feelings, behaviors, and thoughts. How do they understand the way things have evolved in their lives? How do they understand current events? For example, what meaning does a wife give to her husband's working late three or four nights a week? Does it mean he is working hard to provide for her and the children? Does it mean she's lost her attractiveness? Does it mean his boss is overly demanding? Does it mean he is having an affair?

Clinicians listen to whether clients are open to alternative meanings and whether they can hold multiple perspectives simultaneously. For example, can a father understand that although to him his attention to his son's school-work each night means that he cares, to his son the father's inquiries may mean that he is being critical?

Clearly, the components of stories are neither discrete nor static. Thoughts, feelings, behaviors, relationships, events, and meanings constantly interweave and influence each other, and clinicians are always listening for these interactions and influences.

Emphasis

Different theoretical models emphasize different components of the client's story. Behaviorists will emphasize behaviors and their reinforcing consequences. Psychodynamic theorists will focus on client history and development. Cognitive theorists will focus on thoughts as causes of feelings and behaviors. Existential and narrative theorists will emphasize client meaning making. Expressive theorists will focus on feelings. Systemic and family theorists will pay great attention to the context of behaviors and relationships.

In addition, as we discussed in Chapter 2, agencies will present the clinician with information-gathering tools and formats that may shape what the clinician attends to and listens for. For example, evaluation forms for brief treatment increasingly focus on behaviors and behavior change.

At the mental health center, my supervisors were always asking me about how my clients felt and how they expressed their feelings in different situa-

tions by saying things like, "So how did she feel about that?" When I went to work at a health maintenance organization (HMO), my supervisor asked about behaviors a lot more: "What did he do then?" "Is this a pattern or a one-time thing?" I noticed a subtle change in what I focused on with clients. At the mental health center, my clients used to go through boxes of Kleenex; now I notice that my clients hardly use any!

It's not just theories, agencies, or trends that influence how we listen to the different components of the client's story. We recognize that clinicians will sometimes listen more for behaviors, sometimes more for feelings, sometimes more for events. At other times they will listen more for meanings. This flexibility is natural and essential, and it should be guided by client priorities and goals.

EXERCISE 3.12 *Listening to the Story*

Break up into groups of four. Assign roles A, B, C, and D. If possible, videotape or audiotape the conversations. Person A is the first Speaker and Person B the first Listener. Persons C and D are the first Observers. The Speaker talks to the Listener for 2 minutes and describes an event in his or her life. The Listener can respond to the Speaker in any way. Observers take notes on what the Speaker is communicating. After 2 minutes, the Listener should try to report what the Speaker said about his or her context, thoughts, feeling, behaviors, and meanings. The Speaker can correct the Listener, and the Observers can point out any omissions. Watch the video for further feedback. Take 2 minutes to debrief, noting what kinds of things were easier to hear and remember. Rotate roles until everyone has had a chance to be Speaker and Listener. Record in your journal what you learned.

It is important to remember the client's story—both the general message, and the details and nuances. We listen carefully in order to remember what clients have shared with us. We listen to understand, and, with the help of supervision, we use this understanding to develop an appropriate focus, empathy, hunches, and plans. Because clients tell us so much in a short period of time, process notes, audiocassettes, videotapes, and observations are all useful for remembering and reflecting on what the client has shared.

⊙⊙ C L I P 3.3
Verbal
Communication

Listening for Themes and Patterns

People's lives develop rich meaning and complexity, which at times can be organized into themes and patterns. These themes and patterns often reflect some of the client's central organizing schemas. Therefore it is essential that clinicians attend to both the themes and patterns emerging in the client's story and within the clinical relationship. Repeating themes and patterns often signal topics important to explore further.

Themes

Themes are repeated sets of ideas, beliefs, or notions. They may be expressed directly and with awareness ("There I go again, blaming myself"). However, they often emerge indirectly and without conscious recognition, as when a client describes a persecuting sibling in one session, a persecuting lover in another, a persecuting employer in another, and annoyance at the clinician for "running the show" in yet another. Clinicians commonly encounter client themes of loss, betrayal, oppression, injustice, hopelessness, and despair, as well as companion themes of courage, persistence, survival, and resistance to oppression.

Patterns

Patterns are repeated behavioral or affective sequences. Although both themes and patterns may have great impact on clients' daily lives, as with themes, clients may be aware or unaware of them. Some common patterns observed in client stories include avoidance of intimacy, frequent angry outbursts, crying when anxious, addiction to substances or people, and picking inappropriate partners. We also note patterns such as choosing loyal friends, asserting oneself in adversity, protecting vulnerable others, and using spiritual resources.

The clinician pays careful attention to themes and patterns that may arise within the interview. Sometimes a theme or pattern emerges across a series of interviews. These themes or patterns may be things the clinician notes during specific interviews or things that the client reveals over time. Some of the patterns are nonverbal.

E X E R C I S E 3.13 *Say it Again, Sam*

Samuel is a 33-year-old Russian immigrant to the United States who lives in a small town in Ohio. He is meeting with a female counselor to discuss employment opportunities. At the beginning of the interview, while talking about work, Sam said that a person who speaks poor English has no chance of advancement in his current job. Later, while discussing his childhood, he said that he never had any of the advantages of his older brothers, who were bigger and stronger than he. As the session was ending, he said that he was sure that the woman clinician didn't like him because he was a man. How would you describe the underlying theme of this interview? How would you convey it to Samuel?

I noticed that Becky always got teary when she spoke of her mother but seemed strangely cold and intellectualized when she described her father.

For almost six months, I had been working with Johann on problems with self-control at work. It took me that long to realize that in almost every session he would mention alcohol. For example, he would say: "Last night a couple of us went out for drinks"; "The other day we put away a couple of martinis at lunch"; or in describing a picnic at work, he said, "We polished off a keg of beer."

Themes and patterns can also emerge from clinicians. One clinician may have a tendency to always focus on anger rather than on sadness (theme), whereas another may start jiggling his foot when anyone talks about sex (pattern). Clients may observe these themes and patterns in us just as we do in them. Supervision and feedback are important in developing self-awareness, which will inform the clinician's behavior in the interview. We will discuss these issues further in Chapters 9 and 10.

Dana said: "You always look so up-tight when I describe seeing Lynn. It makes me not want to tell you when I see her."

Sonia told me that she could always tell when our time was about to be up, because I would reach for my appointment book while she was still talking.

OO **CLIP 3.4**
Themes and Patterns

Listening to the Relationship

A clinical interview is much more than words exchanged and feelings shared. The nature of the relationship in which the story unfolds is crucial to its evolution. The sustainment of a positive, supportive relationship is thus a clinical goal in and of itself. The clinician therefore pays careful attention to what happens within the clinical relationship, and listens for the thoughts, feelings, and reactions that the interview may arouse in both self and client. In Chapters 9 and 10, we will discuss these complicated relationship dynamics and the skills used to address them. In the next chapter, however, we will discuss the initial development and continuing sustainment of the relationship through clinical support and empathy.

Bridging Linguistic Differences

Throughout this chapter, we have paid careful attention to how cultural filters affect the ways in which clinicians and clients listen to each other. One specific challenge is trying to bridge cultural and linguistic differences when the clinician and client do not share the same primary language.

Talking in a Nonnative Language

The *APA Guidelines for Providers of Psychological Services to Ethnic, Linguistic, and Culturally Diverse Populations* (American Psychological Association, 1990) suggests that "Psychologists interact in the language requested by the client and, if this is not feasible, make an appropriate referral" (p. 6). However, clinical work is often conducted in a language that may not be the client's primary language. For example, a Puerto Rican immigrant with a rudimentary knowledge of English may be asked to speak in English to an Anglo clinician, or even to a Puerto Rican clinician raised in the United Sates whose primary language is English. It can be extremely difficult to communicate complex experiences or emotionally charged issues in a second language— especially when talking about things that occurred before the second language was learned.

> *I remember that when Mercedes and I would talk about things in her childhood, she would often slip into Spanish. At times she would speak in English, talking about how she missed her mother and father. When I asked her to "say it in Spanish," she said, "Yo extraño a mi mami y papi" and burst into tears.*

It can be particularly productive to ask the client to say a particular word in his or her own native language—words that may carry significant meaning and affect.

> *I have a friend who is a very visible, out lesbian. She gives talks around the country about being lesbian. However, she has told me that she isn't "out in Spanish." The word used to denote lesbians in Spanish carries with it such a negative connotation that she can never say it. So, she has never come out to her parents, who speak only Spanish.*

Sometimes neither the clinician nor the client is speaking in his or her native language, which can result in numerous misinterpretations and impatience on the part of both clinician and client.

Using Translators and Interpreters

When the clinician is unable to speak the client's preferred language, it is appropriate (where possible) to refer the client to a clinician who is able to communicate in the client's language. If no appropriate clinician is available, a trained interpreter may be used. Rather than using nonclinical agency staff who happen to speak the client's language, clinicians should be sure that they have access to people who are trained as translators and who know about the counseling process, confidentiality, and the culture of the clients with whom they will be speaking. Untrained translators may be exposed to material that is overwhelming or that they are not prepared to deal with appropriately.

The use of a translator clearly affects the clinician's ability to accurately listen to and understand the client, and it introduces "the additional complexities of a three person relationship" (La Framboise, Berman, & Sohi, 1994, p. 53). The clinician must then attend to what transpires between the translator and the client as well as to what transpires between the clinician, the client, and the translator, respectful of cultural style and nuance (Freed, 1988).

Whenever possible, family members or others with dual relationships or vested interests should not be used as interpreters, since overlapping relationships may affect the validity and reliability of the translation or curtail frank expression of information and feelings.

> *I had a bad experience with an interpreter, which makes me very aware of how carefully you have to prepare before working together with a client. The hospital was attempting to provide counseling support to an unmarried Portuguese teen who had just delivered a baby. Since no one on the staff spoke Portuguese, a Portuguese-speaking priest was invited in to serve as an interpreter. I asked the priest to explain to the girl the services that were available to her in the community. The girl burst into tears. I asked the priest why the girl was crying and he said that he felt it was important to begin by reminding the girl that she had committed a mortal sin for which she must ask God's forgiveness.*

Wong (1987, cited in La Framboise, Berman, & Sohi, 1994) recommends that the clinician meet with an interpreter in "a pre-interview session to build a relationship of trust and to plan the objectives of the interview, the topics to be covered . . . . The clinician and the interpreter should discuss the preferred translation style, whether it be word for word, summarizing or cultural interpretation" (p. 53).

Conclusion

Interviews require careful listening and an accurate perception of what is being transmitted. The clinician carefully attends to the client; listening to the verbal and nonverbal communication; noting behaviors, feelings, themes, and patterns as they emerge in the interview, always alert for both their idiosyncratic and their cultural meanings. It is through listening that the relationship develops and the story unfolds. As we will discuss in the next chapter, accurate listening is not enough. We believe that for effective change to occur, support and empathy are essential.

Suggested Readings

Following are some classic works on the body and nonverbal communication.

Birdwhistell, R. L. (1970). *Kinesics and context.* Philadelphia: University of Pennsylvania Press.

Hall, Edward. (1959). *The silent language.* New York: Fawcett.

Kurtz, Ron, & Prestera, Hector. (1984). *Body reveals: How to read your own body.* San Francisco: Harper.

Schutz, William. (1967). *Joy: Expanding human awareness.* New York: Grove.

Cultural issues in verbal and nonverbal communication are discussed in:

Lum, Doman. (1996). *Social work practice and people of color: A process-stage approach.* Pacific Grove, CA: Brooks/Cole.

The following readings deal with linguistic differences and translators.

American Psychological Association. (1990). *APA guidelines for providers of psychological services to ethnic, linguistic, and culturally diverse populations.* Washington, DC: Author.

Freed, Anne. (1988). Interviewing through an interpreter. *Social Work, 33,* 315–319.

Ivry, Joann. (1992). Paraprofessionals in refugee resettlement. *Journal of Multicultural Social Work, 2*(1), 99–117.

Tien, Liang. (1994). Southeast Asian American refugee women. In Lillian Comas-Diaz & Beverly Greene (Eds.),*Women of color: Integrating ethnic and gender identities in psychotherapy* (pp.479–503). New York: Guilford.

Support and Empathy:
A Sustaining Presence

A Supportive Presence

A *supportive presence* is crucial to the development of a trusting relationship in which meaningful conversation can occur. We shall see that the clinician's caring and support cannot be communicated solely through attending and listening. It can also be consciously communicated by sensitively timed and orchestrated words, gestures, behaviors, and emotional responses—all of which together communicate an active presence and wish to help.

Warmth and Caring

Clinicians must genuinely care about their clients and their clients' well-being. It is only common sense that clients would respond more readily to interviewers who are warm and caring than to those who come across as bureaucrats, technicians, or "cold fish." *Warmth* and *caring* are often conveyed with a smile, a cordial handshake at the beginning of the interview, close attention to what is being expressed or felt, and use of appropriate facial expressions and gestures. There will be individuals who at times may prefer the detached and distant clinician, but even they usually like to believe that the clinician has some feeling of care for them. More frequently, people rate warmth and caring extremely high when asked to list attributes of a potential clinician, mentor, or adviser (Combs, 1989; Rogers, 1958).

Clinicians may have a difficult time judging how to show their caring. On the one hand, they do not want to appear too detached and professional.

On the other hand, if the clinician is too saccharine, or "touchy-feely," clients may feel put off.

> *One of the things I notice when I am teaching first-year social work students is what I call their "singsong" tone. They often say things like "Oh-h-h, I am so-o-o-o-o-o sorry to hear that." It reminds me of the behavior and tone of voice often used with small children and older people. That's why I like to have students hear themselves on tape. It also helps if they can sit in on colleagues' interviews, to hear how different clinicians "really" sound when they're speaking with clients.*

Warmth and caring are relational processes. We find it helpful to look in a mirror or watch ourselves on video to see how we look when attempting to demonstrate warmth and caring. In reality, these feelings do not arise in a vacuum but are elicited by thinking about or interacting with other people, animals, music, and nature.

⊙⊙ CLIP 4.1
Warmth and Caring

EXERCISE 4.1 *Conveying Warmth and Caring*

In class, break up into groups of four. Take turns being the speaker, the responder, and the two observers. The speaker should tell a story about him or herself. The responder should practice conveying warmth and caring. The observers should note the specific behaviors that they think convey warmth and caring. The list could include things like facial expressions, postures, comments, and tone of voice. Also make note of any lapses in warmth. If possible, videotape yourself as a responder so that you can observe the things you do to communicate warmth and caring. Note that each person may experience and manifest warmth and caring in different ways. In your journal, record what you have learned.

Acceptance

Another important element of sustaining presence is *acceptance*. Clinicians must be able to appreciate and affirm clients as people without necessarily condoning specific behaviors that might be harmful to themselves or to others. Carl Rogers (1958) refers to this as "unconditional positive regard." To accept clients as people sounds deceptively simple, but it can be quite difficult when client behaviors either go against societal laws or norms or are in radical conflict with the clinician's personal values or preferred styles of behavior.

Societal Norms

Societal norms are widely held standards of conduct to which all members of a society are expected to adhere. Norms usually dictate what is acceptable and what is not—what the powerful majority in a society defines as "right" and sanctioned or "wrong" and forbidden. Norms are often codified into laws; for example, most societies have laws that prohibit incest, murder, and theft. Usually there are norms that prescribe gender roles, dress, bearing, and speech and that distinguish what is acceptable in public from what is to be confined to private life. Clinicians often see clients who have come to therapy because they have violated social norms or taboos. Sometimes they have broken the law. More often, clients come to therapy because others may believe that their behaviors, although not illegal, violate social norms; for example, the woman who yells and talks to herself in the subway or the man who prefers to wear women's clothes. Clients also come to therapy when they experience a conflict with social norms, such as the married woman who decides not to have children or the man who is struggling with his sexual attractions toward men.

Some norms endure, others change over time: dress and gender roles have changed dramatically in the last 50 years. People from different age groups may hold to "old" norms that may seem outdated. An older man may think it polite to open the door for women, whereas a young woman may be insulted, believing that he thinks women are weak and need help. Sometimes there is a contradiction between what society prescribes as a standard or norm and what actually happens. In the United States, two-parent families are held up as the norm, but this country actually has one of the highest divorce rates and number of single-parent families in the Western Hemisphere. Millions are spent on the "War on Drugs" while millions are also spent on subsidies and research grants to the alcohol and tobacco industries.

Every culture defines its own norms. U.S. society is pluralistic and is composed of many diverse cultures. Problems can arise when differing cultural norms conflict, especially when one group has more political power than another. For example, many Native Americans believe in the power of the dead and may attribute misfortunes to the effects of ghosts or spirits, some of whom they may claim to see. A naive clinician may interpret these beliefs and reported experiences as delusions or hallucinations.

> *An intern reported that the team psychiatrist on the inpatient unit told her to tell a father that he should dress more appropriately when visiting his adolescent daughter. The psychiatrist said that the father was "dressing in a seductive manner with his shirt unbuttoned and gold chains calling attention to his hairy chest." The intern, an Italian American woman, felt this behavior was not seductive but, rather, represented an Italian father's way of dressing up for a Sunday visit.*

Traditional norms in Haiti and several other Caribbean islands may prescribe corporal punishment as an appropriate response to a child's misbehavior and as a sign of caring and concern, whereas the dominant U.S. culture may define the same kind of hitting as child abuse. Lillian Comas-Diaz (personal communication, 1996) states that although corporal punishment may be acceptable in the native country, the parent living in the United States must be educated about the possible consequences of that behavior here.

Finally, while working to improve our understanding of diverse cultures and their norms, we clinicians need to be careful that we do not mistakenly attribute to cultural influence behaviors that may be due to illness, addiction, antisocial stance, or individual style. Clinicians need to be aware of culture-bound syndromes; that is, "recurrent, locality-specific patterns of aberrant behavior and troubling experience that may not be linked to a particular DSM-IV diagnostic category" (American Psychiatric Association, 1994, p. 844).

Personal Values

Individual *values* are cherished beliefs that develop in the context of family and sociocultural influences. Clinicians may value anything from personal autonomy to personal hygiene and find themselves dismayed or offended by clients who do not share their value system. As clinicians, we need to be aware of our values and how they influence our responses to clients in ways that may leave clients feeling unaccepted. Clinicians must be dedicated to being *nonjudgmental*—unconditionally accepting people for who they are without necessarily accepting all their behaviors. The clinician's nonjudgmental stance leaves clients free to confide openly and honestly without fear of rejection, shaming, or reprisal.

> *Eileen, a 48-year-old woman who had always lived with her family, was discussing whether to move out and get her own apartment. I saw her desire to live alone as a healthy one. I didn't even recognize that living independently was a personal value of mine—I thought it was a sign of "mental health." I believed that adult women should be able to separate from their families to develop autonomy. It wasn't until I talked with a colleague that I realized I had to be careful not to let my values influence our discussion.*

As we work with clients and are exposed to diverse situations and beliefs, we often find that our values are challenged and changed. A side benefit of clinical work is that our lenses are inevitably widened so that we both see and appreciate more of the world beyond our own. We ourselves stretch and grow through exposure to differences.

> *I used to see the halfway house as a way station where people were supposed to get it together and then move on. After many years of watching dozens of mental patients bounce back to the hospital after leaving transitional living programs, I came to realize that, for many isolated people, long-term communal living may be the end goal rather than a "halfway" achievement.*

At other times, we may have our cherished values confirmed by the similar beliefs and experiences of clients from diverse cultures, reminding us of the larger, universal community of shared human values.

E X E R C I S E 4.2 *Personal Values*

Think of a time when you found your personal values challenged. Think of a time when your personal values changed. Record each story in your journal. What did you learn about yourself and about others from these experiences? Then, think of a time when you felt forced to go along with values you did not respect. Reflect on that experience and how you might deal with the situation differently now. Why?

Stylistic Differences

Everyone has a *personal style*—individual habits and preferences in interaction with others. For example, when feeling misunderstood, one angry person will raise his or her voice, whereas another will burst into tears. One client may appear quite stoic, whereas another seems to plead for help constantly. One client may wave a pen while talking, another may sit rigidly without moving for the entire session. Personal style is often mediated by gender, class, ethnicity, and geographical region.

Clinicians may find themselves more or less understanding or responsive to particular client styles, looking forward to meetings with certain clients and actually dreading meetings with others.

> *Usually I can be accepting of most of my clients' behaviors, but Maddie's whiny tone really grated on me. I had to use every trick in the book to remind myself of her pain so as to stay attentive to her story and not just shout, "Stop whining!"*

> *Joanne, an intelligent and competent teacher, spent most of the session time asking my opinion of family and life issues, rather than giving her own. I found this extremely annoying as I knew it to be unnecessary, given her capacity to figure things out. But I came to appreciate that in her family, one never gave an opinion in front of an authority figure—it was considered disrespectful. It took a while for her to perceive our situation as different and exempt from her family's rules.*

Clinicians, too, have unique personal styles and preferences. Some are more formal and businesslike, others more relaxed and down to earth. Some retain a serious demeanor, whereas others take a lighter touch. Some readily reveal themselves to clients; others prefer a more "blank screen" approach to the work. The important point about personal styles of clinicians and clients is not that they match perfectly but that they are not so discordant as to constantly distract from the focus of the work or be offensive to each other. It is the clinician's responsibility—not the client's—to try to make the interviewing ambiance as harmonious and supportive to the client as possible. Uncomfortable presence makes for uncomfortable relating and working and can wordlessly signal lack of empathy and attunement to the needs of others.

Norms, values, and personal styles are all interrelated and can be hard to sort out, one from another. Supervision is often a good place to explore our attitudes and values so that we can learn to be accepting of our clients, even if we don't accept a particular behavior. Although the development of openness, tolerance, and true acceptance of others is a lifelong task, it is also a clinician's ethical responsibility.

EXERCISE 4.3 *Clients I Might Find Hard to Accept*

Following is a list of clients with different characteristics. In your journal, rank-order them from the easiest to the hardest for you to accept. Discuss what made each one easy or hard for you to accept. In class, you may want to discuss in small groups what kinds of clients you would have a hard time accepting and what steps you might take to become more accepting.

Woman having an abortion

Person who is a crybaby

Drug-addicted mother

Client who hates professionals

Client who yells in the session when angry

Religious zealot

Husband who is abusing his wife

Transsexual

Person who is a bully

Clergyperson sexually involved with a parishioner he or she is counseling about loneliness

Man who makes racist statements

Person who is very critical

Gay adolescent

Clinical Repose

The clinician's anchored and relaxed presence acts as an island of calm and allows the client to stay self-focused without being distracted by the clinician's needs or anxieties. This repose is central to supportive presence. It provides a clear but unobtrusive *holding environment* for the work and the relationship. Clients come to know that they can count on the clinician to remain centered and steady regardless of events and developments. Even in the face of the unexpected, clinicians try to remain as calm and reliable as possible. As noted previously, the clinical environment is portable and can be re-created almost anywhere in order to establish safe and supportive conversation. We are really speaking here of a *clinical repose* that is developed with experience and tends to relax, reassure, and open others to process because it gives them confidence in the helper's dependability. Such repose is expressed by a relaxed and open posture and gaze and a calm and confident manner in proceeding.

In attempting to learn how to create a supportive presence, students often complain that they lose their natural warmth and spontaneity. They feel that the deliberateness of the clinical role and the restraints imposed by other-centeredness make them self-conscious and interfere with their natural responsivity. At first, their newly adopted professional tone or detachment may cause loved ones to begin to say, "Quit therapizing me!" With time, experience, and good models, clinicians are able to combine informed awareness and appropriate self-control with genuine warmth, caring, and acceptance in a way that feels more comfortable and natural.

E X E R C I S E 4.4 *Clinical Repose*

In your journal, describe your view of your own clinical repose and how well you are able to maintain it in spite of things that occur in interviews. Discuss any ways in which your clinical presence is different from your manner when you are just being yourself in your private life. Note any things that disrupt your clinical repose. How will you be working to enhance your repose and presence? In thinking about repose and presence, what have you learned about yourself? Is your clinical presence beginning to alter the way you carry yourself in your private life? Have people commented on that?

Genuineness

To be effective, support has to be *genuine*—sincere and free from pretense or hypocrisy. As one of his six necessary and sufficient conditions for change, Carl Rogers (1957) speaks about "genuineness or congruence." By congruence, Rogers means that "the therapist is willing to express and be open about any persistent feelings that exist in the relationship. It means avoiding the temptation to hide behind a mask of professionalism" (Rogers & Sanford, 1985, p. 1379). Barbara Okun (1997) writes about the need for clinicians to be honest: "Clinicians can communicate honesty by being open with clients, by answering questions to the best of their ability, and by admitting mistakes or lack of knowledge" (p. 40).

While attempting to communicate a supportive presence, clinicians need to avoid fake smiles, counterfeit approval, and false reassurance (such as "Don't worry—things will get better"). Many clients can spot faking easily because they have often been manipulated by the pretenses of others. They may not comment because they need the approval or services that the clinician can offer. Perceptions of clinician inauthenticity undermine confidence in the clinician and impede the development of a trusting relationship.

There is a difference between genuineness and "total honesty." A wise French saying, "Toute verité n'est pas bonne à dire," translates as "The whole truth is not always good to say." To create a supportive presence, we need to be selective, always considering the impact that our remarks and behaviors have on our clients. We don't always say everything we think, but we do think about everything we say. And, what we do say, we have to mean.

Clinicians are always in role. While we have to be ourselves, authentic in our role rather than hiding behind it, we also have to be deliberate. For example, we might think that a diagnosis of a particular kind of cancer puts a client at high risk of dying, but we would not say that. The clinician's goal is to accompany the client in the moment of his or her experience, not to be wizard or mind reader.

Availability

Clinicians further support clients by making themselves easily *available*. They need to be physically and psychologically accessible. As we discussed in Chapter 2, clinicians indicate their willingness to join and work with clients by setting up their offices so that they are welcoming, by having hours that fit with clients' needs, by being available by phone, or by being flexible in setting the frequency and length of sessions. In addition, clinicians demonstrate their availability by being culturally responsive and able to provide services in the language of the client's choice. In sum, every effort is made to reduce feelings of distance or alienation.

> As a social worker in the rehabilitation hospital, I needed to meet with the children of Rachel, a woman in our hospital recovering from a serious stroke. I'd been seeing one daughter each week for 30 minutes or so to provide support as she began to screen nursing homes and come to terms with her mother's chronic disability. When two more daughters became involved, I began to meet with everyone together, including Rachel, for an hour. I had to switch our meeting time to the early evening to accommodate their work and home schedules. I planned our meetings for Wednesdays so that it would be easy for them to stay for the stroke education group that met on Wednesday nights.

A number of factors constrain the amount of time that clinicians can see clients face to face, such as a short-term therapy approach, financial and insurance limitations, and long-distance travel. Clinicians need to be flexible in finding additional ways of being available to clients—in person, by phone, by letter, and, today, even over the Internet or by fax, e-mail, cassette recordings, or videotapes. The use of cell phones, fax machines, and computers presents the clinician with the difficult challenge of ensuring confidentiality. These forms of communication are accessible by others, and therefore sensitive material should not be transmitted by these means.

There may be times in the relationship when the clinician offers the client more opportunities for contact, as when the client is going through a particularly difficult time or when the clinician or client believes that the client will make productive use of additional contact. Proposed increases in contact should be reviewed with supervisors in advance, since they can have unforeseen consequences. Most clients respond favorably to a goodwill offer of additional visits or "other times you can reach me." Some, however, may abuse the availability, experience it as seductive interest on the part of the clinician, or feel too dependent after additional calls or visits. The clinician notes the use the client makes of the added contacts and responds accordingly by discussing any untoward effects of this extension of self and role. We will discuss this further in Chapter 9.

It should be noted that in emergencies or to support clients under duress, clinicians may accompany clients to emergency rooms, court proceedings, hospital admissions, school evaluation meetings, and the like. In Chapter 8 we will discuss accompanying clients as a form of clinician influence. Visiting incarcerated clients can also be supportive under well-thought-out conditions. Clinicians always try to consult with supervisors or senior colleagues on the implications of activities with clients outside the usual format of the work.

> *I visited Maureen in jail two days after she stabbed her husband in front of her two boys. I knew she would be beside herself with guilt and shame, and possibly suicidal. She was also new to the area and had no friends. My supervisor suggested I take her some personal items like comb, brush, and lotion and some magazines to pass the time. She could not believe I would come "to such a place, to see a person like me." I also went to their court hearing and then out to lunch in the neighborhood with her and her husband after he dropped the charges. The agency provided the money for all of these services, seeing it as building the family's view of themselves as "mattering." We really began our deeper family work after that. No one had ever given them the time of day.*

Many other services and arrangements can be set up to support clients between interviews so as to diminish feelings of isolation or vulnerability. The clinician can establish a "safety net," which can include family members, friends, on-call staff or hotlines, brief inpatient hospital stays, attendance at Alcoholics Anonymous (AA) or Narcotics Anonymous (NA) meetings, day treatment, sheltered work, respite care, and the like. The art in this work is matching the service to the client in order to maximize good fit and follow-through. Positive attitudes of network providers, readiness to help, availability of translators as needed, affordable transportation, and well-coordinated schedules all make a difference as to whether "supports" feel truly supportive or not.

Validation

Validation occurs when the clinician endorses and appreciates the realities of the client's story. The clinical encounter may be the first opportunity people have had to feel that their stories are moving and believable and that the details ring true to a witness.

Another supporting and validating technique used to undercut a client's sense of isolation or differentness is *universalizing*—framing our response in such a way as to locate the client as one of a universe of people sharing similar feelings, experiences, or opinions.

Examples of Universalizing Responses

"A lot of other people share that feeling."

"Who wouldn't be nervous in a dark parking lot late at night!"

"Most working moms like yourself have the same fear you do about being laid off or losing their benefits if they take a maternity leave."

"Join the crowd."

Universalizing is not always useful. Some clients may need to feel unique in their experiences or perceptions—the only "specialness" they have known. Such clients may respond to universalizing with irritation or disappointment, communicating a feeling that the interviewer just doesn't understand their unique situation. Others may have experienced aloneness, alienation, or differentness for so long that simple reassurances from the clinician about the commonality of their experience are insufficient to break up this core sense of an alienated self. To them, the clinician may appear naive or inattentive to their deep levels of distress. As with all techniques, we watch carefully for the client's response and may want to note and explore it further.

Identifying and Affirming Strengths

Clinicians who hold a strengths perspective recognize clients' courage or persistence against great odds. Recognition and confirmation can build self-esteem and initiative. Clients often come to see that the strengths used in one situation are often transferable to other seemingly insurmountable crises of the moment, making problems seem more resolvable. *Identifying and affirming client strengths* furthers the development of the supportive presence.

⊙⊙ CLIP 4.2
Affirming Client
Strengths

Examples of Strengths Perspective Responses by Clinicians

"It's amazing how much you got done with almost no support."

"You said you 'ran out on every relationship you ever had'—but you've come to see me for three months straight now, and this is a relationship. This relationship counts; it's a very important exception to your stated pattern, and it suggests to me that you do not in fact 'run out' on every relationship. Maybe we could take a look at when relationships work for you and when they don't."

"I notice you whizzed right over the statement that for the first time, when you felt like drinking this week, you increased your AA attendance. That was such an important step. I'd like to hear more about how you made that change happen."

"You say you're embarrassed to talk to me over and over again about your job achievements, but I like to hear about them. I think it's wonderful that things are working out for you now, and frankly, I think you deserve a little more support for your successes than is out there for you right now."

Provision of Concrete Supports

Clinicians in both agency and private practice often demonstrate their support for clients by helping them *access needed services*. Professional attention to the deleterious effects of poverty, economic dislocation, and institutionalized bias has increased clinicians' appreciation of the importance of providing for the basic human needs of individuals and families. These needs include food, clothing, shelter, adequate financial support, transportation, pathways to education or training, and access to opportunities for recreation and affiliation. Abraham Maslow (1968) outlined a hierarchy of human needs with concrete needs at its foundation. He postulated that unless these basic human needs are met, people will understandably not develop much beyond the level of profound despair and so may not feel secure enough to take action in their own behalf. It is unrealistic, if not cruel, to ask desperate people to merely sit around reflecting on their psychological lives and perspectives.

The provision of needed resources can be a critical factor in building trust and in developing a therapeutic alliance. Clients often experience the clinician as more respectful of their struggles when the clinician actively helps them obtain needed services such as food stamps, housing, referrals to job training, and so on. The clinician is then perceived as more appreciative of the exigencies of daily life and the bureaucratic snares that often await the person seeking services. A word of caution: While clinicians may at times directly provide clients with needed services or resources, client "resourcefulness" is best developed when clients learn how to exercise their own knowledge and skills in behalf of themselves and their loved ones. We agree with the wise saying that if you give a hungry person a fish, the recipient eats for a day, but if you teach him or her to fish, he or she can eat for a lifetime—if there are fish!

Clinicians are ill-advised to impulsively offer concrete help if such offers are motivated by rescue fantasies, the wish to be liked, or a client's demandingness. Such moves frequently backfire, leaving all parties feeling used or betrayed. It is also unwise for clinicians to lend their own money (as opposed to helping the client obtain funds) and give rides in their cars (because of the risk of injury to the client if there is an accident or if a suicidal or psychotic client jumps out into traffic).

Advocacy

There is another very important kind of support intrinsic to the work clinicians do with people: *advocacy* on behalf of client rights and opportunities. Such advocacy takes place when clinicians join with others in political activities and movements in the community to achieve greater rights, protections, and opportunities for all people, including but not limited to our clients. As advocates we also inform agencies or practice groups of important services or amenities that are not available to clients. Clinicians need to work together with colleagues and community groups to improve the conditions within which services are delivered. Advocacy also occurs when clinicians struggle with insurance companies or other payers to get the proper amount and kinds of services for clients. All of these activities have the potential to heighten morale and hopefulness and to energize the clinical work.

Empathy

Supportive presence is good for starters, but it is not enough to carry clinical process forward from its beginnings of cordiality, interest, and openness. The clinical relationship cannot move forward without *empathy*—the ability to immerse oneself in another's experience without losing one's own sense of self. Empathy requires that the clinician see and experience the world from the client's subjective perspective while maintaining the perspective of an outside observer. It thus requires a constant oscillation between observing the client, feeling and thinking as if one *were* the client, and then feeling and thinking *about* the client's experience. In addition to what it contributes to supportive presence, empathy provides the clinician with important human experience and information on which to base hunches that will inform future clinical work.

Empathy is a complex process that is often misunderstood. The following clarifications may be helpful:

1. Empathy is not sympathy. Sympathy is what I feel *toward* you; empathy is what I feel *as* you.

2. Empathy is much more than just putting oneself in the other person's shoes. Empathy requires a shift of perspective. It's not what I would experience *as me* in your shoes; empathy is what I experience *as you* in your shoes.

3. Finally, empathy requires a constant shifting between my experiencing *as you* what you feel, and my being able to think *as me* about your experience.

E X E R C I S E 4.5 *Experiencing Empathy*

In your journal, record a time when someone really understood you, when they seemed to know exactly what you were feeling—a time when you felt someone's empathy. Describe the experience to your colleagues. How do you think that person knew so much about what you were feeling? In your journal you can also keep a record of your reactions to those experiences in which you felt empathy coming from a role-play counselor.

Empathy in Human Relationships

Jean Baker Miller and her colleagues at the Wellesley College Stone Center have written about the development of empathy and mutuality in relationships (Jordan, Kaplan, Miller, Stiver, & Surrey, 1991). They suggest that empathy is developed through mutually engaging exchanges that begin in infancy. Infants and children experience pleasure when they feel they are being accurately seen and heard by their caregivers. They internalize and practice the engaging skills of observing and feeling with others. They receive feedback and praise in relation to the accuracy of their empathic responses, reinforcing their pleasure and increasing their attempts at empathy. Likewise, their caregivers feel and show similar pleasure when on the receiving end of the child's budding caretaking behaviors or when delighting in the child's playing nurse, Mommy, or helper.

> *My 3-year-old daughter noticed that I was sad and she patted my back and said, "Mommy, you're sad today. . . . Do you want my teddy bear?" I said, "Yes, sweetie, I am sad. You are a very good girl to try to take care of Mommy."*

The accuracy and appropriateness of joining with the experiences of others are fine-tuned over time. Basically, one learns empathy by experiencing empathy, by being on the receiving end of empathy. The experience of being accurately seen and heard by another has few equals. Those who have been denied or shortchanged in their experience of empathy *from* others often show little or tenuous empathy *for* others. Those who have been overwhelmed by requests for empathic caretaking may manifest "compassion fatigue" (Figley, 1995). In either situation, people may be less likely to reveal themselves to or care much about others.

Developing Clinical Empathy

Empathy is a developmental process that can be consciously fostered and strengthened in adulthood in a number of ways. To be able to think and feel as another person would feel, we need to have a lot of experience with other people, and we need to learn about the range of reactions that people have to specific situations. We can gain this knowledge by enriching and expanding our own life experiences and by learning about human diversity through experiences with others who are different from ourselves.

A simple technique that can be useful in establishing empathy with another person is the psychodramatic process of *getting into role*—taking on the physical and psychological characteristics of the other. We assume the other's posture, manner, tone, and intentions, as well as the dynamics of their personal history, family, and cultural experiences.

EXERCISE 4.6 *Becoming the Other*

Think of an important person in your life, perhaps a member of your family. Get into the role of that person. (For example, let's assume you have taken the role of your sister Jen.) Of course, you can take the role of anyone you want. Now, tell the group your name. (In the instructions, we'll use "Jen," but you can play anyone.) Assume the body posture, tone, and manner of Jen. What are you wearing? Jen, think about how you look, dress, feel, and speak. Remember your history, family, and culture. Give a brief monologue about yourself to the group, Jen, and then let the group interview you in role for 5 minutes so as to learn more about you. Videotape the monologue.

While you are in role, group members may ask you questions about how you feel about current social issues, what is important in your life, or about the relationship between the person you are role playing and you; for example, between Jen and her sister.

Group members may help each student stay in role by using the role name. (For example, "Jen, how do you feel about . . . ?" or "Jen, is that how you speak?" or "Is that how you hold your body, Jen?")

After you do your role play, talk with the group about the experience. Watch the video together. In your journal, record what you learned about the other person when you took his or her role. Did you learn anything about yourself? Did you learn anything about your relationship with that person?

This exercise was easy because you are familiar with the person you were asked to play and you have a history of interaction with him or her. You have a wealth of information about that person on which to draw. Similarly, clinicians need some basic background information about the people they work with in order to build empathy, since it is a relational process and cannot occur in a vacuum.

EXERCISE 4.7 *Information Builds Empathy*

Play Leti. Notice that you can't do it without some basic information about Leti that will help you get into her role. Write down what kinds of information you would want to know about in order to empathize with her. You might want to compare the information that you would want to know about Leti with the information that others would want to know. Note the different kinds of information different people seek. You might want to know her age, ethnicity, living situation, and other important circumstances before even trying to empathize. Discuss with others the things that help you, personally, to empathize with someone, and the things that make empathizing harder for you. Record your reactions in your journal.

One of the tasks of the initial interview—indeed, of all interviews—is to gather *necessary and relevant information* (see Chapter 5). Sometimes it is easy to gather information: from an intake form; the initial telephone call; or comments from friends, family members, or referring persons. Many times clients themselves readily provide continuing information with which we can identify and empathize. When clients are silent or do not talk easily or readily, we still use the empathic process by imagining ourselves as the other and feeling why it is we are expressing ourselves through silence rather than through speech. Shulman (1992) regards silence as an important form of communication and speaks of "reaching into silence" as an important technique in expressing empathy and reengaging the client in verbal exchange.

Students often ask, "How can I be empathic with people whose experiences I've never had and can scarcely relate to?" (Examples could be pregnancy, imprisonment, death of a child, or people from other classes or ethnic backgrounds.) To be empathic, we need to both broaden our knowledge of the wide range of human experience and, quite simply, open our hearts.

Clinicians need to learn to strengthen empathy by trying it out with many different kinds of people and getting differential feedback from them regarding the accuracy and timeliness of these empathic responses. Under the pressures of school or work, it's often easier to socialize with people whose backgrounds and experiences are similar to your own. However, it is important to push yourself beyond the familiar and to expand the network of those with whom you interact. In-class exercises and group assignments are designed to enhance your knowledge of other people's experiences and perspectives. Hopefully, in the process, you will increase your capacity for empathy with a widening range of people in varying situations.

> *As a southerner, I had been taught that Catholics were under rigid papal control, and that if Kennedy were elected president, he would be taking orders directly from the pope. I laugh now to think how incredibly naive this was. It wasn't until I came to social work school and actually became friends with a number of Catholics that I realized that many of my Catholic friends were freer from religious strictures than I was as a southern Methodist. It was also the first time I befriended people of color and worked with people from the inner city. My ideas changed so much as we all shared our stories in role plays, over lunch, and hanging out after work.*

Reading the professional literature in courses and conferences is another way to better acquaint ourselves with the conditions and experiences of many different people. This professional reading can be augmented with novels, plays, autobiographies, and the like. Educational and commercial films, videos, plays, and documentaries offer additional opportunities for learning. For example, the film *Hoop Dreams* may be useful for developing empathy with some inner-city black families; while the film *Philadelphia* may help people grasp the struggles of some gay men with AIDS.

EXERCISE 4.8 *Expanding Your Capacity for Empathy*

This week, read or watch something you think will expand your capacity for empathy. It could be a story about a person with a mental illness, a family from a different culture, or someone struggling with an issue with which you are unfamiliar or uncomfortable. Record in your journal why you chose the topic you did and what you experienced and learned from it. Also discuss what it would be like for you to be *in* this situation, rather than reading about or watching it.

Clinicians can also broaden their human experiences by volunteering in the community: for example, working at a meal site, senior center, or homeless shelter; helping with a neighborhood campaign for better schools or voter registration; marching for an end to domestic violence; or joining candlelight vigils. Here we refer to the "expanded role" or "broader role" of the clinician in working for peace, justice, equity, and basic rights for all.

> I did my master's thesis on working with people who were dying. However, it wasn't until many years later, when I volunteered at AIDS Action Committee, that I had any idea of what it might be like to face my own death. Meeting each week with men who had just discovered that they had a life-threatening illness made me much more sensitive to the issues and feelings around death and dying. I moved from "knowing" to "experiencing."

EXERCISE 4.9 *Empathy Role Plays*

Take the role of each of the people described in the following vignettes.

> You are Janelle, a 23-year-old African American mother of two children who has moved to a new neighborhood.

> You are Kieran, an Irish Catholic college junior, and you have just been told that you have been cut from the Notre Dame football team.

> You are Kim Soong, a 16-year-old adopted daughter from Korea, and your parents just told you they are getting a divorce.

> You are Frankie, a 78-year-old widower, and your daughter told you it would be best for you to live in a nursing home.

> You are Rosalie, a woman being stalked by her boyfriend.

In your journal, discuss the following: What helped you get into each role? Did you have similar experiences on which to draw? What information and experiences were helpful in taking on each role? Which role was hard to get into, and why?

In the preceding exercise, you may have noticed that it was easier to get into some roles than others. It's often harder to get into a role in which we have to take on negative or uncomfortable feelings (such as fear, shame) or an identity discredited by others (gay, welfare recipient, drug user). Empathy can also be difficult if the client's experiences arouse some unfinished business or personally charged issues for the clinician. Clients often notice when clinicians tighten up or detour around such issues.

> *When my client began expressing her sadness about her mother's death, I noticed that I did not want to feel her sadness. Prior to the interview, I had just been at the hospital, visiting with a good friend dying of cancer. The moment my client cried, I actually stood up and said, "Please go ahead, don't let me interrupt, I just have to shut the window, it's freezing in here." When I returned to my seat she changed the subject without skipping a beat.*

Communicating Empathy in the Relationship

We move from *feeling* empathic to *being* empathic by converting our perceptions, feelings, and intuitions into postures, gestures, sounds, words, and behaviors. The basic methods clinicians utilize to communicate support and empathy include supportive sounds, mirroring, and empathic echo. These methods incorporate two important components. First, the clinician is the *caring other* who offers supportive responses as the client reveals his or her story. Second, the clinician is the *empathic other* who reflects back content, affect, and themes and patterns in the client's story from the client's perspective.

Supportive Sounds

Clinicians demonstrate their presence and close attention by making periodic use of *supportive sounds*, such as "ohhh," "mm-hmm," "uh-huh," "yes," "ah," and "I see." These brief utterances mark our active involvement in the client's narrative and are often gently interjected during long narrations by the client. They indicate to the client that we are listening and following the story closely, and they can encourage the client to continue talking.

Example

Client: It hurt so much when I was dismissed like that.

Clinician: Awww . . .

Client: I didn't want to give my boss the pleasure of seeing me cry.

Clinician: Mmm . . .

Client: I have some ideas about what to do next, though.

Clinician: Good. I'd like to hear them.

Responses must be genuine to be effective, and every effort is made to avoid speaking in a repetitious, hackneyed, or "singsong" manner. In the example just given, a minimal interviewer response suffices to show caring and presence while keeping the clinician out of the way of the story so that the *client's* voice is exercised and validated.

> One of the first times I listened to myself on tape, I noticed that I kept saying "right" to the client. It wasn't that I was agreeing with her, it was my way of saying "uh-huh." I realized the danger of using that phrase when she said, "My husband is a pain in the ass," and I said, "Right." I suddenly worried that she would go home and tell her husband that her counselor agreed that he was a pain in the ass!

Mirroring

Mirroring is a physical form of reflection. In mirroring, the clinician matches the client's posture, facial expression, and gestures. For example, if the client is leaning forward, the clinician may also lean forward; if the client is frowning, the clinician may also frown. Mirroring helps the clinician develop empathy for the client's perspective, and it communicates that the clinician is closely following and is "where the client is." We are always careful not to mimic the client or interfere with the natural flow of productive conversation. Interviewers who imitate or copy the client's every movement can make the client self-conscious and distract attention from the whole person and the emerging details of the story. Mirroring thus involves art as well as technique, and it is a matter of nuance and subtle responding.

As rapport and synchrony build between interviewer and client, their postures will often become more congruent or synchronous with each other. Kadushin (1997) notes that the client can also unconsciously begin to parallel the clinician's posture, tone, and nonverbals. Clinicians can use this knowledge about synchrony to shape interviewee behaviors—using relaxed posture and comfortable gaze to calm and soothe an overexcited client, for example, or using exuberant facial expressions and gestures to energize someone about a hard-won success.

E X E R C I S E 4.10 *Mirroring*

Watch any ongoing conversation between two people and note how the participants mirror each other nonverbally. Is the synchrony present from the outset? If not, how long does it take to set in, and what forms does it take?

Empathic Echo

Empathic echo refers to a verbal reflection of the client's story—that is, behaviors, thoughts, contexts, affect, and meanings. For purposes of theoretical discussion, clinicians often distinguish between content and affect, although the two are always interacting at some level. *Reflection of content* involves making statements that accurately represent the client's statements about behaviors, thoughts, and interactions. Reflection of content can also involve making statements regarding the context or situation in which the client's story is embedded. *Reflection of affect* involves making statements about the feelings that may wrap around or suffuse the client's content.

Gerard Egan differentiates between basic empathy and advanced empathy. Basic empathy is the skill of joining the client's perspective. In discussing his concept of advanced empathy, Egan notes that "as skilled helpers listen intently to clients, they often enough see clearly what clients only half see and hint at" (Egan, 1994, p. 180). In advanced empathy, the clinician reflects the meaning beneath the surface of the client's awareness. We agree with Egan that one can reflect content and affect for reasons other than to convey basic empathy. As we will discuss in later chapters, the clinician can choose to reflect some parts of content or affect to increase clients' awareness of patterns and themes, to confront, to explore, or simply to move the conversation ahead. Our concept of the empathic echo is similar to Egan's concept of basic empathy. In the empathic echo, the clinician attempts to reflect content and affect that is the most crucial to the client. The goal of reflection in the empathic echo is to have the client experience the clinician as joining his or her perspective.

Empathic reflection of content. Reflection of content may seem simple, but it is a lot harder than it sounds, and it involves clinical judgment. The interviewer has to decide whether speaking is appropriate at the moment, and, if so, whether to reflect the words themselves or their presumed meanings. We don't always use the same words as the client; more often we paraphrase the client using similar words and phrases that hopefully convey the same meaning.

Examples

Client: I had my one-year anniversary at AA.
Clinician A: You had your one-year anniversary in AA. (same words)
Clinician B: You haven't had a drink in a long time. (different words)

A risk in using words other than those of the client is that we may choose words that do not convey the same meaning the client intended. In the example above, Clinician B's view that one year is a long time might not correspond with the client's perspective. For the client, the one-year anniversary may be small compared to his cousin's 22 years of sobriety. Also, having one year in AA does not necessarily mean that the client hasn't had a drink in a year.

Reflecting content is further complicated by the fact that people don't often talk in single sentences, conveying only one idea. Human communication is usually multilayered, and the clinician is constantly making judgments about which of the many pieces of shared content is the most important to reflect at the moment. At different times in the interview or in the working relationship, the clinician may reflect and emphasize different pieces of client content in order to challenge, help expand awareness, or develop new perspectives on problems. At this point, we are using reflection as part of the empathic echo; we are trying only to demonstrate empathy and support, so we need to reflect what we believe the *client* sees as the crucial content. Other content is stored for future consideration.

Example

> *Client:* I had a terrible day. The bus was late, my daughter was sick, and the boss yelled at me for being late for work again.

There are six pieces of content that could be reflected following this client's statement:

1. Terrible day
2. Late bus
3. Sick daughter
4. Late for work
5. Not the first time late for work
6. Boss yelled

The clinician is free to reflect any of these pieces of content, and three different clinicians might all choose different reflections, depending on the stance or focus each wants to sustain.

Examples

> *Clinician A:* Your daughter was sick, the bus was late, and you were yelled at by your boss for being late again. It was a terrible day.
>
> *Clinician B:* You had a terrible day.
>
> *Clinician C:* What a lot of things to cope with in one day!

Clinician A decides to reflect all of what the client said, to acknowledge hearing it while leaving the conversation leadership to the client. Although this may be useful in letting the client know that the clinician heard all that was said and simply wishes the client to continue, just repeating back time after time everything the client says can feel tedious and meaningless to both client and clinician. Too many repetitions can dull the liveliness of spontane-ity and make the clinical conversation feel too far removed from ordinary exchange. Rarely does anyone just repeat back what someone else has said.

Clinician B notes to herself that the client was late for work "again," which may be an important piece of information to pick up on later—especially if it signals a pattern undermining the client's achievement of stated goals. However, since she is attempting an empathic echo, she reflects what seems most crucial to the client in the moment of this encounter: the "terrible day." She will store the information about being late for work, the boss's yelling, and the daughter's illness, perhaps to make use of them later. Clinician B uses the *first* piece of content because in this instance she feels that it captures the gestalt of the entire communication. At other times, clinicians will reflect the *last* piece of content in clients' narratives, just as an encouragement for clients to go further.

Clinician C's response is a *summary comment,* using words that are different from those of the client. Such a response is an attempt to reflect content *and* tone so as to express and build empathy.

EXERCISE 4.11 *Empathic Reflection of Content*

Read the following client statements. List the pieces of content—the different ideas—in each statement. Which pieces might you reflect in order to show empathy or support for the client? Reflect the content in two ways:

1. By using the client's own words
2. By paraphrasing the content or meaning of what the client said

Client A: I am trying to choose between a career with the military or with the police. The military will give me a chance to see the world and experience other cultures. I can also get my B.A. degree for free. But my father and my uncles are all cops.

Client B: I just found out that my aunt is having her kidney removed. My uncle is 86 and is really worried about her. He has high blood pressure and diabetes. I have to find out about nursing care for both of them.

Client C: The kids at school are picking on me. I am the only girl in the shop class. We have to make a model for a toolshed, and no one will be my partner. If I can't get a partner, I will fail.

Note that you are only reading this and that your experience of the exchange might be different if you actually heard the client's statements, replete with nonverbal, paralinguistic, and metacommunicative clues. Now, instead of reading each statement to yourself, pair up with a colleague and take turns making each statement. Note differences in tone, emphasis, speech rate, and other paralinguistic cues as the speaker and the content change.

Empathic reflection of affect. Clients can tell us directly how they feel, as when a client says "I'm so proud . . .," or "I am scared," or "I am so sad that. . . ." Sometimes, though, the words clients use to describe their feelings are ambiguous; for example, "I was upset that I got fired." The term *upset* could mean that client was sad, worried, angry, embarrassed—any number of things that we can only imagine unless the client elaborates the meaning.

Often the clinician is left to guess what the client feels, using a combination of any prior knowledge of the client's habitual patterns; the literal words spoken; and with what tone, emphasis, facial and body movements, or feelings the words are spoken. Clinicians need to develop a capacity to recognize when feelings are arising, to discern one feeling state from another, and to decide when and when not to focus on feelings. They also need to familiarize themselves with the variety of ways in which clients express feelings, coming to appreciate local, cultural, and idiosyncratic styles and influences.

Examples

> *Client:* I'm so pissed off at my brother for telling my mom I'm pregnant, when I wanted to tell her myself.
>
> *Clinician A:* You're pregnant and your brother told your mother.
>
> *Clinician B:* You're mad at your brother.
>
> *Clinician C:* You're disappointed that you didn't get to tell your mother you're pregnant.

Clinician A decided to reflect content only. She noted two pieces of content: that the client was pregnant and that her brother told her mother. She did not reflect the client's feeling, perhaps because of the way the client expressed herself: "pissed off." The clinician may have felt uncomfortable reflecting that term or uncomfortable about getting more anger into the room by focusing on it. Other clinicians might feel that unless the angry feelings are acknowledged and validated, attempts to focus intellectually on content will not get very far because the client is "so pissed off."

Clinician B reflected that the client was angry with her brother. Note that this clinician used the word *mad* to reflect the client's feeling. Clients may at times use words that we feel uncomfortable reflecting. We have found that it is wiser not to fake comfort; it works better for us to paraphrase the client than to use terms with which we're not comfortable. For example, adolescents can use extreme language for purposes of group belongingness or to test or shock adults. Clinicians may try to assume this style and end up seeming and sounding very disingenuous.

Clinician C did not reflect the feeling that the client directly expressed—anger. She reflected what she felt the client might also be feeling—disappointment. So, even when clients directly express feelings, clinicians attempting empathy may pursue other feelings that, although unspoken, may also be crucial to the client's perspective in the moment.

Each of the preceding reflections takes the conversation in a different direction. Clinician B's response might lead to a focus on the client's relationship with her brother, whereas Clinician C's might lead to concerns about talking with her mother. All the approaches have merit: they are attempts at empathy.

E X E R C I S E 4.12 *Empathic Reflection of Affect*

Go back to Exercise 4.11 and reflect the affect that might go along with the content of each client's statement. Again, note the difference when you *hear* communication rather than read it, that results from the addition of multiple clues to intent and meaning.

The empathic echo is more than simply an echo of specific words or feelings. In reflecting either content or affect, clinicians carefully attempt to reflect the way clients understand or make meaning of their situations, feelings, behaviors, or thoughts. We thus reflect not only *what* is said but also *how* it is said—its tone and coloration, and the metacommunication and paralinguistic cues we listened for in Chapter 3. We use the empathic echo for several reasons: to show we are listening, to increase the client's feeling of being attended to closely, and to increase the client's feeling of being understood. The empathic echo allows the client to correct any misconceptions the clinician may have.

 CLIP 4.3
Empathy

Empathic Failures

Because clinicians are human, there inevitably will be times when we miss the boat empathically and reflect the wrong content, feeling, or meaning. At other times, clinicians may drift from the moment and miss a very important theme or feeling altogether, all the while appearing to listen and nod attentively. We have found that clients often do notice when we drift away, and they may signal this awareness by asking, "Now, where was I?" or "What was I talking about when I got off there?" as though *they* were lost, not us! Sometimes interviewers confuse one client's story with another's and make a remark about an event or loved one unrelated to the client, hurting the client's feelings. The client may feel, "I'm indistinguishable from all the others."

There is an increased likelihood of empathic misses when the client and clinician come from different ethnic or sociocultural backgrounds (Comas-Diaz & Jacobsen, 1991). Even within the same cultural or ethnic group, people can act on faulty assumptions or generalizations. Empathic failures can also occur when the clinician overidentifies with or idealizes the client, or feels some antipathy toward the client. In addition, empathic misses may occur when the client is particularly difficult or when the client demeans, attacks, or sabotages the clinician.

Psychodynamic theorists postulate a process called *countertransference* in which the clinician unconsciously sees the client as representative of an important figure from the past and behaves toward the client as though the client *were* that person. A countertransference distortion would negatively affect the clinician's ability to be empathic, since empathy requires the ability to accurately perceive and join with the client's perspective. We will discuss the psychodynamic concepts of transference and countertransference in greater detail in Chapter 9.

Clinicians make use of detailed process recordings, video- and audio-tapes, and supervision to understand and, hopefully, to change personal feelings, beliefs, and reactions that interfere with empathy and caring. Group supervision is very useful in the mutual sharing and spotting of overidentifications, scapegoating, aversions, and other behaviors that negatively impact on clinician empathy. Personal therapy is highly recommended when clinicians continue to have problems with caring, sustainment, and empathy. If they continue to have difficulties with empathy, they may need to conclude that clinical work is not a suitable undertaking for them.

Learning from Empathic Failures

It is good to remember that even when our reflections of content and affect are misguided or wrong, the process attending these errors can be extremely important in modeling for clients that mistakes can occur without destroying relationships. Both client and clinician are reminded that the important step in maintaining connection is not the perfection of the participants but the work of sorting things out together in a mutually trusting and accepting bond. Moreover, mutuality is heightened because the client gets to educate and correct the clinician about what was actually said or what is happening between them, so that the customary power imbalance in clinical work is somewhat mediated through this *two-way feedback*. We listen for empathic failures, acknowledge them with grace, and thank clients for patience, reactions, and feedback helpful to correcting the course.

 CLIP 4.3
Empathic Failure

Example of Empathic Failure and Correction

Client: My child has gone off to college. It's really a change in my life.

Clinician: You must feel very sad now that your last child has left home.

Client: Not really. I actually feel relieved to finally have time to spend on myself.

Clinician: So you don't feel sad. You feel relieved, and perhaps excited, that there are new opportunities for you.

Client: Yeah, it *is* very exciting.

I was seeing a client who had been abruptly let go from her company during a downsizing. She said she was incredibly anxious. I started to reflect how worried she must be about economic issues—how she would pay the rent, where she would get a new job, etc. We spent almost the whole session talking about that. The next week she came in and said that what really had been bothering her was how other people would perceive her. I had missed the point of her anxiety. I immediately acknowledged that I had been thinking that she was worried about money when she was worried about something else. At first I felt bad. Later, my supervisor pointed out that it was great that she corrected me. I didn't have to be perfect. I had created an atmosphere where she felt comfortable telling me when I was wrong. We really were a team working together. I was trying and she was helping me so that I would really understand her.

Conclusion

In this chapter we have reviewed the basic elements that sustain clinical work: support and empathy. The clinician communicates support through a reliable clinical presence that provides genuine warmth, caring, acceptance, and validation and that affirms client strengths. Effective clinicians also demonstrate their support by being available, by providing concrete services, and by advocating with and for their clients.

Empathy is the ability to join the perspective and experience of the client—to feel with and as the client—while maintaining the position of an observing and communicating other. Clinical empathy can be expressed through supportive sounds, mirroring, and empathic reflection of content and affect. But as we saw in the clinical examples, clinicians may not be empathic, and attempts at empathy may fail. The conscientious clinician uses every opportunity to promote and sustain the clinical relationship. In the next chapter we will discuss methods clinicians use within this relationship to help clients further elaborate their stories.

Suggested Readings

This is a classic work on the helping relationship.

Rogers, Carl. (1958). The characteristics of a helping relationship. *Personnel and Guidance Journal, 37,* 6–16.

There are a number of excellent works on the process and complications of empathy, including the following.

Book, Howard E. (1988). Empathy: Misconceptions and misuses in psychotherapy. *American Journal of Psychiatry, 145,* 420–424.

Comas-Diaz, Lillian, & Jacobsen, Frederick M. (1991). Ethnocultural transference and countertransference in the therapeutic dyad. *American Journal of Orthopsychiatry, 61,* 392–402.

Jordan, Judith V. (1991). Empathy and self-boundaries. In Judith V. Jordan, Alexandra G. Kaplan, Jean Baker Miller, Irene P. Stiver, & Janet L. Surrey (Eds.), *Women's growth in connection: Writings from the Stone Center* (pp. 67–80). New York: Guilford.

Pinderhughes, Elaine. (1979). Teaching empathy in cross-cultural social work. *Social Work, 24,* 312–316.

CHAPTER 5

Exploration and Elaboration

The clinician understands that supportive ambiance and empathy alone are not sufficient to help clients better grasp their situation and bring about the changes they desire in themselves or in their lives. In the following chapters we will explore a variety of ways clinicians work together with clients to create change: using exploration, developing hunches and new perspectives, changing old behaviors and learning new ones, using the clinical relationship as a venue for change, and moving to action. In this chapter we will begin by discussing exploration and elaboration.

Levels of Exploration and Elaboration

Few narratives, especially ones shared with a relative stranger, emerge full-blown all on their own. In addition to creating a supportive relationship, safe space, and congenial tone, the clinician uses the techniques and strategies of *exploration* and *elaboration* to elicit and expand on the story. Exploration helps both clinicians and clients. It helps clinicians gather new information, clarify ambiguities or uncertainties, raise new issues, and attain a deeper and more accurate understanding of the client. It helps clients expand their stories, note and elucidate their meanings, and develop new perspectives. Exploration and elaboration are important to every aspect of clinical work. They are central to the assessment process as clinicians clarify and prioritize presenting problems and assets. However, exploration and elaboration are not limited to the assessment phase; they are also crucial in establishing working agreements and in planning and implementing interventions.

Arnold Lazarus (1971) was the first to describe layers or circles of personal territory. He suggested that people keep their most private thoughts in an inner circle, shared with few others. Dusty Miller (1996) further proposed that interview conversation itself has outer, middle, and inner layers or circles. The *outer circle* houses the opening—sometimes surface—exploratory conversation between people who are just getting to know each other. Outer circle exploration occurs early in the interview as the client is assessing the clinician's trustworthiness, respectfulness, and reliability. The goals of this outer level of exploration are to develop knowledge of the presenting situation and to establish a relationship of trust and collaboration by talking about subjects that do not push the client too quickly into forbidden or overly distressing topics. Outer circle talking is characteristic of intake and brief interviews. It focuses on clarifying the reasons for referral, eliciting the strengths and vulnerabilities of the client and his or her systems, fleshing out client demographics, and spelling out interviewer-client roles and agreements on how to proceed.

The *middle circle* houses more revealing exploration of deeper-level content, conflicts, and feelings as the relationship develops and both client and interviewer feel themselves on more secure ground. A shift to the middle circle involves more focused exploration, which may elicit more painful detail, reflection, and affect. Here the clinician may begin to raise topics not yet broached or elaborated on by the client. Whereas the earlier focus often tends to be more about information, middle circle exploration usually elicits more complicated feelings and meaning. Often, more is shared about significant or previously undisclosed behavior patterns, relationship issues, and situation dynamics.

The *inner circle* houses feelings and content about frightening, taboo, or shame-bound areas. This level of exploration brings people into areas of the story that may have been previously unshared with others or may have been unknown even to the clients themselves. At this level of conversation, clients often discover things about themselves and their relationships with others of which they previously have been unaware. Often a good deal of embarrassment, reluctance, hesitation, and confusion is manifest at this level. Only after trust and talking are well established do most people risk the maximum exposure of the inner circle.

The following examples demonstrate outer, middle, and inner circles of conversation in response to clinician probes. Although the clinician's questions and the client's responses all move from outer to inner circles, often the client's responses will have more to do with where the participants are in the interview or in the relationship than with the specific questions the clinician asks. In this chapter we will discuss ways clinicians can deepen the level of conversation by helping clients explore and elaborate on their stories.

Examples

Outer Circle Talk

Clinician: Can you tell me something about your work?

Client: I work as a painter for a large painting company. I'm the supervisor for a crew of four. I like the outdoor activity and being my own boss.

Middle Circle Talk

Clinician: You mentioned things you like . . . are there things you don't like?

Client: Well, I find it hard to be the boss sometimes. I'm not really comfortable telling people what to do. I hate it when someone screws up and I have to get after them.

Inner Circle Talk

Clinician: Where do you think this "hating to get after people" comes from?

Client: I always hated being bossed around myself. I was the youngest boy in the family and my four older brothers were always on my case. I guess I feel that I never want to come across as a bully and make people feel as bad as I did. I never thought about that before. . . . It's weird how something that happened when I was a kid could affect me at work today.

Levels of conversation and exploration are not discrete, and they do not appear in neat sequences, one right after the other. More often, clinicians and clients will subtly shift between levels within each interview and from interview to interview. Most interviews begin at the outer circle in order to "warm up" participants to further exploration and discussion and then move, when comfortable, to deeper levels of elaboration. Inner circles of communication usually aren't reached until a level of trust has been established between the participants. It is not unusual for clinical interviews to stay at the outer and middle circles for several sessions. In fact, some clinical relationships stay almost entirely at the outer and middle circles and still get very important work done.

Depth and intensity of exploration should always be guided by clinician awareness of cultural norms, customs, and taboos. Lum notes that Valle (1980) suggests that clinicians begin with friendly conversation, or "platica."

> Latinos are accustomed to mutual extended discussion, which is a recognized form of relationship building. "Platica" stresses mutuality and reciprocity, meaning an open and free exchange of information between two parties. Helper-initiated friendly conversation about the weather, humorous incidents, or recent activities sets the stage for development of a relationship. (Lum, 1996, pp. 121–122)

During times of crisis, both clinicians and clients may move rapidly to inner circle conversation without necessarily building the relationship first. Accelerated questioning is often appropriate when there is limited time available and an urgent need for prompt intervention. Such accelerated probing often occurs in mandated protective service evaluations; for example, where a child's insufficiently explained burns, an elderly woman's black eye and broken arm, or a mentally ill person's delusion of flying between buildings are all cause for direct, persistent exploration to protect people from further harm.

Other clients may also move quickly to inner circle conversation, believing that this is what "therapy" is all about, and pushing ahead without sufficient awareness of the impact that too much self-disclosure may have on them. Almost all of us have been involved in such situations at some point in our careers: overwhelmed clients canceling for a period of time, for example, or never coming back, feeling too exposed. Clinicians need to be aware that while one frequent goal of clinical work is to deepen the level of conversation, such a deepening is only one goal among many. An equally important goal is to maintain the safety of the clinical experience so that clients do not feel overwhelmed by revealing too much, too soon. Usually, we also try to move conversation to the middle or outer circles before the interview ends, so clients aren't left feeling overwhelmed or exposed as they return to community roles and responsibilities.

> A mentor told me never to do emotional surgery on people if what they needed was a transfusion, and never to do emotional surgery in the session without leaving enough time to suture the client back up before leaving, so they don't go out alone and have an emotional bleed with no tourniquet in sight.

It is important to note that beginning clinicians often confuse "going deep" with succeeding as an interviewer. In reality, good clinical interviewing can occur even when the interview does not move beyond the outer circle of conversation. The purpose and goals of the contact, and the time and resources available, usually have a great influence on the level and duration of clinical conversations. "Success" is most often measured by the realization of agreed-upon aims and goals, not the number of painful subjects covered. Indeed, the thoughtful clinician tries to introduce *momentary intervals of respite* into intense exploratory conversation, carefully helping clients move back and forth between immersion in material and somewhat more detached review. Respite protects the client from being overwhelmed and also allows the clinician to check in with the client to ensure that the process feels okay to continue.

> Lupe came into the Rape Crisis Center for her second interview after being assaulted at her high school homecoming party. This time she did not hold back and talked for almost 20 minutes straight, graphically describing the attack, and with a whole lot of crying. This was a different girl than I saw last time, and I think she would have cried and talked the whole time if I

hadn't stopped her. At about 20 minutes, I asked if we could stop for a minute so she could catch her breath and check in with me about how it was to share all this with me. First she cried quietly for a time. Then she let out a huge sigh. She held herself and rocked a little. I said we could take our time, there was lots of time for the story to come out. She said she wasn't used to talking so much and apologized for "making me listen to all this." I said this is what we're here for, so women can speak out in safety. She nodded and leaned back against the wall. She said she didn't know what she would have done without this place. In a bit, she described a nightmare no one else wanted to hear.

The rest of this chapter focuses on techniques clinicians can use to help clients explore or elaborate their stories and move, where appropriate, between conversational levels or circles.

Techniques of Exploration and Elaboration

There are a number of techniques that can be used in exploration and elaboration. Those we find most useful are questions, prompts, silence, reflection (including underlining and summarizing), refocusing, and initiating new topics.

Questions and Questioning

Asking questions is one of the most reliable and effective techniques for gathering information, deepening discussion, or broadening focus. Clinicians ask questions about the client (the client's thoughts, feelings, behaviors, and relationships), about other people (what the client reports that other people feel, think, or do), about the client's circumstances and the larger social contexts with which the client interacts, and about the clinical relationship itself. In general, interviewers routinely ask more questions in the engagement and assessment phases of work. Here the aim is to elicit a working sketch of the story and its participants, their strengths, resources, and stressors as guides for more immediate decision making and planning. This use of many questions early on is particularly true in managed care settings, in which engagement, assessment, planning, and intervention all occur in the first contact. Detailed early questioning has also historically characterized crisis intervention work (such as protective service evaluations and emergency room interviews). A lot of gentle questioning may also characterize initial contacts with clients who present for help but have difficulty expressing themselves.

Asking questions may seem to the novice interviewer an easy, even routine, matter. In reality, asking appropriate and timely questions is one of the hardest clinical skills to be mastered. Good questioning requires sensitivity to where the client is; exquisite timing as to the fit between the question, the moment, and the people present; and conscious self-containment to avoid asking numerous tangential questions that may readily come to mind as the narrative unfolds. Beginning interviewers frequently either ask too many questions in order to fill out mandatory forms or because they don't yet know what else to do, or ask too few because they feel intrusive in asking or embarrassed to go more deeply into sensitive or forbidden areas.

The clinician's attitude toward questioning is often influenced by family and cultural norms and taboos. For example, clients and clinicians both may have been taught that asking personal questions is prying. We stress again how essential it is that clinicians become familiar with the communication norms and styles of the many different cultural and social groups—understanding the norms of both our own cultural group and those of the clients with whom we work. Teresa La Fromboise notes, for example, that Native American clients may feel more comfortable and more responsive if the clinician demonstrates cultural sensitivity and uses self-disclosure before asking personal questions (La Fromboise & Dixon, 1981). Many cultures still educate members not to share feelings with outsiders, not to discuss conflicts outside the family, and not to disclose in-group information that could damage group members or weaken group cohesion.

The clinician's attitude toward questioning is also influenced by his or her training. Clinical theories vary regarding the importance given to questioning, and some mentors and supervisors encourage active exploration by the clinician, whereas others do not.

Closed-Ended and Open-Ended Questions

Questions can be closed-ended or open-ended. *Closed-ended* questions are more focal and can usually be answered with a word or two, after which the client characteristically ceases talking and waits for the next question from the clinician. Closed-ended questions often begin with interrogatives, such as "do you," "are you," or "have you," and hint at what the interviewer expects the response to be. In contrast, *open-ended* questions give the client more opportunity or flexibility in responding and elaborating. Because they keep the client in the driver's seat of the conversation, open questions are usually preferred by clinicians. Open-ended questions usually begin with interrogatives like "what" or "how," but they need not.

Examples

Closed-ended:	"Do you live alone?"
Open-ended:	"What is your living situation?"
Closed-ended:	"Did that make you sad?"
Open-ended:	"How did you feel about that?"
Closed-ended:	"Did you hit him back?"
Open-ended:	"What did you do then?"
	"What happened then?"

Note that in the last question, two different open-ended questions were offered. While both allow the client to elaborate the story of being hit by another person, the first is more directive in that it focuses specifically on the *client* and what he or she *did* in response. The second question is more nondirective and allows the client to proceed in any direction he or she wishes. The client could say what he or she did, or what he or she felt, or what someone else did or felt.

E X E R C I S E 5.1 *Opening Up Closed Questions*

In small groups, take each of the following questions and think of all the ways you could phrase it as an open-ended question.

"Did that make you feel guilty?"

"Would you stay put or run if he threatened you?"

"Is our work together a help to you?"

"Are those tears telling me you are sad?"

"Are you relieved to have her gone?"

Problems with closed-ended questions.   The use of closed-ended questions introduces a number of problems. First, these questions give the client little opportunity or encouragement to expand on the theme at hand, since they often suggest monosyllabic answers such as "yes" and "no." Second, closed questions (as well as too many questions in a row) keep the initiative with the interviewer and disempower the client, who will quickly be conditioned to expect just to answer one question and passively await the next. Reducing the client to the role of mere respondent may inadvertently replicate the experience of far too many clients who historically have been made to feel that they are the objects rather than the subjects of their own lives and stories.

Moreover, closed-ended questions often suggest the answer the interviewer expects or prefers—for example: "Did that make you mad?" "Was that when he hung up?" "Are you nervous about our meeting?" The client who sees the interviewer's preference within the question may feel worried about differing with the clinician's point of view or may feel irritated by the clinician's "mind reading." In the earlier example, the question "Did you hit him back?" could convey to the client that hitting back is what the clinician thinks the client would or should have done when hit.

There are times, though, when clinicians *need* to use closed-ended questions. Such questions are essential when agency routine or necessity requires that the clinician get a great deal of information in a very short time in order to determine immediate eligibility for needed services. The clinician may go through a symptom checklist (such as, "Do you have a sleep disturbance?"), a benefits enrollment form ("Do you have other sources of income we haven't covered?"), or an emergency room family history ("Has anyone in your family had problems with alcohol?").

Furthermore, if someone is rambling agitatedly or is getting out of control with fear or confusion, a series of organizing closed-ended questions can often provide much needed structure and calming, as in the following sample conversation:

Example of Purposeful Closed-Ended Questioning

Clinician: Do you have a place to sleep tonight, Aaron?

Client: No, no! Do I look like I have any place?!

Clinician: Is there anyone I can call to let know you're okay?

Client: Nobody, I don't want nobody to know . . .

Clinician: Do you have any money to buy dinner with while I look for a bed for you?

Client: No . . . I'm flat out.

Clinician: If you're hungry, I can get you a voucher for a cafeteria meal.

Client: (Relaxes and sits back) Okay . . . I could stand something hot for a change. Could somebody go with me, though? This is my first time here . . .

Clinician: Can you sit here with me while I make a couple of calls to find a bed? Then I can go with you to the cafeteria.

Client: Yep . . .

E X E R C I S E 5.2 *Interviewing Using Questions*

Divide into teams of three and take turns interviewing each other about your day. Have the observer note all the questions and review them to see how many were open-ended and how many were closed-ended. You might try to interview again using only closed-ended, and then only open-ended questions. Discuss anything from this exercise that you want to keep in mind when asking questions. Record what you learned in your journal.

Tried-and-True Questions

Certain questions remain useful over many decades of experience; they just seem to get easily and directly at the things we need to know in order to assess, plan, and act wisely in our clinical roles.

Examples of Tried-and-True Questions

"What brings you here to see me?" (reasons for coming)

"Why are you seeking help *now*?" (timing of request)

"How did you think I might help?" (anticipation of the experience)

"What would you like to get done today?" (client as the driver)

"Where would you like to begin?" (client as the driver)

"Can you tell me more about your situation?" (elaboration of person-situation)

"Who else is available as a support or help in this?" (situation dynamics)

"Who, if anyone, is making things more complicated just now?" (situation dynamics)

"Have you ever spoken with a professional before? If so, how did it go?" (vision of the work)

"Are there other things you haven't mentioned yet that would be important for me to know?" (elaboration)

"What will we look for, to know that the changes you want have actually taken place?" (concretizing desired outcome)

"What do people say about your coming to talk with me?" (work dynamics)

"What's it like for you to be talking about these things with me?" (relationship building, checking in)

"Is the work moving in the way you hoped it would?" (checking in)

"How does the work we're doing compare with what you thought it would be like?" (checking in)

"Are there any other things that should be on our menu of things to talk about?" (double-checking)

"Is the pace we're going at okay for you?" (checking in)

"Would you let me know if, at any time, we go too fast or get into things you're not comfortable talking about?" (checking in)

"Does what I'm saying make sense?" (clarifying)

"Could you put that in other words so I can understand it better?" (not knowing)

"Can you say more about that?" (elaboration)

General Principles Regarding the Use of Questioning

1. *Questions should be intentional.* Clinicians should know why they are asking what they are asking. Clinical questions always have to have a purpose, and the clinician should always be aware of the possible effects that each question might have on the client.

2. *Clinicians need to be sensitive to cultural attitudes toward questioning.* Every culture, and most families, inculcate norms regarding who can ask what, of whom, in what order, and which questions should be asked only in private or without certain members present. It is imperative that clinicians develop cultural sensitivity and competence in asking questions

regarding such subjects as class, sex, money, serious illness, addictions, and family violence. As previously noted, members of the family or culture are the most expert interpreters of their own meaning systems, and they can be asked directly about preferred customs and styles in providing needed information to outsiders like clinicians.

3. *Questions should be well timed.* Clinicians should know why they are asking what they are asking *now—at this particular time* in the interview. The clinician must think about whether it is possible to get the same information by another means that will not disrupt client flow; often it is simply a matter of waiting for the client to disclose more information. Clinicians also need to be aware of the degree of trust present in the relationship before asking sensitive questions.

4. *Too much questioning makes the clinician the director.* As previously stated, gentle guidance and data-gathering questions are inevitable in emergencies and in initial sessions with clients not used to clinical work. As the work evolves, however, the clinician wants the client's thinking and voice to strengthen through maximum encouragement, participation, expression, and initiation of topic or focus. This potential for strengthening is lessened by too many clinician initiatives.

5. *Questions can interrupt concentration.* While questions are often necessary and helpful, it's important to remember that every question, no matter how well intended, interrupts the natural flow of the client's narrative. Few things are more maddening than attempting to tell something to another person and being constantly interrupted by questions that throw the narrator off beat.

6. *Flexibility in data gathering is essential.* Sometimes we're forced by necessity to ask lots of questions immediately, in order to get information necessary to make decisions by the end of the meeting. Even in such a situation, the clinician may alter a planned agenda if the client sits down and bursts into tears, comes in and starts shouting at the clinician, or describes an impending crisis or a personal success. Usually the clinician will explore briefly what's happening, rather than abruptly refocusing the conversation in order to get preplanned questions asked. Data gathering merely for filling out forms should come only after showing concern and support for the client, and a data-gathering agenda should always give way to situational or psychological emergencies. Clients are more likely to broaden or deepen their stories when they feel calm, safe, and understood.

7. *Good questions can be supportive and therapeutic, as well as useful for gathering data.* Questioning can serve many purposes: to help the client expand the story or to gain new perspectives; to provide more information or help clarify ambiguity for the clinician. Questions can also be used to support or underline client strengths or to reflect empathy. For example, "How have you managed so much at once?" is both a real

question and an affirmation of client strength. "Will your remarkable courage hold up through this long court process?" performs a validating function, as does a question such as, "You mean there's even more that's happened to you?"

8. *Difficult questions should be introduced carefully.* Kadushin (1997) suggests that the impact of difficult questions can be mitigated by the use of prefaces or lead-ins that help clients save face, that "universalize problems," or that "raise a client's self-esteem in preparation for dealing with a question which is apt to be self-deflating" (p. 261). For example, the clinician might preface a question by saying: "So many moms have told me they feel alone and pushed to the wall when they strike out at their children. What were you personally feeling before you hit Kendra Lee?"

9. *Too little questioning can make for drift, or leave the client at a loss for direction.* Although it is possible to conduct an interview in which the clinician doesn't ask a single question, sometimes the clinician needs to help the new, unfocused, or disorganized client by asking gentle questions in plain language designed to keep things on track when the client starts to wander. A new client may start to talk about her worries about being a mother for the first time, then describe a new mother she saw on TV, then talk about how much cable TV costs, and then talk about the things she watches on cable in the evening when the baby's asleep. While none of these subjects is "bad" and all are pieces of information about the client and her experience, goals of the session will determine to what degree the clinician may reintroduce the original topic by gently asking questions that redirect the client back to it.

The clinician may also need to ask questions for purposes of clarification or to get more information. Too little questioning can occur when the interviewer thinks personal questions are becoming too intrusive or does not want the client to feel pushed too fast to reveal difficult material. At other times, the clinician may not ask questions for fear of seeming unempathic ("If I ask a question, she'll think I haven't been following closely and have forgotten her details"). Sometimes the clinician's own unresolved issues may prevent timely exploration of personally sensitive material.

My supervisor urged me and urged me, but I just could not ask that lady more details about her divorce right then, and I wasn't ready to have my supervisor or others at work know I was splitting up with my wife then, in much the same way my client was splitting up with her husband. I would go into each session with a plan to ask Ms. Morales more about what had happened, and somehow, the time would just zoom by and it would be the end of the session and I hadn't asked her.

10. *Follow-up questions are often necessary.* Clinicians need to stay with a line of inquiry long enough to mine it sufficiently for details about content, meaning, or feelings. Sometimes the clinician should ask more follow-up

questions regarding something the client has said, but the clinician doesn't ask them. Perhaps the clinician feels he or she should know the answer or has been told the answer before and is embarrassed not to have remembered it. Some interviewers are embarrassed to ask clients what they mean by things, fearing to appear ignorant when in the not-knowing position.

11. *Answers to questions can be both verbal and nonverbal.* Clinicians need to listen to both the verbal and nonverbal answers that clients give. Sometimes there are discrepancies between the verbal and the non-verbal. Any discrepancies in clients' answers are stored away as potentially important pieces of information for possible future explo-ration. We also listen for discrepancies between clients' stated inten-tions (for example, "I'm going to AA every night next week") and their actual behaviors, which can be known only over time, through exploration ("I only got there once"). Clinicians also need to attend to apparent patterns and themes that emerge in client answers to questions. For example, the repeated exclamation "Am I stupid or what?!" following descriptions of habitual behaviors definitely would bear exploring further. So would statements like "There I go again" and "I can't believe I let that happen!"

12. *Clinician questions can be both verbal and nonverbal.* Raising an eyebrow, cocking one's head, responding wide-eyed to statements—these and many other lighthearted responses of the clinician can act as questions to which the client can respond immediately and with goodwill. These clinician responses represent a warmer, less formal style of probing, and they are best used within the context of a solidly established working relationship.

13. *Clinicians need to be aware of what they are* not *asking.* Clients often notice clinician patterns the same way clinicians notice client patterns. They often note, sometimes subliminally, which topics clinicians don't ask about (sex, money, violence). It is not unusual for clients to protect clinicians by not bringing up subjects around which the clinician has shown uneasiness or embarrassment. It is all too easy for clinicians to say that clients are not talking about certain issues, only to discover through examination of process recordings or videotapes that the clinician is not asking about these issues either.

14. *Questions can be used as defenses or weapons, by both clinician and client.* They can be used to try to diminish or shame the other so that the questioner feels more powerful once again. The following are examples of hostile questions that aren't seeking the answer they appear to solicit.

> "What is the point of all this?"
> "Is this really what we're here to talk about?"
> "Haven't you asked me that enough times?"

"Are you finished yet?"

"You mean you don't know after all this time what the 12 steps are?"

E X E R C I S E 5.3 *Asking Hard Questions*

Break up into small groups and list topics that you personally find difficult to explore. Practice asking the other members of your group two questions about one of your least comfortable topics, those that you'd find hard to ask a client. Give each other feedback to assist in reconstructing questions or style so that the questions come across more comfortably. Did your questions elicit what you anticipated? Record what you learned in your journal.

Problematic Types of Questions

"Why" questions can be problematic because they often sound judgmental—and they often are. "Why did you do that?" may leave the client feeling defensive. "Why do you feel that way?" can leave the client feeling as though their feelings are strange or unnatural. Although at times it might be helpful to ask clients to think about motives for their behaviors or feelings, we have found that "why" questions rarely work. We prefer to use phrases such as "How do you understand that happening?" or "What do you think caused it?" or "As you look back, what do you think was going on?"

Pseudo-questions are often directives or commands disguised as questions. For example, a parent might say, "Are you going to do your homework now?" when he means "It's time to do your homework." A clinician may begin a session with the question, "Did you want to pick up where we left off last time?" when she is suggesting, "Let's pick up where we left off last time."

Double questions occur when the clinician asks the client to respond to more than one question at a time. A confused look on the client's face often indicates uncertainty as to which question to address. Double, and even triple, questions are not unusual in interviewing.

Examples of Double Questions

> *Clinician A:* Tell me about your week. How are the kids doing in school? What's going on at work?
>
> *Clinician B:* So, are you feeling more depressed? Are you having fights?

Tangential questions veer from the main topic, taking side roads without good reason. This can happen when the clinician either is curious about an unrelated detail or doesn't have a clear focus or direction in mind. The clinician who goes off on too many tangents can create an aura of hopping around aimlessly or of being superficial.

Examples of Tangential Questions

Client A: I've had the hardest day! We're putting out a new computer program, and everybody was so stressed out.

Clinician A: What kind of computer program is it?

Client B: My mother's new boyfriend moved in with us last week. I don't like him very much.

Clinician B: What day did he move in?

Ratatat questioning barrages the client with one rapid-fire question after another. The questions often impart pressure and don't leave time for in-depth exploration. They may all be on one topic or they may shift from topic to topic, so that no subject is pursued long enough to develop any real depth or meaning. Again, the aura of the meeting is one of superficiality or lack of clear direction or interest on the clinician's part.

Example of Ratatat Questioning

Note that these are all closed-ended questions as well.

Clinician: Where did you go to high school?

Client: Sacred Heart.

Clinician: When was that?

Client: '63.

Clinician: Was it a big school?

Client: Pretty big. I was—

Clinician: Did you date while you were there?

Client: Not really.

Clinician: And after that, did you date . . . later on, I mean?

I told my supervisee that I thought she was covering so many subjects in her interviews that it didn't give clients enough time to really get into anything in depth. She didn't agree, so I asked her to videotape her next client session and then watch the interview with a tablet handy so she could count up the number of new subjects introduced by her questions. She was astonished to find that she had asked 37 questions in 45 minutes and had covered a wide array of subjects. She was surprised by both the number of questions she asked and the number of topics introduced.

Prompts

Prompts are brief responses by the clinician that encourage the client to continue with the story or to add to what has been said. Prompts are often given in the form of questions or brief utterances that pick up on the client's last remarks. Prompts are meant to be minimal and to signal the clinician's close following of the story and interest in details. Some clients respond well to prompts; others may feel they'd prefer the clinician to just sit quietly and listen unobtrusively.

Examples of Common Prompts

"Say more about that."

"Could you please expand on that?"

"I'm not sure I quite got that . . . could you say that again in different words?"

"And then . . . ?"

"Please continue . . . "

"Was there more you wanted to say?"

Silence

The clinician's judicious use of *silence* can help the client explore and elaborate. Silence can also be uncomfortable for both the clinician and the client. However, sometimes the best way to encourage the client to tell his or her story is simply to leave room for it to unfold. Clients may use silences to reflect on what has been said, to make choices about where to take the story next, or to experience reactions to what is happening in the moment. Sometimes clients may simply not know what to do or say next. If the clinician is too quick or too active in ending a silence, clients—especially those whose experience has already undermined initiative—may be conditioned just to sit and wait for the clinician to direct the process.

Reflection

In Chapter 4, we discussed the use of reflection to build empathy. Reflection can also be used in a number of ways to further exploration. Reflection can be used as a *probe* to encourage the client to explore a specific area further.

Reflection avoids the problem of too much questioning. Rather than asking a direct question, the clinician can indicate a line of inquiry by reflecting back a specific part of the content or affect in the client's story, thus encouraging continued discussion of that topic. Carl Rogers, the founder of person-centered counseling, was a master at using reflection, prompts, and silences to help his clients elaborate and expand on their stories.

Examples of Reflection

Note that each clinician helps the client explore or elaborate, and each takes the story in a different direction while encouraging the client to amplify.

Client: You know, I'm not feeling bad for a man of 50. I have my health, an okay relationship with my wife—although she wouldn't agree. Although my best buddy just died, I still hang out with a great group of guys. We go bowling every Friday.

Clinician A: You're feeling that your relationship with your wife is "okay," but you don't think she'd agree.

Clinician B: Your best friend just recently died.

In the *dot-dot-dot* reflection technique, the clinician simply repeats back the last thing said and hangs it, unfinished, in midair for the client to complete. Dot-dot-dot is a very useful technique in any conversation where the client loses track for a moment. It's an unfinished sentence of reflection that, if written out, would appear as triple dots indicating an invitation to complete the sentence.

Examples of Dot-Dot-Dot Reflection

"You came home, fed the puppies, and then you . . . ?"

"You were saying that after you got your GED, you would . . . ?"

"First we talk about Glen; then we . . . ?"

Underlining is a special form of reflection. The clinician underscores important content or experience by the strategic use of verbal or nonverbal emphasis. This emphasis is often rendered through tone of voice, facial expression, or emphatic gesture.

Examples of Underlining

"So you *did* talk to your partner after all."

"You felt *angry* that your sister didn't lend you the money."

"But I *want* you to give me feedback on this work."

CLIP 5.1

Questions,
Prompts,
and Probes

In *summarizing,* the clinician pulls together the major ideas, themes, or patterns that have just been discussed and reflects them back to the client. At the end of the interview, summarizing is often used for closure. During the interview, summarizing can be used as a prompt to help the client further elaborate the story. Summarizing is, of course, also a form of reflection, as the clinician sums up what has just been discussed. In pure reflection, we usually repeat back only one thing the client has just said. In summarizing, we usually reflect back many ideas or themes just expressed, but they are now reflected back in condensed form.

Example of Summarizing

Client: I don't know whether to adopt a baby from China or to wait on this list and try to get an American child. It could be years and I'm not getting any younger.

Clinician: Mm-hmm . . .

Client: My parents want me to wait for an American child. They say you never know the kind of experience a baby might have in overseas orphanages. You could be in for a lot of medical expenses.

Clinician: So they want you to wait?

Client: Yeah, but my friends are even worse. They say I shouldn't wait or I will be too old to handle a child. As it is, I'll be 60 by the time the child graduates from college.

Clinician: I see.

Client: Well, there are going to be lay-offs at work and some of my colleagues keep telling me I should be worried that I will lose my maternity benefits.

Clinician: (Summarizing) So it sounds as if a lot of people have ideas about what you should do—your parents, your friends, and the women at work.

Client: Yeah, and what's important is that *I* figure out what *I* want.

EXERCISE 5.4 *Using Reflection Techniques to Explore*

In small groups, experience what it is like to interview without using any questions. Each person will try using only reflection techniques: prompts, dot-dot-dot, underlining, and summarizing. In the large group, discuss any advantages and disadvantages of using no questions when interviewing.

Refocusing

When the client has left a specific topic or theme that the clinician deems important, the clinician can use the technique of *refocusing*, which involves returning the client to a desired topic by gently inserting that topic into the conversation once again. Sometimes clinicians interject when the client takes a breath, but sometimes we may just have to gently intrude upon a long stream of conversation in which no breaks are apparent.

In today's fast-paced managed care environments, which emphasize brief clinical interventions, the need for highly focused interviewing assumes increasing importance. Where once clients might be encouraged to muse on whatever subjects they elected to address, it is important today to keep the clinical conversation focused on the stated objectives of the interview. Feeling comfortable with refocusing assists in this effort, and comfort can be developed only by using the technique under supervision. We have found the following interjections to be useful in refocusing.

◖◗ C L I P **5.2**
Refocusing

Examples of Refocusing

"I'm wondering if we can get back to the topic of . . . "

"Getting back to the requirements of your probation, do you have to . . . ?"

"Earlier we were talking about . . . "

"Forgive me for interrupting, but I'm not clear what this has to do with our work on your sobriety."

"How is that related to the issue of . . . ?"

"Let's continue with what we were talking about earlier."

"Excuse me, but our time's almost up, and we haven't designed the next steps you wanted to map out today."

Initiating New Topics

At times we follow the client. At other times, our acquired knowledge of human behavior and person-in-situation dynamics suggests potentially fruitful areas for further exploration, not as yet introduced by the client. The art of exploration involves learning (1) when to follow and just accompany the client on the journey unfolding, and (2) when to introduce and explore new areas.

Examples of Introducing New Topics

"I realize I don't know anything about your relationships with your siblings."

"We haven't talked about how you handle your anger."

"We've discussed your home life but not much about work. Could we talk some about that today?"

Important Factors in Effective Exploration and Elaboration

Good exploration concerns itself with many complex issues. While seeming so easy at the outset, effective exploration calls for good timing. The clinician must also be sensitive to the client's tolerance level for both the topic and the depth of exploration, to the client's cognitive capacity and expressive style, and to the state of the clinical relationship. Clinicians need to accumulate knowledge of the many ways of encouraging and eliciting a story: how to use tried-and-true methods of exploration; how to ask questions in the client's language and style; how to maintain a "not-knowing perspective"; how to cushion intensive exploration with sustainment; and how to appreciate and use resistance. Finally, clinicians need to know when to stop pressing for more.

Sensitive Timing

Why am I asking this particular thing, at this particular moment, in the visit or the work?

Every interviewer has had the experience of asking something that gets no response, that gets a look of puzzlement, or that goes over like a lead balloon. Typically we'll say after the meeting, "I wish I had waited till the client brought that up herself" or "I wish I hadn't interrupted him with that question, which wasn't as important as what he was saying—it really threw him off." *Timing* has to do with *what* and *how much to ask, when to ask it,* and *whom to ask.* Part of developing a timing instinct has to do with noticing how different people react to exploration, and noticing which behaviors of the clinician seem to broaden or deepen the conversation instead of shutting it down or causing undue discomfort. The sharing of personal information is framed and timed differently for everyone and is very much shaped by family and cultural norms and taboos. With experience and supervisory feedback, skill develops in judging the timing of exploration with each particular client.

Timing has to be considered within each interview, as well as across the sequence of all interviews. It is important to note from first contact how readily and under what circumstances clients share personal information and how accurately and realistically the story seems to be unfolding. Many clients will indicate right away, by opening up or closing down, how they feel about questions and probing and around what topics it is easier and harder for them to explore. Their behavioral cues assist the clinician's judgments about the timing and dosage of further inquiry. Indeed, these cues can be used to focus further tentative exploration, as when, for example, the clinician might note that the client looks down and blushes any time dating or sex is mentioned. The client may then elect to say more, may elect to look down and blush again, or may elect to simply stare at the clinician and await her lead. Each of the responses is useful new information.

An important challenge for the clinician is to begin to notice the client's patterns and styles of responding to exploration, and to watch carefully for what evolves *following* an exploration. A spontaneous deepening of conversation often does indicate growing trust and readiness to share at a more personal level. More deepening or opening up of content or feelings often signals to the clinician that the timing is right to risk middle circle and inner circle exploration. It's vital that the clinician attend carefully to the client's response to any question or probe, to be ready to pick up on the response or just store it away. Respect for a client's need to ebb and flow—to have good days and bad—is imperative. No one is "on" all the time in clinical work, neither the clinician nor the client. Sometimes clients will signal problems with the clinician's timing by saying things like, "You don't usually push me on stuff like this . . . you usually let me take my time. Why are you pushing me today?"

Even when trust and safety are well established and evidenced by increased client participation levels, certain material will always prove more difficult to elicit and develop. Just which material will prove difficult will differ from person to person and from culture to culture. Again, it is crucial to *watch what evolves once exploration begins*. Clients often manifest unreadiness to proceed with further exploration by protesting the need for it, questioning or criticizing the questioner, demeaning the topic, changing the subject, or abruptly cutting the session short.

> *I remember Junior just getting up and walking out without a word when I brought up his wife's charging him with incest and asked his reaction to the charges. Later he told me by phone that he found the question "shocking and disgusting," and that if that is what I think of him, then he would like to work with someone else in the program.*

State of the Clinical Relationship

Is the relationship strong and trusting enough to bear the questions I'm about to ask? Knowing this client, what is the most respectful way to explore this material?

The level of trust and comfort between clinician and client greatly determines the timing and the substance of exploration. In a good working alliance, all that may be required to forward exploration is a supportive, empathic milieu and some initial broad questions that set the frame of meetings. The client takes it from there, in his own style, at her own pace. But people new to each other have to feel each other out, testing for comfort and safety. For example, a lesbian client might not come out to her clinician until the latter has demonstrated trustworthiness and acceptance around other focal issues. The clinical encounter is a fishbowl in which both parties become known to each other in conscious and unconscious ways: the former by listening and watching, the latter by intuitive "radar" honed over years of human interaction. Gradually, as we have seen, safe and sound work together builds trust, increasing relaxation, and synchrony.

Every relationship, however, has its ups and downs, and no less so the relationship between clinicians and clients. Clients may at any time balk or react to exploration in unaccustomed ways, perhaps because of increased outside stress or illness, unexpected behaviors on the part of the clinician, or misinterpretation of the clinician's intentions. Again, new topics may have been introduced that suddenly reveal to both client and clinician an unexpected level of sensitivity, apprehension, or shame. Similarly, the clinician may balk at material brought up by the client, leaving both parties feeling awkward and uncomfortable. No conversation just rolls along without some stumbling points.

The ongoing work of a good relationship is to first acknowledge and then together sort through such stumbling points. Rough spots are not a disaster; in fact they offer possibilities for relationship building and the deepening of conversation. The clinician may want to just say simply, "Say—something's just happened . . . let's stop a minute and talk about it. I think it's important not to just let it go by." Here the clinician demonstrates the value of "examining the moment" and models the skill of addressing things directly, with great caring (see Chapter 7).

Client's Readiness to Explore Charged Areas

Will the material I am about to pursue make things better or worse for the client? If worse, whose interests are being served by this inquiry?

As clinical conversations develop, all decisions about exploring charged areas are based on the accumulating assessment of the client's capacities, vulnerabilities, and tolerance for varied content and affects. Our overriding intent is to do nothing that will harm or needlessly intrude on the client. For example, a time of increased client stress is not the preferred time to go on fishing expeditions into painful areas, stirring up themes or feelings that will only add to the stress already besetting the client. Clinicians are always thinking about what is in the client's best interest at any given moment, weighing the appropriate challenge to new learning against the price to be exacted emotionally.

We prefer the gradual introduction of deeper-level exploration, carefully monitoring and often discussing the client's reactions to advancing exploration. We understand that both clients and clinicians can be traumatized by the detailed recounting of overwhelming stories (McCann & Pearlman, 1990), and we proceed carefully, always asking at the outset of each new session how the client experienced the last session, both just after the session and during the time since. Coping levels and resources (or the lack of) give us important clues as to client readiness and capacity to continue exploring.

Client's Cognitive Capacities and Expressive Style

Can I put this in her metaphor or language? How would he or she say it to me, if our positions were reversed?

The kind of exploration and elaboration we do also depends on the client's intelligence, educational level, and cognitive capacities, including accuracy of perception, reality testing, judgment, logic, abstract and concrete thinking, use of fantasy, insight, and general quickness of mind. Cognitive capacity can be affected by: lack of adequate nourishment, stimulation, soothing, and modeling; trauma; limited educational opportunity; and messages from others that thinking is dangerous. Always trying to "be where the client is," the clinician tries to frame prompts, reflections, and questions in a style that follows that of the client, insofar as this feels natural and appropriate to the participants. We generally try to avoid jargon and esoteric language, although we have sat in many meetings where professionals seem to need to use these forms to assert power or expertise. We try to keep language immediate, simple, encouraging, and respectful of each client's style.

Using the client's *metaphor* (a word or phrase that stands for another similar concept) creates a sense of close following and respect for the way the client frames the world. Sometimes we might purposely want to praise the client's special metaphors as a way of making things very clear, or as being a real gift that not everyone has. At other times, we listen for frequently used metaphors (such as "This is part of my journey," "I'm digging myself in deeper," or "I'm in a stew") and without noting them out loud, simply use them in the conversation:

Examples of Metaphors

"Do you have to take *this* much baggage on your journey?"

"If I were going to dig myself out, I might start by . . . "

"Tell me more about the vegetables in this particular stew . . ."

Joining the Client's Style without Losing Professional Self

Am I staying true to my professional self while exploring this story? Am I different with this client than I usually am with clients? If so, why?

Educational and class differences can negatively affect the language that clinicians use with and about clients while exploring and elaborating the story. More than once in our careers, we have observed clinicians making fun of the vernacular of poor people, nonnative English speakers, or people who are poorly educated. On the other hand, we have noticed colleagues using more pomp, jargon, or flourish in the presence of clients who are famous or wealthy. Furthermore, many clinicians seem to feel that it is all right to ask poor or disempowered people anything, while at the same time they may feel extremely uncomfortable and apologetic probing the lives of the rich and famous.

Clinicians may also make mistaken assumptions about groups of people and not explore things as frankly as is appropriate. They may not ask a lesbian woman if she is having safe sex, for example, or ask a "good Catholic girl" if she ever had an abortion, or ask a longtime widow in her seventies if she thinks of dating again.

Maintaining the Not-Knowing Position

"I'm not really sure what he meant by that; I need to ask. . . ."

"There's a lot about this situation that needs clearing up. I need to explore further before I come to so many conclusions. . . . "

"I haven't asked about subject x for a long time. I should ask, to see if anything has changed since we last talked about it."

A not-knowing perspective has two important aspects: (1) it's okay not to know; and (2) we never really know—only the client does.

New learners often think they need to show that they know a lot in order to retain credibility with clients. Comfort with not knowing is absolutely essential for eliciting the client's story. When we do not adequately grasp clients' situations, they will often say things like "I'm not sure you really get what I mean" or "See what I'm saying?"

Surprisingly, saying "I don't understand" is often more useful than saying "I understand" for eliciting more information. "I understand" or "Yes, I know" from a clinician can be interpreted by clients to mean "enough said," whereas "I'm not sure I understand what you mean" invites the speaker to elaborate more fully, even in different words. We can have brilliant hunches, but we never really understand things until clients spell them out more fully for us; even then, clients may add material later on that gives completely new meanings to situations or events. No matter how much we think we "understand," we must always remember that the client is, and will always remain, the expert on his or her own life.

Sustaining Techniques to Cushion Intensive Exploration

What can I do or say at intervals so that inquiry feels less intrusive and so that the client feels less vulnerable?

Clinicians attend to the timing and dosage of inquiry and try to ensure that feelings of relief and support outweigh any potential feelings of vulnerability or threat from overexposure of personal information. *Checking in* is a sustaining technique in which the clinician is really asking how things feel or seem to the client after a period of exploring. Check-ins emphasize to the clinician the importance of the client's feelings, observations, and participation generally. They are like the periodic reading of the road map together, or the joint taking of the temperature of the meeting. "What's this like for you?" and "How are you doing with this?" are two standard ways of checking in. Another is, "Have we talked enough about this for now . . . should we give it a rest for today?"

Another sustaining technique during elaboration work is *crediting client strengths,* especially those shown in sharing the story and unfolding its layers in spite of any pain or risk involved. Variants of "It takes courage to do what you're doing" serve to accredit clients, as long as the clinician is authentic in giving the credit.

Slowdowns can also be quite sustaining. They are the verbal equivalent of tapping the brakes and are often framed thus: "Take your time now, there's no rush" or "You needn't rush this . . . give yourself the time you need." Here we model patience and carefulness with self, which is novel for many clients.

Validation of the difficulty of disclosure can also feel quite sustaining: "This is hard, and I respect your willingness to do it." At other times we might say, "You've talked about some really painful things today, and I can appreciate the exhaustion from it that you're describing."

Appreciating and Using Resistance

I need to see the responses of the client to my inquiry as her best means of protecting herself and her loyalty systems at the moment. The main thing the client is "resisting" is having familiar things taken away or tinkered with in ways that do not yet feel safe. I had best slow down or change course.

When seemingly sensible exploration hits a stone wall of silence, protest, denial of relevance, or refusal to respond, clients are signaling a need for caution and a wish to protect the known in the face of the unknown. Clinicians have historically labeled as "resistance" most refusals to follow the clinician's leads or suggestions. (In psychodynamic theory, the term *resistance* refers to the unconscious defenses against the emergence of painful or forbidden material.) Over the years, resistance came to imply failure or weakness in the client: something wise and good from the clinician was being unwisely refused by the client. With the demystification of the clinician's role and the increasing empowerment of clients has come a greater appreciation of people's needs to protect themselves when faced with apparent threats to stability or needed secrecy.

When the client balks at further elaboration, the clinician might honor and define the balking as sensible: "I think you're absolutely right to stop here for now. It's good to see you being careful of yourself and not just plunging into topics because I suggest them. I agree with you. I don't think we should go anywhere near this topic right now, and I want you to keep on waving me off of anything like this that seems absurd or hurtful." Again, this technique works only when the clinician believes what he or she is saying. Another response to balking is to simply say something like "I can see that what I asked doesn't feel right to you; can we stop a minute and talk about it?" This is an example of examining the moment, a skill we will discuss in Chapter 7.

Enough Is Enough

I need to let this line of questioning or exploration go—at least for now.

Sometimes when clients balk, it may be wise to go down another path or to try exploring with different words, on another day, or when clients may signal readiness by introducing a topic akin to the topic refused earlier. Sometimes clinicians get "on a mission" and pursue a hunch or an agenda, unable to let go. Such persistence may be forced on the clinician by a mandated protective role, as when the clinician has reason to fear for the client's safety. It may also arise from the clinician's own needs to be right, to prove a hunch, or to please a supervisor who is pushing for material about which the client is not forthcoming. Interns and new employees are especially vulnerable to pressure from their supervisors and consultants to go after information that, in face-to-face contacts with clients, may feel impossible or unwise to obtain. Pressuring clients usually makes no sense, feels very unempathic, and often ends in power struggles, cancellations, and termination of work. Sometimes it ends with the client going to the agency director and requesting another clinician. So, it's good to recognize when enough is enough, and to let go and move on, unless there is imminent risk of harm to client or to others.

⊙⊙ CLIP 5.3
Sustaining
Techniques

Conclusion

Exploration and elaboration help the client put ideas and feelings into words, so that assets and problems are clarified in ways that make goal setting, planning, and problem solving possible. Information gathered and hunches evolved will be distilled into the purpose and focus of work together. Questions, prompts, silence, reflection, refocusing, and initiating new topics are important skills in exploration. Sustaining, watchfulness, and sensitive timing all cushion the sometimes painful process of elaborating the story.

A final point: Remember that the clinician clearly influences the conversation by the areas she or he chooses to explore, by the topics to which the clinician responds and does not respond, and by the ways in which the clinician frames exploration or elaboration probes. Good clinical work requires a constant monitoring of the clinician's behaviors, acts of commission and omission, and attempts to understand these actions. Process recordings, clinical notes, and the use of audiotaping and videotaping will help clinicians monitor their use of influence so that they can use it intentionally and appropriately—not only in exploration and elaboration but throughout all clinical work.

Suggested Readings

Anderson, Harlene, & Goolishian, Harry. (1992). The client is the expert: A not-knowing approach to therapy. In S. McNamee & Kenneth Gergen (Eds.), *Therapy as a social construction* (pp. 25–39). Newbury Park, CA: Sage.

DeJong, Peter, & Miller, Scott D. (1995). How to interview for client strengths. *Social Work, 40*(6), 729–736.

The following reading discusses how to ease clients into more trusting and revealing conversations.

Miller, Dusty. (1996). Challenging self-harm through transformation of the trauma story. *Journal of Sexual Addiction and Compulsivity, 3*(3), 213–227.

Saleebey, Dennis. (Ed.). (1997). *The strengths perspective in social work practice.* New York: Longman.

See especially Chapter 6, "Exploration, Not Interrogation" in:

Wachtel, Paul. (1993). *Therapeutic communication: Principles of effective practice.* New York: Guilford.

Assessment and Working Agreements

The hospital social worker meeting with a family around a health crisis . . . the counselor doing case management in the drug treatment program . . . the outreach worker talking to a teen mother on the street . . . the psychologist doing individual therapy with a woman who has anxiety attacks—all must have some kind of a working agreement with their clients in order to proceed with the work. Working agreements can be formally written and contractual, or they may be informal, unspoken shared visions of what the relationship and the work will be like. Most working agreements probably fall somewhere in the middle, having some clearly spelled out understandings and goals and some quiet, shared hopes and intuitions about how things might work out.

Whatever the level of formality and concreteness, working agreements are usually composed of at least four parts: (1) assessment, (2) the setting of goals, (3) the negotiation of contracts to meet these goals, and (4) plans for the periodic evaluation of the work. Throughout, the clinician is continuously engaged in building the relationship and hypothesizing about the client's story and the tasks to be accomplished.

Influences on the Working Agreement

While discussing and working out agreements with clients, it is important to note that insurance companies, the clinician's employer, or legal institutions can intrude on or shape clinical activities. Managed care plans, agencies under religious auspices, or school boards, for example, may have fairly substantial say over what interventions or treatment will be allowed, and for what duration. Since most clinical codes of ethics require that clinicians advocate for client rights and services and hold their service to clients primary above all other objectives, clinicians today face many dilemmas as clinical work comes under the increasing control of *third parties*. Certainly, financial considerations more and more shape working agreements and the selection of treatment modalities (Snowden, 1993).

The clinician's *theoretical orientation* also influences assessment, goal setting, contracting, and evaluation. The clinician with a behavioral orientation may focus on assessing specific client behaviors, their antecedents and consequences; set goals that focus on behavior change; and evaluate treatment effectiveness in terms of behavioral change. The psychodynamically oriented clinician may assess the client's developmental history and may set goals that are based on the attainment of insight. The cognitively oriented clinician may look for distorted patterns of thought and set goals that help clients either block negative self-thoughts or alter faulty cognitions. The systemic clinician may assess the client in the context of multiple relationships and systems and set goals that focus on changing communication patterns, structures, or dynamics in these systems. Often clinicians will draw on useful principles from several theories as they tailor their approaches to particular clients' needs, capacities, styles, and preferences.

The state of the goal-focused relationship between clinician and client— often referred to as the *working alliance*—will greatly influence the amount and kind of information that the clinician seeks and the client offers. The development of trust, safety, and confidence in the relationship will affect all levels of the working agreement.

Although influenced by third parties, theoretical orientations, and the strength of the working alliance, all clinicians engage in the tasks discussed in this chapter: assessment, goal setting, contracting, and evaluation of interventions.

Assessment

We use the skills of exploration and elaboration to help us assess or make sense out of the person's story. Assessment involves gathering and analyzing information about the client, the story to date, and contextual or larger system influences affecting the client and the story. As Doman Lum notes, "The term 'assessment' denotes appraisal of the value or worth of a person and situation. Assessment comes from the root 'asset,' which is an item of value or a resource owned" (1996, p. 199). Six classic questions are often used by interviewers to organize their assessment agendas: *Who? What? Where? Why? When? How?* These questions can be used at two levels.

The first level concerns the *process of the assessment* itself. We start with "Why?" because the "why" of assessment often predicts "whom" and "how" the clinician assesses.

Why am I doing this assessment? Why has the client presented for help or why was the client referred?

Who is "the client"? (The client could be a person, family, group, organization, or larger system.) Who should be involved in the assessment process? Who made the referral?

What do I want to know? What information should I gather?

How should I gather this information? What methods will be most useful to get this information?

Where should the initial assessment take place—in the office, home, street, shelter?

When will I have enough understanding to begin to plan and contract?

At the second level, the answers to these questions form the *content of the assessment.* The questions here are asked in a different order:

Who are the main participants in the successes and problems of the people or systems I am assessing?

What are the presenting problems, strengths, resources, and needs in this system? What are the potential barriers? What incentives for change can be identified? What will change look like when it is achieved?

Where do the successes and problems most often manifest themselves, and where will effective interventions most likely occur?

Why is the client presenting at this point in time, and why would the client be interested in continuing beyond the initial meeting?

When did major influencing events take place, and when did the problems begin? When did problems reach the level of precipitating a contact with professionals? When in the client's life am I entering the story?

How can I or others help at this time?

Formal Clinical Assessment

Clinicians are often asked to do formal, reasonably structured assessments of individuals for the purpose of diagnosis, treatment planning, or research or to determine eligibility for specialized services such as disability assistance payments, residential placement, or inpatient treatment. Clinicians doing formal assessments often evaluate the individual's physical health and well-being, strengths and resources, psychosocial history, cognitive functioning, affective range and management, social functioning, problem-solving ability, and expressive style. Box 6.1 contains a sample assessment outline. (See Hepworth, Rooney, & Larsen, 1997, for more thorough discussion of formal assessment.)

B O X 6.1 *Sample Assessment Outline*

Client name, address, and telephone number

Demographic variables including gender, age, religion, cultural identity, sexual orientation, relationship status, employment or means of support, education, and training

Significant others (names, addresses, phone #)

Presenting problem

Family background

Significant developmental history

Health and physical status, including medications

Cognitive/intellectual capacities and skills

Behavioral assessment

Emotional/affective state

Biopsychosocial stressors

Client's strengths

Assessment of person in situation, including natural networks, community supports

Clinical assessment need not be limited to individuals. Clinicians routinely conduct family assessments in which they evaluate the structures, roles, communication, and overall functioning of the family as a whole, as well as the more specific transactions between family members. A clinician may also assess the dynamics of a classroom, an activity group, a neighborhood gang following a member's death, and so on (see Chapter 10 of Hepworth, Rooney, & Larsen, 1997, pp. 276–316, for a more thorough discussion of family assessment). At the macro level, professionals may also assess an agency, institution, organizational structure, or community—even systems of ideas and related behaviors, such as sexism or racism (see Chapter 4 of Netting, Kettner, & McMurtry, 1993, pp. 64–92, for a more thorough discussion of macro-level assessment).

Formal assessments often involve the collaboration of a number of clinical colleagues with specialized knowledge and diagnostic skills. The sum of their investigations and hypotheses, often pulled together in a team meeting, constitutes a *diagnostic formulation*—a summary of the client's strengths, resources, and problems to be solved, which serves as the basis for goals and interventions. (Health and mental health settings may require a formal DSM diagnosis of individuals.) Clinicians also assess the client's motivation for change and the work necessary to achieve it. Assessments usually provide tentative prognostic statements regarding expectations for the short, medium, and longer term of the work to follow. The assessment usually outlines any important implications for intervention suggested by assessment findings and hypotheses, from which will then flow recommendations for interventions. Formal assessments are often repeated (both during and at the conclusion of clinical work) to evaluate effectiveness of interventions.

From an ecological perspective, it is essential that, as a part of ongoing assessment, clinicians continuously listen for overt and covert barriers to the realization of client potentials. Clinicians analyze the intrapersonal, interpersonal, and societal forces that may hinder the client's problem-solving abilities, growth, and development. For many years, clinical assessment focused almost exclusively on the *intrapersonal*—the individual's characteristics, behavioral patterns, or intrapsychic dynamics. Most clinicians now prominently focus on the *interpersonal*, assessing the client's family support, work relationships, friendships, spiritual connections, and social networks. We believe it is essential that the clinician consider the impact of such larger social forces as poverty, language barriers, racism, sexism, and other systems of oppression as potential barriers to the client's growth and development (see Garbarino & Abramowitz, 1992, for a further discussion of how larger systems impact on clients).

In training, when I saw the documentary True Colors, *I realized for the first time the way that racism affects the daily interactions of African Americans in the United States. Watching two men (paired for similarities on education, age, dress, social skills) as they spent a week in a midwestern town doing exactly the same things, revealed how the fact that one was black and the other white affected every aspect of their daily lives—from walking into a department store to browse to renting an apartment.*

Methods of Assessment

Formal clinical assessment uses a variety of methods, including the following:

1. *Interviews* (self-report data and the clinician's experience in the interview, interviews with family members and relevant others)
2. *Observation* in lab, natural setting, or life space
3. *Testing* (including intelligence tests, personality tests, symptom checklists, appropriate medical tests)
4. *Review of life records* (previous treatment notes, school records, health reports, and other written documents)

Clinicians need to explain their methods of assessment and obtain signed informed consent forms for any procedures or assessment activities to be undertaken, as well as obtain permission releases for any information to be obtained from others. Box 6.2 contains a sample release of information form.

Techniques of Assessment

As discussed in detail in Chapter 5, the techniques of exploration and elaboration are particularly useful in assessment interviewing. These techniques include questioning, prompting, probing, reflecting, summarizing, underlining, refocusing, and initiating new topics. While most clients come to professional encounters expecting to have to answer questions, reveal information, and share ideas about their situations, many have no idea of how the process of disclosure and exploration will actually *feel*. They may have impressions from others or from the media; but, just like the clinician, they will have to carefully feel their way into the process of making themselves known as they feel more comfortable with the clinician. In so doing, they may feel pressure to consider the feelings of significant others who have a stake—spoken or unspoken—in the process. What is revealed during the assessment process may have major consequences and can affect relationships, economic supports, living situations, custody rights—future prospects of all kinds. No wonder, then, that apprehension and caution can manifest itself during exploration.

The techniques of *sustainment* are crucial to assessing, in order to ease the way (see Chapter 4). For example, assessment may proceed smoothly until the clinician asks for permission to send off for records from a psychiatric hospitalization. A client response such as, "So you think I'm mental, too?" can signal sensitivity to what the clinician thinks or to being judged, stigma

---

B O X 6.2 *Authorization for Release of Information*

Client Name: _____ Date of Birth: _____

Prior to the release of any information, we wish to make you aware that this request may include results of an HIV antibody or antigen test, or records that contain such information, which may be covered by MGL c.241 CMR 180.300. This information may not be copied or transferred to anyone other than the recipient noted above.

Your medical record may contain information about your identity, diagnosis, psychiatric treatment, mental health history, alcohol and drug addiction history, and sexually transmitted disease history. You are here granting permission to release this information to the specified provider or facility.

I hereby authorize _____ to:

1. Obtain From:

      Name: _____

      Address: _____

      City/Town: _____ State: ____ Zip: _____

   Send To:

      Name: _____

      Program: _____

      Agency: _____

      Address: _____

2. Furnish to Other Provider/Facility: Name: _____

      Agency: _____

      Address: _____

      City/Town: _____ State: ____ Zip: _____

3. The specific information as indicated below:

☐ Admission/Intake Note   ☐ Lab Reports

☐ Discharge Note/Summary of Treatment   ☐ School/766 Reports
   to Date   ☐ Birth Records

☐ Psychological Test Report   ☐ Verbal Client Status Update/Treatment

☐ Substance Abuse Treatment Records   Coordination

☐ Health Reports/Records   ☐ Other (specify)

This authorization shall be considered valid for this express purpose only and will automatically expire ninety (90) days from the date of signature.

_____ ,   _____ ,
Signature of Client or Legal Guardian   Date

_____ ,   _____ ,
Witness   Date

left over from the experience of mental illness, or concern about what the record will reveal. Here the clinician might stop to explore what meanings the client attached to the request for hospital records, giving the client a chance to express concerns or even perhaps to share past experience in which having a hospital record worked against him or her. Sympathetic appreciation of the concern, as well as universalizing the fear of stigma and negative consequences, might be quite sustaining here.

Example

Client: So you think I'm mental, too?

Clinician: Many people worry that once someone learns of their hospitalization, they will be viewed as mentally ill.

A latency-age child might be embarrassed to have his play therapist, an admired psychologist, come and observe him in the classroom as part of the assessment process, worrying about being seen at his most problematic (given that the therapy referral was based on distractibility and impulsivity in the classroom). The clinician might want to spend a few moments exploring this sensitivity and its attendant fantasies of what would occur in the visit. Then some time might be spent *educating about the usefulness of assessment,* of getting to see firsthand how things are for the child in the class, and exploring the things that might be making it hard for the child to focus and learn. Similarly, before including testing in the assessment process, a clinician would educate the client about the test and about the nature, purpose, and process of the testing situation, then elicit client reactions to all of this information.

Another useful technique might be *encouraging the client to assess the clinician* as part of the assessment process. Usually in assessment, the clinician asks the client many questions, which can leave the client feeling "in the hot seat." Reminding clients that they are also evaluating the clinician can heighten the sense of collaboration and shared responsibility.

Sometimes during an assessment interview, I will say to the client: "I've gotten to ask you a lot of questions. Is there anything you would like to ask me?" Clients often ask about my training, or about what I think will happen in our work. Sometimes they ask if I think I can help them. If they don't ask anything, I might say, "Sometimes clients want to know if I've had any experience with the kind of problems they're bringing in."

When I am going to do an assessment observation in a classroom, I often let the child come behind the one-way mirror and watch me as I interact with some of the kids. I say to them, "You can watch me, and then I'll watch you ... and then let's talk about what we see."

All Interviewing Requires Assessment

While formal assessment procedures are most frequently required in hospitals, outpatient mental health clinics, and forensic and protective services evaluations, many clinicians work in situations or settings that do not require formal assessment protocols. No matter the setting or task, clinicians must always do some kind of assessment before planning and acting in concert with or on behalf of clients. Street workers may not use a formal standardized test, but they are making assessments of client strengths, weaknesses, styles of interaction, even cognitive abilities. As we noted in Chapter 3, the clinician is also always listening for content, affect, and themes and patterns in the client's story. As clinicians come to appreciate the importance of understanding before responding, assessment becomes second nature.

> *As a social worker, I am always thinking about the "person-in-situation" context. Even when friends ask for advice, I find myself asking all sorts of questions as they talk. I find I am trying to figure out all kinds of things that might be influencing the situation.*

Principles of Assessment

1. *Assessment is an objective and an outcome of initial conversation, as well as an ongoing process guiding clinical interchange.* It begins immediately when people meet, and it is continuously threaded into ongoing interchange as the story deepens and broadens. The more we know, the more we want to ask or to understand. Moreover, people and their situations change fluidly over time; little remains fixed. Knowing this, we realize that situations and dynamics always merit reexamination along the way, as information, people, activities, and relationships can all change.

2. Although assessment seems to focus narrowly on the client, *full assessment includes evaluation of the clinician, the relationship, the appropriate services, the surround, and the interface between all of these elements.* For example, the clinician may ask, "Is this the agency or setting that can provide the best resources for this particular client?" We also continuously assess the motivation of the clinician and the agency to make sure that they are persisting, advocating, and caring about the people they are committed to help.

3. *Assessment should be culturally responsive.* Both the methods used and the areas explored should be sensitive to cultural differences. Guilmet and Whited (1987) suggests that the intake interview with Native American clients should avoid direct questioning and consist of a supportive conversation about the clients' needs, thus requiring more time than usually scheduled. Sue and Sue note that "White counselors tend to view their client's problems as residing within the individual rather than society" (Sue & Sue, 1990, p. 72). Romero states that "the majority of mental health

problems exhibited by Chicanos are not pathological. Rather they result from a combination of socioeconomic stresses that are compounded by poverty, racism, oppression, [and] lack of access to educational and legal systems and institutions" (Romero, 1983, p. 91). Thus, the clinician should assess the effects of oppression, racism, bilingualism, ethnic-identity conflicts, and so on. In working with immigrant families, Lum (1996) suggests using Congress's (1994) culturagram (Figure 6.1), which illustrates the complexities of family culture.

4. *The more methods and strategies used to assess, the more balanced the understanding we are likely to develop.* Where feasible, we like to observe—or at least ask in detail about—functioning across many domains. The woman who stays with a batterer and does not currently "appear" to be able to protect herself or her children from harm may be a leader in her church's women's group or a helpful suicide hotline responder. Perhaps we don't think to ask her what she does in her free time because we've already assumed she doesn't have any. By the same token, observing an adult at a neighborhood meeting or in a home visit, or observing a child in gym or in a classroom, may provide much more clarity about skills and limitations than office interaction ever would. Test information may provide us with new insight into the cognitive

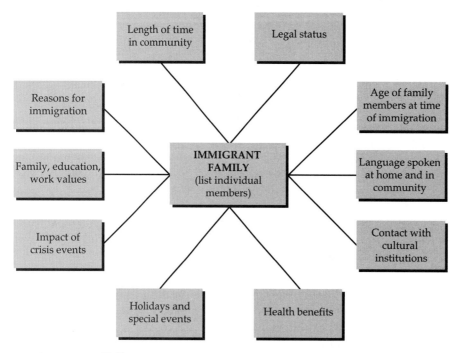

FIGURE 6.1 *Culturagram*

Source: From *Social Work Practice and People of Color,* Third Edition, by D. Lum, p. 219, Brooks/Cole Publishing Company, 1996.

strengths of a client so that we may plan our intervention to fit his or her cognitive style. A physical exam could reveal diabetes, which might be one alternative explanation for the symptoms that the client defines as "anxiety attacks."

Several helpful tools are available to capture and reflect client experience, relationships, and themes or patterns. The *genogram* reflects multi-generational family relationships and patterns. The *ecomap* maps the ecology of the client's positive, negative, and reciprocal versus unbalanced relationships with significant others. The *Life Chart* provides a birth-to-present time line of dates and ages at which major life experiences impacted the client, positively or negatively (see Hartman, 1978, and McGoldrick & Gerson, 1985, for more detailed discussion of the use of these tools).

5. *Multiple perspectives help in assessment.* We cannot always include as many participants in the assessment process as we would like, but we do understand as clinicians that the more perspectives we include, the greater the likelihood of adding new dimensions to our understanding. Events are experienced differently by all parties to them; each will put an interesting spin on the story and, in doing so, flesh it out usefully. Often we make the mistake of limiting the number of people in the room for purposes of control, focus, or expediency. Remember that we often sacrifice information and valuable relationships for control.

I'd never met with a family before, and I found seeing the parents and their five adult children awesome. The dad had had a heart attack, and the mom was depressed thinking that he looked older and more tired and might die suddenly. The adolescent kids seemed a little sullen and critical of him for "making Mom wait on you hand and foot." There was a little 4-year-old who ran around the room distracting everyone, so for two or three meetings I had her play outside with the secretary. My supervisor suggested I bring the little girl back in next meeting, and this time ask her what she thought of daddy being sick at home. She looked straight at me and blurted out, "Daddy squished our brother." Mom tried to silence her and looked so uncomfortable. I asked how come. She looked at dad, who paled, but said it was okay. Mom then told me that ten years before, dad had come home for lunch, and in backing out of the driveway to return to work, he ran over and killed their 2-year-old. Mom said it broke everyone's heart. No one knew what to say next . . . me either.

6. Cyberneticists first noted that *what is observed is altered by the presence of the observer and the activities of observation* (Maturana, 1978; von Foerster, 1981). The interviewer has to keep in mind the influence that he or she has on the behaviors of clients, and the reciprocal influence they have on him or her.

We were doing interviews on videotape for a research study. Children were observed for two weeks by two different evaluators. When Randy was in the room with Bonita, she was active, made eye contact, and explored the room. On those days when Susie was with her, Bonita sat down in a corner and didn't make eye contact. Needless to say, Randy and Susie each had very different evaluations of Bonita. We also observed that Susie was less active with Bonita than she was when we observed her with other children. We really got a sense of what our teacher meant when she talked about "reciprocal influence."

7. The assessor can also be altered by the process of assessment. *Clinicians can be drawn into or "inducted" into systems they are assessing,* becoming a participant in them, which can undercut their capacity to see, experience, and accurately report the system to outsiders or other colleagues. This blurring of roles can occur when clinicians overidentify with client systems, have strong needs to rescue, or get caught up in unwitting reenactments of old unresolved scenarios of their own.

   A couple of years ago I was supervising a student, Nadine, at the Department of Family and Children's Services. When one of her clients came to the agency, I thought I could smell alcohol on the client. It became obvious to me that the student was ignoring the fact that the mother was drinking again. When I pointed it out to Nadine and questioned her about why she thought she missed it, she said that she probably didn't see it because she was hoping that the kids would have some stability. If the mother was drinking again the kids would be sent to separate foster care families. Nadine, just like the kids, really wanted to believe that this time the mother would succeed in sobriety. I thought it was possible that Nadine might have also come from a family where the kids were taught to pretend parents weren't drinking when they actually were.

8. *Where we carry out our assessments also influences the kinds of data we gather.* People are often much more comfortable in their own natural settings than in office or agency settings. On their own ground, they may be more comfortable and open. On the other hand, people threatened in their own environments may at last relax in an agency, where they feel safe and protected.

9. It is important to remember that *the clinician is seeing the client only at one particular moment in time.* At that moment we are seeing but one frame of an entire movie. The clinician needs to remember that the client who today looks well put together may have been very distressed five years ago. The client who is struggling to get an entry-level job today may have been a physicist in his country of origin the year before. Therefore it is helpful to make sure that the clinician obtains as much information as possible about the whole story to date.

   When I started working for the state, I had to go 20 weeks without pay because of Civil Service complications. I was new in the area, without resources, and it was suggested I apply for temporary public assistance, which I reluctantly did. The intake social worker was incredulous that I was a social worker needing public assistance. I could see she didn't believe me by the frown on her face. I gave her the name of the financial director at my agency to validate my application. She called and got the facts while I sat there. At no time did she show one ounce of care for my plight. I got food stamps and left feeling very embarrassed. It left me very much more understanding of how clients feel judged.

Furthermore, the clinician usually meets the client at a highly stressed time. As we noted previously, the act of seeking assistance from strangers can be very stressful for people and can cause clients to regress from previous better levels of functioning. At such times, people can present their stories with more urgency, anxiety, and disorganization than we might see under different conditions. Were the clinician to enter the story at a different time or see the client at a less stressed point in the client's life, the clinician might gain a different perspective.

When I was working in a detox setting, we were encouraged not to give alcoholics a personality diagnosis until they had been abstinent for a year or so because their functioning could look so much healthier once they were off drugs for a while.

An elderly, psychotic woman without family available came into the hospital unable to offer a coherent story. It looked as if she would be transferred out to a state hospital locked unit. However, a nurse took a liking to her and asked me to look in the transfer record from the acute hospital and see if there was anything else that could keep her in rehab. By examining the detailed notations in her transfer record, I was able to determine that she had been a senior seamstress for almost 50 years and was nicknamed "Golden Fingers" for her dexterity. She had always lived independently before her diabetic complications and surgery. Hearing this detail reminded the team that there might be strengths here, once medication helped clear cognition. Sure enough, once clear, this lady proved to be very spunky and verbal and had a longtime taxi driver friend who worked with the team and found her an accessible first-floor apartment in her old neighborhood. People had mistaken her confusion for permanent impairment. So had she.

10. As previously noted, *the "assessor" is also being assessed* by the client, whose estimation of the clinician will greatly affect what is shared and owned by the client.

Lara was a 19-year-old single mother of a 1-year-old son in our Transitional Living Program. She was usually cast as a shy "outsider," and people wondered why she was so shy. One day, as we were hanging out in the kitchen, she told me that she had been attracted to women for a couple of years and that she was afraid that other mothers would find out. She was worried that people might think she was an unfit mother. I thought "No wonder she's so quiet. She's scared." I asked her what made her tell me. She said she had been watching the way I interacted with the other mothers and I seemed to be pretty open to different things.

11. *Research informs clinical assessment,* just as it does clinical practice. The clinician uses available research data on human behavior to inform assessment. For example, the clinician who is familiar with the research showing that lack of economic resources often prompts women to stay in battering situations will ask abused women about their financial supports. The clinician who knows that people who suffer from depression often have, among other symptoms, fitful sleep and early morning awakening will include questions about changes in sleep patterns.

12. *Real understanding* involves more than data gathering, for it brings the heart as well as the mind to bear, and it *involves the intuition as well as the intellect.* Intuition is a "sixth sense" combination of autonomic bodily reactions, perceptions, and insights in reaction to experience.

As a social work instructor, it is often hard to explain to students how to hone intuition and the sensing of things that cannot be rationally explained or aren't empirically derived. I often describe it as getting a "flavor of" something, or "having an internal beeper go off." I don't want to just have students learn to "listen to their gut"; but, on the other hand, if we don't pay attention to it at times, we can really miss important clues for further assessment. Sometimes it involves goose bumps on the arms, a "funny feeling" in the chest or gut, hair standing up on the back of my neck, or a welling up of things I can't name but that I feel are for sure at work in the room or in the person's life. Sometimes I think this ability to "sense" things is a gift that one is born with and can't just be implanted. But I do believe that intuition is nurtured and validated through clinical experience and life experience in general.

Communicating Assessment Findings

Both during and upon completion of an assessment, the clinician should attempt to discuss the findings with the client. This includes sharing with the client the results of any tests or information obtained through interviews with others and reviews of life records or any other material or experience with the client. In sharing this information, the clinician is careful to include a discussion of the client's strengths, normal developmental issues and challenges, and other areas for potential work. Communication should be direct, in plain language, and interspersed as needed with support and empathic comments. The clinician seeks feedback from the client, listening for thoughts and reactions that may differ from those of the clinician, and exploring these further. The discussion of the assessment process helps

⊙⊙ **C L I P** **6.1**
Assessments

clients and clinicians as they attempt to set up goals and contracts for their working relationship.

Goal Setting
Desired Outcomes

Goals express the *desired outcomes* of the working relationship agreed upon by clinician and client. Working from a strengths perspective, the clinician is always interested in (1) what clients do well and want to sustain or enhance, and (2) what issues need to be addressed or what problems need to be solved. In the assessment process, clinicians and clients assess what skills and resources might be used or developed to help clients reach their goals.

Goals are informed by future images of how clinicians and clients would like things to be, and goals can be either short term or long term. *Short-term goals* are those that need be accomplished relatively quickly, whereas *long-term goals* may take more time. Clinicians can ask clients about their goals by asking *future-oriented questions* such as:

"How would you like things to be different?"

"What goals do you have for our work together?"

"If our work were successful, what would be changed for you?"

"How would things look if they were the way you wanted them to be?"

While exploring problem areas presented by clients, clinicians also ask clients what is working for them—what they would like to keep. Sometimes, at point of intake, the client and related others may be so caught up in worried or unhappy feelings that positives are left out of their reports or are disqualified as having no real meaning or present relevance.

Example

Clinician: Have you ever had any moments when you're not feeling "out of it"?

Client: No . . . um, well, at the gym when I'm working out I feel better.

Clinician: What is it about working out that helps?

Client: I don't know. I get out of myself, I guess.

Clinician: Anything else about the gym?

Client: I guess I'm with people. I talk to the other guys some days. I don't feel so alone.

Specific and Concrete

Goals flow from assessment findings, and they have to be *specific* and *concrete* in order to provide clear directions for ensuing work together. As often as possible, goals should include outcomes that are observable or measurable and can be used in assessing the effectiveness of interventions, including clinical work. Clinicians often ask questions such as:

"What would things look like if you were to achieve your goal?"

"How will we know when we have achieved the goals you want?"

Sometimes the client comes in with a very concrete and specific goal: "I want to score 10 points better in my basketball games" or "Can you help me get into the Jobs Program?" Often, however, clients come in with goals that are abstract or are generally stated: "I want to feel better." The clinician then needs to help the client be more specific and eventually formulate more concrete goals.

Example of Helping Clients Set Concrete Goals

Clinician: If therapy were successful, what would be different?

Client: Davey wouldn't be so depressed.

Clinician: What would we be able to observe that would show us that Davey wasn't so depressed?

Client: He would smile more.

Clinician: What else would you notice?

Client: He would play with friends after school instead of just hanging out at home alone.

EXERCISE 6.1 *Turning Abstract Goals into Concrete Goals*

In your journal, record some goals that you have for yourself. See if you can turn these general goals into specific concrete goals with measurable outcomes.

Partializing and Prioritizing

Clinicians help clients partialize goals; they help clients break major goals down into component parts called *objectives.* There may be many objectives within each goal. For example, recovery from alcoholism is a broad goal within which there may be a number of specific objectives: to recognize a problem with drinking, to attend AA meetings, to develop friendships with people who are sober, to live in a stable home environment. The clinician has to help clients take broad goals and partialize, or break them down into component parts. In doing so, we take unitary concepts like "feeling more independent" and identify their defining components.

Example of Partializing Goals

Clinician: What goals do you think we should have for our work together?

Client: I want to be more independent.

Clinician: How would that look?

Client: I'd have my own place, my own spending money and schedule.

Clinician: What kinds of things would need to happen for you to be more independent?

Client: I would have to improve my English and get a job.

Often clinicians and clients can see problems as so enormous and lacking in definition that they can feel burdened and overwhelmed. A feeling of hopelessness can suffuse the work. By breaking goals down into concrete objectives and talking about them in simple, everyday language, tasks can feel much more achievable and hopeful.

EXERCISE 6.2 *Partializing*

Following is a list of goals that clients might have for their work with a clinician. See if you can partialize them into smaller objectives. In your journal, write down the broad goal, and for each goal make a list of component objectives. Discuss your list with your fellow students in class.

Freydia is a 27-year-old mother who has been using crack cocaine for four years. Her children, ages 7 and 9, have been removed from her care by DSS and are currently living with her mother. Freydia comes to the drug program saying: "I want to get my children back."

Thomas, a 20-year-old college sophomore, drops out of school. He has just been diagnosed with schizophrenia. His mother has brought him to the day center saying she hopes that "somehow he will be able to get back to college."

Rad is a 49-year-old refugee from Bosnia. He was an engineer in Sarajevo but now he is cleaning buildings at night. He does not speak English well. He wants to get certified as an engineer and get a job so he can bring his family to the United States.

The clinician helps the client *prioritize* goals and objectives, ranking them in order of their urgency or importance. The ranking of priorities has to take into account client capacity and motivation to work on selected tasks within and between visits, the likelihood that achieving selected objectives will have positive consequences, and the availability of resources that might be required to achieve those objectives.

Sometimes, the client and clinician may prioritize a relatively easy goal or objective so that the client can experience mastery, which will fuel further efforts. Every effort is made to *stage the work* so that, where possible, small successes build on one another.

Example

Clinician: What would be your first step in becoming more independent?

Client: Get a job first, I guess, then I can pay my bills.

Clinician: What kinds of things would you have to do to get a job?

Client: Well, I would have to go out on interviews.

Clinician: Are there steps you would need to take before that?

Client: Well, first I guess I would have to start reading the want ads . . . I'd have to start buying the paper first.

Priority setting is also affected by the needs and feelings of others in the client's family or social system. Different stakeholders may have different goals. For example, Davey's mother wants him to smile more. Davey may want his parents to stop fighting, or Davey may want to have his mother less concerned about whether he smiles or not. The parents of Thomas, the young man with schizophrenia, may stipulate that he can live at home only if he stops smoking in the house. Giving up smoking may not be Thomas' goal at all, but since he needs to live at home, realistically he will have to change his priorities and accommodate his parents' wishes; perhaps all can agree that Thomas can smoke on the back steps. It may even turn out that this "smoking" issue masks other fears regarding Thomas' condition.

The demands of the larger society can also intrude on priority setting. Freydia, the woman who wishes her children back, might set getting sober and getting work training as priorities. However, in conversation with the clinician, Freydia realizes that she is going to have to include a DSS-mandated six-week parenting course in her priorities.

EXERCISE 6.3   *Prioritizing*

Go back to Exercise 6.1 in your journal. See if you can list the strengths and resources that will help you meet the specific goals. Then prioritize the specific goals and objectives. In class, share your goals, objectives, and priorities. Remember to set priorities:

◆ that you want
◆ that are attainable
◆ with the resources available

 CLIP 6.2
Developing Goals

Once assessment and goal setting have taken place, many clinicians write up formal *treatment plans* in which the specific long-term and short-term goals and objectives are prioritized and specific interventions are laid out.

Contracting

Contracting involves the developing of working agreements between clinicians, clients, and any significant others vital to the realization of goals and objectives. In general, contracts:

1. enumerate the goals
2. describe the roles and responsibilities of all involved parties
3. include the interventions and methods that will be used to attain the goals
4. describe the frequency, duration, and length of the meetings, and, if applicable, the costs and payment arrangements
5. include the means for evaluating the work or measuring progress toward the specified goals
6. include a provision for how the contract can be renegotiated
7. discuss the consequences of failure of either party to carry out their agreed-upon responsibilities, as well as how to handle unanticipated complications

While contracts can be informal or formal, clinicians are increasingly moving to more formalized contracting arrangements based on treatment plans. *Formal contracts* are highly specific and concrete in order to clarify responsibilities and minimize drift and ambiguity. They enable both client and clinician to judge whether they are accomplishing what they intend. Formal contracts are often written, and they may list each goal and its component objectives, specifying particular tasks and anticipated time lines for achievement of each objective. This form of contracting is intended to result in a more structured *treatment by objectives.*

Issues in Contracting

1. *There are individual session contracts as well as overall contracts.* The clinician and client may agree during the session to focus on certain subjects and

to table others. Or they may agree at the end of one session that next week's meeting should include all of the children and be held at the homeless shelter so that the clinician can better appreciate the conditions under which the family is struggling to maintain itself.

2. *Contracts should include all stakeholders insofar as possible.* Others significant in the client's life may be involved in the process, and so may other service providers who have a stake in the desired outcomes. The wise clinician makes sure that all of these others are included in the contract in some way. If they are not, we may lose significant input, misattribute problems, weaken alliances, or cause others to impede implementation of the contract. In constructing a contract with the young teen mother who lives at home, the clinician should involve the family in order to support them and to be sure that they will be able to provide the teen with transportation to the center. The adjustment counselor who wants to set up a behavioral program for the disruptive child should make sure that not only the classroom teacher but also the principal, the school, and the family sign on. Charles Garvin and Brett Seabury (1997) note the pitfalls of the "corrupt contract," a situation in which the various agreements among different individuals are not coordinated, are in conflict, or are deliberately negotiated to be inconsistent: "Corrupt contracting can be avoided if all the significant individuals in the service process are brought together in the beginning and periodically thereafter to discuss their various impressions, intentions, and responsibilities" (p. 165).

3. *Contracts should be specific.* The more specific the contract, the more able the parties are to determine whether they are carrying out their roles and moving toward the specified goals. If there are specific steps (such as sobriety) that must be taken before other steps can be taken, those should be spelled out in the contract.

   In the adolescent drug treatment program, the kids have specific behavior contracts that are determined each morning at group meeting. The goals are written up and posted in the dining room. Privileges such as watching TV or playing basketball are earned by achievement of these daily goals. The kids also contract to attend daily group therapy and family meetings weekly.

4. *Contracts should be mutually constructed.* Both client and clinician should participate in developing the contract, each contributing ideas and preferences as to what should be done and how. Each should be able to specify what is expected from the other.

   There are times when the client may not want or may not be able to be an equal participant in the construction of the contract. For example, the involuntary client—such as the man who is forced to see the probation officer—may not have many choices about the contract; he may be told who he has to see and what he has to work on. In negotiating the contract, it is helpful if the clinician can give the client room to negotiate something, such as the time of the meeting. Contracting can be prefaced with the idea that almost everyone has things to talk about or hope for, and since the client is obliged to attend, why not put the time to use on something the client is interested in or concerned about?

When working with members from oppressed groups—the poor, immigrants, those who do not speak English—the clinician recognizes that the client may be fearful or be feeling powerless, and so may be unable to negotiate a contract but instead will simply agree with whatever the clinician suggests. As Wynetta Devore and Elfriede Schlesinger (1996) note, "the skill of helping people who feel particularly defeated to recognize and believe that they can play a part in determining why and how something is to be done is one that needs to be continually sharpened" (p. 209).

5. *Contracts require informed consent.* Clients need to be aware of the potential risks and benefits of the work. The woman who is coming to the clinic because she is depressed should be informed that when people change their behavior and are less depressed, this often impacts on their relationships with others. Her partner, friends, and family may begin to respond to her differently, and she may want to make other changes in her life. This could be seen as either a benefit or a risk. Optional treatments and their benefits and risks should also be discussed with her.

   In addition, clients need to know what other options and resources are available to them to meet their desired outcome. The couple who is seeing the counselor about marital difficulties should also be informed about other resources, such as pastoral counseling, couples groups, or marital enrichment groups, which they may choose instead of, or in addition to, counseling.

   At times clinicians work with children or with adults who are not able to give informed consent because of mental retardation, cognitive impairment, or mental illness. In those circumstances the clinician is both legally and ethically bound to get consent from legally authorized guardians. However, even in these instances, the clinician should explain the contract to the client in as clear and detailed a way as possible.

6. *Contracts should be flexible.* Brett Seabury speaks of the dynamic nature of contracting, recognizing that people, resources, and situations change (Garvin & Seabury, 1997; Seabury, 1976). The clinician and client should be willing to renegotiate the contract in response to changing circumstances, emerging information, or client growth.

   Gemma and I had a contract that we would work for 12 sessions to help her control her angry outbursts in the classroom. After 5 meetings, she seemed to really be managing this well. We talked about what we should do with the remaining sessions and decided that she would like to work on becoming less shy. I decided to continue to meet with Gemma even though she had accomplished the original task. Gemma enjoyed our meetings and would be disappointed if they stopped before scheduled. I thought that to end now would not reinforce Gemma's hard work and that it might even result in more angry outbursts on Gemma's part in order to continue our relationship.

7. *Contracts should be realistic.* Contracts must take into account the resources, capacities, motivation, and opportunity that people and agencies have to meet the contract requirements. Setting up a contract in which a teen mother is expected to come to the agency twice a week for parenting group meetings is unrealistic unless the agency is sure that there is transportation available and that child care is provided.

   Max resisted having a regularly scheduled weekly appointment, feeling he had been locked into something he couldn't control. So at the end of each session I'd ask, "Would you like to come again?" We would wind up with the same appointment each week. It was unrealistic for me to expect him to commit to a long-term relationship.

8. *Contracts should be upheld.* For example, if the contract contains a specific prohibition against using substances while in the homeless shelter, the shelter worker needs to stand firm, even if it means refusing shelter to the client for the night. In such a circumstance, caring clinicians can offer the client detox or a referral to a "wet" shelter—one that houses those who are actively drunk or on drugs.

   Holding clients to contracts is one of the hardest things for beginning interviewers to do. Clinicians are highly motivated to help others and may feel reluctant to say "no" or apply limits. Many have reported in supervision that they fear losing the client if they do not bend the rules or look the other way. Others fear the anger that can arise in clients when clinicians remain firm in the face of challenges to agreements made in the client's best interest.

   Clinicians also need to be held to their part of the contract. Being late, canceling appointments, not providing agreed-upon resources or services are violations of the contract that should be addressed. Clients may have a difficult time in confronting clinicians about their failures to meet their part of the contract. Regular review of the contracts allows both clinicians and clients to comment about adherence to the contract.

⊙⊙ CLIP 6.3
Establishing
a Contract

EXERCISE 6.4 *Exercises in Contracting*

In class, role-play the scenarios in Exercise 6.2 (Freydia, Thomas, and Rad). See if you can negotiate written contracts that follow the principles outlined above. Decide who should be involved in the contract, and make sure that your contract is specific, mutually constructed, flexible, and realistic. Include a section on informed consent. Think of any circumstances that might require you to readjust or adapt the contract. Role-play the renegotiation.

Evaluation

As we noted in Chapter 2, evaluation is an ongoing part of all clinical work. Clinicians examine their work session by session to assess the effectiveness of the specific focus, techniques, or uses of self. Progress and process notes, weekly assessment measures and scales, audiocassettes, and videotapes are all helpful in this process. We review our work on a regular basis with supervisors or with outside consultants with particular expertise. In addition, agencies or insurers often require monthly progress reports or quarterly summaries for management to oversee the quality of care. In some settings these evaluation reports will be required even more frequently.

Finally, there is a process of evaluation at the end of the working relationship. Clinician and client may use formal outcome measures or may simply review the relationship, the work, and what has been accomplished. As managed care and quality assurance become more prevalent, clinicians are more frequently asked to demonstrate the effectiveness of their interventions.

Common Elements in Evaluation

While measurement of progress and effectiveness will take differing forms, instruments or procedures usually have some common elements.

1. There is an *assessment of baseline functioning*, enumerating patterns or problems targeted for change. It is on this functional baseline that change goals will be developed, contracts made, and hoped for outcomes evaluated.

2. Some form of *progress measurement* is used consistently. This can include informal discussion of the work and its effects; the periodic reuse of original assessment measures; or the use of other evaluative measures, such as a symptom checklist that tracks specific behaviors or feeling states over time.

3. Measurement of progress often occurs at *specified intervals,* and certainly at the end of the contracted work together.

4. In addition, there can be *follow-up evaluations* to see whether gains or changes have been maintained or whether further services are needed.

Principles of Evaluation

The questions one asks in assessment *before* intervention are very similar to the questions one asks in evaluation *after* intervention. These include the who, what, how, where, and when issues that can complicate the process of evaluating progress, outcomes, and postintervention maintenance of well-being.

1. *Evaluation is influenced by who does the evaluating.* A risk in evaluation is that clinicians, for motives of self-preservation, may be biased toward finding positive changes and outcomes. Clients can also be inaccurate reporters, since they have invested time, energy, and money in the work and quite understandably want to believe that they and their situations have changed. They may also wish to please or reward their clinicians by putting a positive spin on developments and suppressing questions or doubts. Outside observer-evaluators, including family members, may also be differentially motivated to see positive or negative results, depending on the effects that outcomes have on them. For all of these reasons, it seems most efficacious to use multiple reporters in the evaluation process.

2. *Evaluation should focus not only on problems but also on the strengths of clients and their related systems.* Naturally, evaluations focus on changes in the frequency and duration of the problems targeted for intervention. Just as in assessment, evaluation must also focus on the frequency with which previously identified strengths and resources are used and new strengths and resources are developed.

3. *Evaluation should utilize a number of evaluation methods.* Clinicians often utilize standardized tests and self-reports, such as logs and journals, to help clients monitor the effectiveness of their work together. Sometimes direct observation is possible. For example, if a teacher wants a child to be less aggressive with other students or wants the child to engage with more people in interactions, an objective observer can actually record the change in behavior frequency before, during, and after an intervention aimed at behavior change.

4. *Whenever possible, evaluation should occur in real-life settings.* It is possible for a client to make changes that are observable in the clinical setting but do not necessarily generalize or translate to broader areas in his or her life. For example, a client may learn to be more assertive in the office or even in the classroom, but not in the playground or at home. The clinician who evaluates the work solely by looking at assertive behavior in the classroom might consider the intervention successful, whereas the clinician who looks at behavior in many settings may report a mixed picture, pointing the way toward specific further work.

5. *It is essential that there be follow-up evaluation.* Follow-up evaluation can occur one month, two months, or even years after the initial intervention. Such follow-up enables the clinician and client to reevaluate the long-term effectiveness of the work. At times, follow-up evaluations can serve as "booster shots" to the original work, helping clients to remember and continue to build on the positive outcomes of their work.

E X E R C I S E 6.5 *Evaluation*

Using the cases in Exercise 6.4 (Freydia, Thomas, and Rad), describe the methods you would use to evaluate the effectiveness of your work together. Address the who, what, how, where, and why of evaluation.

Conclusion

To develop a working agreement, clinicians and clients engage in assessment, develop specific goals with component objectives, construct clear and realistic contracts, and measure progress and outcomes using a variety of reporters and procedures. They work collaboratively with the client and significant others in the client's life to determine a clear, concise, and consensual working agreement.

In designing interventions, clinicians rely on their training and theoretical orientation; their experience with the clients; their assessment of the client's motivation, capacity, and resources; and their sense of the time and the professional resources available. They also utilize the professional literature and the findings from clinical efficacy studies that examine and compare various treatment intervention outcomes for specific problems and populations. Many clinicians use a number of the same basic skills, regardless of the clinician's theoretical orientation or the specific intervention strategies to be used. In the next chapter we will discuss these intervention skills.

Suggested Readings

Cowger, Charles. (1997). Assessing client strengths: Assessing client empowerment. In Dennis Saleebey (Ed.), *The strengths perspective in social work practice* (pp. 59–73). New York: Longman.

Greene, Gilbert J., Jensen, Carla, & Jones, Dorothy Harper. (1996). A constructivist perspective on clinical social work practice with ethnically diverse clients. *Social Work, 41,* 172–180.

Hartman, Ann. (1978). Diagrammatic assessment of family relationships. *Social Casework, 59,* 465–476.

Lum, Doman. (1996). *Social work practice and people of color: A process-stage approach.* Pacific Grove, CA: Brooks/Cole. (Chapter 6 includes useful information on culturally responsive assessment.)

McGoldrick, Monica, & Gerson, Randy. (1985). *Genograms in family assessment.* New York: Norton.

CHAPTER 7

Gaining New Perspectives: Helping Clients See Things Differently

Clinicians' preferences may vary widely as to the specific theories that guide their work and the particular modalities or interventions they choose. In spite of these disparities in theoretical and practice models, clinicians often draw on a fund of basic skills to be used in implementing their interventions with clients. In this chapter we will elaborate on those skills commonly used to help clients develop new perspectives. Developing new perspectives often affects clients' feelings and emotions, as well as their cognitions.

When people come for help, they often feel "stuck." They may experience or view things in fixed and often immutable ways and may feel distressed or hopeless, seeing few, if any, options to their situation or perspective.

> As a boy from a poor, nearly abandoned part of a large city, LeShon thought he had only two options open to him if he was going to "get somewhere": either be an athlete or run drugs with his cousin. The idea of staying in school and going on to college was completely foreign to him, as no one in his family, neighborhood, or playground group ever had. His nickname for me was "Pipe Dreamer."

Others may hold tenaciously to a view that feels right to them, and their limited ability to see alternatives may be problematic in helping them approach the future differently.

> Angie came from three generations of women who married alcoholic men who beat them when drunk. The women had all stayed in their marriages, believing that "marriage is for life." All of their children had needed counseling for depression or substance abuse, and when I talked with Angie in detox,

she was getting ready to return home to Dougie, an active alcoholic. She hoped that her own sobriety would act as an example for Dougie, and that by sticking by him she would influence him to go with her to AA. She said: "I've got to think of Dougie; I can't just think of myself."

One of the major tasks of clinicians is to help clients develop new *perspectives,* or simply envision other potentials that may maximize strengths or effect change. *Perspective* refers to viewpoint: the position you take as you envision self, others, and the world. If you change where you stand, things can look quite different. For example, a tree looks very different to you when you're flying over it than it does when you're lying beneath it. Similarly, an alcoholic home can look different to its members than it does to an outside observer, who may focus chiefly on symptoms rather than on the connections between people or on time-honored intergenerational, cultural, or gender norms. In both instances, stance affects perspective and vision.

Clinicians frequently work with clients to assist in the development of new dimensions to their understanding—other possibilities that may not have been presented to them, that they may not have previously considered, or that they may have been afraid of entertaining. When clients can safely begin to see things from new perspectives, they often begin to feel or act differently; they may even feel and act for the first time in many years. Having a multiplicity of perspectives gives clients options from which they may choose those that they find to be most useful to them. Some clients will need help to change to more positive and hopeful perspectives regarding themselves, their prospects, and potentials. Others will need help facing harsh realities and discovering resources of which they were previously unaware. The simple encouragement that clients receive to explore, express, examine, challenge, and try out a range of ideas and feelings can itself be novel and inspiring.

Accentuate the Positive

People seeking help often have self-doubt or feel very bad about themselves or their prospects. They may see themselves as "loser," "sick," or "hopeless," very often in reaction to things they have taken in from others regarding self or situation. These views may be expressed quite directly or may lurk beneath an exterior of bravado or mock acceptance.

I ran a group for young adults with schizophrenia, and one night I asked them what music best represented the way they felt about themselves. One young man said that the Beatles' song "Nowhere Man" was the song that he identified with. Another responded sadly, "Fool on the Hill."

While recognizing and appreciating the client's perspective, it is imperative that the clinician simultaneously maintain a positive outlook and convey this actively to the client. Here we *do not* mean ignoring or minimizing the client's very real pain by making simplistic statements like

"Let's look on the brighter side." Rather, we mean that, after empathizing with the client's experience of "being nowhere," the clinician tries, when the moment is right, to elicit or highlight instances of efficacy or agency, with special attention to those abilities the client may not recognize or may trivialize as irrelevant. We seek out and reflect an alternative view of the client—a technique we refer to as *acting as positive mirror*. We reflect and comment on small achievements the client may have overlooked or undervalued, and we emphasize the positive connections that clients may already have in their lives.

We believe in *teaching a transferability of skills* in a way that builds a sense of competence and hope. We suggest that what works in situation A could well work in situations B and C.

> *Zarita was down on herself for "being out of control" at home with anxious obsessions that drove her husband crazy. We explored her work as a clerk-magistrate at the court, where she had been through every imaginable thing with unflappable cool: bomb scares, threats to her life from convicted felons, unexpected fights erupting in court, and so on. My anxiety went sky high as I heard her examples from court, and I shared this with her. She explained that her family had always put huge importance on dignity and self-control in public. At home, though, both parents yelled at each other and at the kids, would slam doors, cry—"the works." I said I could appreciate more where these two sides of her came from: the "cool and collected" one in court, and the "out of control one" at home. She had never appreciated how in control of her reactions she was at work and was very pleased to see it. "But how," she asked, "can I bring the collected one home?" We went on to identify the skills she used in court to calm herself ("count to ten" or "take deep breaths") and then visualized an upsetting scene at home in which she could practice using the same skills.*

We also accentuate the positive when we help clients *construct positive future visions*. The beginning clinician is often tempted to give the client false reassurance to assuage the client's pain (such as "Everything will be fine" or "I'm sure that if we work on this, we can make things better for you"). Interns may not readily understand why this type of reassurance is "false," since they are told to maintain and share an optimistic viewpoint with clients. By false reassurance, we simply mean that, given the complexities of everyday life and the changing nature of people and situations, we cannot predict either the future or the utility of imagined interventions.

Rosy expectations may be unbelievable to despairing clients. Such expectations may be incorrect or inappropriate to the moment or situation at hand, especially with clients from families or neighborhoods where poverty, violence, and lack of opportunity and support appear unremitting. What is required instead is the complex skill of *communicating appropriately timed hopefulness* while maintaining a balancing empathy for the pain and "stuckness" of the moment. We usually empathize in the moment, then later quietly shift to some potential in the person or situation.

Stevie was a 20-year-old mother of two girls who had just been denied custody of them because she had hit them while she was drunk. She said she now had a record of child abuse that would likely be checked every time she went for child care jobs, and child care was the thing she always thought she could do best for a living. I asked how it was for her to think that what she'd loved best might be out of her reach in some instances now. I said it sounded like she'd felt alone and down for so long that it must seem futile to hope for anything. She blew off some more anger and then started to cry and said, "I might as well just give up." I said I could see why she would feel that way, and that it was an awful feeling, to want her girls and her work back, and yet to want to give up sometimes. She nodded.

To be effective, clinicians have to *build on here-and-now connections and achievements* to help the client develop realistic hopes for a more positive future. This future image may not be totally or even primarily positive, but it is important that clients identify islands of possibility that serve to fuel hope for the work.

(Stevie's story continued): After things had subsided a bit, I reminded Stevie that she had told me earlier of wanting to complete her night school diploma and try for LPN training. This seemed to me within reach while the kids were still in foster care, and I said so. I then said that I had seen other folks like herself get some support and ideas from talking with me like we've done today. I told her that I would love to see her try it, to see if it added anything to help her think through the times she feels so lost and alone. It might not, but on the other hand, what if it did? Stevie said she would consider it, but the main thing she wanted today was to find out if she could visit her two girls in foster care on their birthdays. I asked how she wanted to go about finding out. First she asked if I would call ("Who wants to talk to a con?"). Then she laughed and said, reaching for the phone, "If I can call my sister a million times a day to ask if she's seen my boyfriend, I can work the phone to ask about my kids. If I can't use the phone, how am I ever going to get an LPN job?"

Creating Alternative Perspectives

As we noted previously, at times clients have a fixed perspective and find it difficult to explore alternative views. Sometimes clients have been exposed to only one way of thinking about things, and their thinking reflects that one way and little else. Sometimes clients are aware of alternative views but are manifesting loyalty to family, cultural, or religious precepts by adhering inflexibly to a perspective, even though it isn't proving useful to them in attempting to resolve tensions or problems at hand. At times, clients who have been dominated or silenced may simply enjoy holding on to a perspective in order to enjoy a rare opportunity to affirm their own way of thinking. Moreover, some clients will feel threatened by alternative perspectives that may feel unfamiliar or risky.

At times clinicians will want to *introduce alternative perspectives* to broaden clients' sense of possibilities, to heighten and encourage a spirit of curiosity and exploration, or to counter the automatic thinking that we all tend to do under stress. Clients may have a variety of reactions to the introduction of novel explanations or ways of thinking about people and situations. Although some clients welcome new points of view and feel stimulated by them, not everyone will be delighted to explore ideas different from their own.

> *Takis and I had met a few times to talk about his experience in hospice. In about our fourth meeting, I asked him if he had any faith, or any belief in anything beyond himself that he could call on to help him through this time. He looked at me with a good deal of sarcasm and said he hoped I was not going to introduce "some kind of spiritual crap" into his quiet little corner here. He said he was raised strictly in the church but had been an atheist for a long time.*

> *Polly Mae had been talking about what a loser her mother was. She was an alcoholic who had spent most of Polly's life in and out of the hospital. Polly hated having such a poor role model and disidentified with her mother. At one point, I noted that at times her mother really seemed to have a way with people. Polly at first said this made her afraid I would be on her mother's side and would be taken in by her like everyone else. After a minute or two, she said, "You know, she was good at working people. I think I have a little of her skill but I hope I put it to better use."*

There are many ways to introduce or stimulate new perspectives. Some are things that the clinician and client can do together when they meet. Others are suggestions for things that the client can do outside of the meeting.

Questioning and Brainstorming to Elicit New Perspectives

Clinicians can help clients elucidate new perspectives by simply asking questions such as: "How else could we see that?" "Can you think of any other way to explain this?" "What other kinds of things could be going on?"

Sometimes a simple technique of listing alternative explanations or possibilities is useful. The clinician and client can decide to *brainstorm* together, making a list of numerous alternative explanations, sometimes recording them on a flowchart. No idea is evaluated or judged; they are all simply put on the table (or chart). Later the clinician and client can review the list to see if any of the perspectives are useful.

Exploring New Perspectives through Role Plays

Role plays are a useful technique with many applications. In Chapter 4, we discussed using role plays to help the clinician gain empathy for the client. In the next chapter we will discuss using role-play techniques to help clients do things differently. Role plays can also be used in a number of ways to help clients gain new perspectives.

Play out the other side.   The clinician may take a position that plays out the other side of an issue, struggle, or ambivalence: "Tony, you said that you'll never find another job now that you are in a wheelchair, but there are lots of jobs I could imagine for you." When the clinician plays the other side, there is a risk that the client will get into a "stuck opposer" role, rejecting any alternative the clinician presents. On the other hand, the clinician must be aware that some clients will quickly defer to what they perceive to be the superior knowledge of the clinician. One way to avoid such dilemmas is to reverse things and have the client play the other side: "Tony, I know that right now it seems impossible for you to think of being able to get another job. If you could take the other side for a moment—pretend you are an optimistic champion of people with disabilities—what kinds of things might you say to a guy who thinks he'll never get another job because he's in a wheelchair?"

Take the role of the other.   When talking about a relationship, people are often so wed to their own point of view that they have a hard time appreciating another's perspective. Role playing the other can help clients broaden their views of a relationship and offer new insights about another person. The clinician might give the following instruction: "Jeremy, we've been talking a lot about your perspective on your relationship with your brother Hugh. Let's try having you play Hugh for a moment so you can get some insight into how he might see things. Sit in the chair over there. When you do, you become Hugh. (Client moves to other chair.) The clinician can then interview "Hugh," asking such things as "How do you feel as Hugh?" and "Hugh, what do you think about Jeremy?"

Play the outside observer.   Clients sometimes can get a better perspective if they feel more removed from the situation. The clinician can help clients see things from a different angle by asking them to "bystand" the situation: "If you were an outsider, viewing this situation from afar, what different ideas might you have about what is going on? Or if you were reading a novel about these people, how would you understand their story? Would you have any observations about the central characters?"

Using Videotape to Expand Perspective

One useful way of helping clients take the observer role to get new perspectives is through videotaping clients as they interact with family or group members or with the clinician. Client and clinician can watch the video together and discuss new ideas that may emerge or things they might have missed during the interview. Clients can also take home videotapes and play them back to see if they gain any new perspectives while literally observing themselves. The clinician might ask the client to make notes on observations or reactions that can be addressed during the next meeting. These new perspectives may include observations about the clinician and the relationship, as well as about the client.

Contact with Others

Contact with other people can assist clients in redefining themselves and their stories. Clients can be encouraged to open themselves to the novel, often liberating ideas of others by joining self-help groups such as AA, Parents Anonymous, and Breast Cancer Support. In communities of color, the black church, an Asian neighborhood, a family improvement association, or the tribal council can all provide opportunities for clients to think about their problems and issues in new ways and gain greater perspectives. We often see rapid changes in thinking following group participation. Clients can move from lonely, discouraged isolation, to more hopefulness and self-acceptance. More hope and self-regard almost invariably lead to thinking more imaginatively and energetically about life situations and possibilities.

Developing New Metaphors

Richard Kopp (1995) defines metaphors as "mirrors reflecting our inner images of self, life, and others" (p. xiii). He believes that cultures, families, social groups, and individuals structure reality through use of guiding images (metaphors) and, by helping clients change the negative or powerless metaphors that structure their versions of reality, we can help them move more rapidly toward positive change. He gives an example of a woman who was helped through questioning to shift from describing her husband as an out-of-control locomotive and herself as a tunnel to describing herself as a "derailer" of locomotives. Kopp is discussing a theory of therapy that he calls "Metaphor Therapy"; however, we believe that the skill of helping clients develop new metaphors can be used by all clinicians to help clients broaden their perspectives.

> *Marisol said that trying to date in this country was like swimming with sharks. We talked at length about the risks of dating strange men in a big city. She was used to scuba diving in her country, so I compared our meetings to scuba lessons where she could identify the safety equipment she needs and she could enjoy the coral reefs (club scene) while learning to tell the beautiful fish from the predators.*

Culturally responsive clinicians are aware of the rich metaphoric traditions of the clients with whom they work, and can use these metaphors in helping clients enlarge their perspectives. Those working with Native American clients, for example, may make use of some of their traditional stories and "sings."

A word of caution: Just as we need to be certain that our clients understand the meaning of our words, we have to be particularly careful that they understand the meaning of the metaphors we are using.

⦿⦿ CLIP 7.1
Developing New
Perspectives

> *The other day the clinic director called me into his office to discuss a complaint he had received about me from a family I was seeing. I was surprised that the family had complained because I thought we were doing well. The family had told the director that I showed them no respect. They told the director that as far as I was concerned, their son's problems "could just go up in smoke." When I thought about it, I realized that during our last meeting I had suggested that "we put Frankie's problems on the back burner for a while" while we focused on some other issue in the family. "Putting something on the back burner" to them meant "letting it go up in smoke."*

Developing Working Hypotheses or Hunches

Another way that clinicians help clients develop new perspectives is by sharing ideas or hunches about content, affect, themes and patterns, or relationship dynamics of which the client may be unaware. *Hunches* are informed guesses or working hypotheses about the client and his or her situation.

Gerard Egan (1990) coined the term *advanced level accurate empathy* to describe the process of hypothesizing from experience with the client. For Egan, hunches are based on empathy with the client around themes or feelings the client may not yet have verbalized or even understood. Lawrence Shulman (1992) refers to this process as "tuning in to indirect cues from the client" (p. 56). Following the work of Theodor Reik (1948), others have referred to the activity of hypothesizing by means of empathy as "listening with the third ear." While we like to think of developing working hypotheses and hunches as trying to understand the unspoken, we must remember that until the client confirms or disconfirms our hunches, we are at risk of misunderstanding or misattributing meaning. Our hunches must always be tentative, awaiting the client's affirmation or denial.

As noted earlier, clinicians often refer to hunches as intuition, and some clinicians talk about "getting this feeling" when they are with someone, experiencing their intuition as a sensory or visceral event. We believe that clinical intuition and hunches are actually derived from a number of sources.

1. Working hypotheses or hunches can come from *clinical theory or research.* If a client has recently lost a loved one due to death, the clinician may have a hunch that the client may have trouble sleeping, based on research demonstrating a correlation between grief and sleeping problems. The clinician who is trained in psychoanalytic theory may have a hunch that a person with a snake phobia may have some repressed unconscious conflict with her father, whereas a cognitive-behavioral

therapist might posit a conditioned association between a snake and an anxiety state.

2. Working hypotheses or hunches can come from *clinical experience in general.* The intern working with the client who has recently lost a loved one might have a hunch, based on accumulated practice wisdom, that the client may react sensitively to the intern's announcement of an upcoming vacation.

3. Working hypotheses or hunches can come from *clinical experience with the specific client.* As the clinician gains information and understanding about the client and his or her situation, hunches develop more easily. These guesses are informed by the clinician's growing knowledge of the client's idiosyncrasies, of the themes and patterns in the client's story, and from information gleaned from the clinical relationship itself.

4. Working hypotheses and hunches come from *knowledge about larger social issues,* including political and socioeconomic conditions that might impact on the client. The clinician might consider that health care policies that limit hospital stays for new mothers might increase the anxiety of the pregnant woman who is about to give birth for the first time.

5. Working hypotheses or hunches can arise from *personal experience and beliefs.* The clinician who is in recovery from alcoholism may be more prone to see clues indicating alcoholism than would other clinicians for whom alcoholism is a more distant issue.

6. Working hypotheses or hunches can involve "reading between the lines." The clinician may develop hunches about things that are unspoken but seem implicit in the client's story.

Example: Wally

Wally is a 60-year-old computer programmer who has had four sessions with the EAP counselor of the computer company where he has worked with moderate success for the past 20 years. The company is downsizing and is offering faithful employees like Wally an adequate early retirement package if they will leave within a month. If they opt to stay on board, they will have to move with the company to one of two distant states, with no clarity about future security. Wally wants to move and even seems excited about it, but he reports that his wife does not want to move. She said that if he doesn't want to retire, he should just get another job in the community where they currently live. He states that his two sons are in computer businesses in nearby towns and seem settled here with their families. His youngest son has just had his third child, and his oldest son has two young infants. His wife, Evelyn, is a paralegal who can probably get work anywhere, but she prefers to stay near the boys and the five grandchildren. The EAP counselor has offered to have a meeting with Wally and his wife to talk about the options, but Wally has said he would rather not bring Evelyn in.

Some Hunches about Wally

Hunch 1: Wally seems willing to sacrifice family ties for job security.

Hunch 2: The reason Wally is asking to be seen alone is that he may have a secret that he has not shared with his wife or children. Furthermore, he may be coming to see the counselor about the "secret" under the guise of asking for help about his job situation.

Hunch 3: Wally is depressed and wants to make a change in order to feel better.

Hunch 4: Wally feels that he has no choice and must move if he wants to continue working.

Hunch 5: Wally is attempting to protect his wife by not including her in the counseling sessions.

Hunch 6: Wally would welcome the opportunity to put distance between the couple and their children and grandchildren.

Discussion

Hunch 1: Based on theory. The clinician is familiar with life-cycle theory, as well as with recent literature on gender differences. She has learned that men in Wally's age cohort frequently use work achievement as a way of obtaining meaning and purpose, whereas women frequently use family and other relational connections as a way of developing a sense of self-worth. The clinician thinks that Wally's concerns about premature retirement are causing Wally to sacrifice family ties for job security, in direct conflict with Evelyn's wishes to be near family.

Hunch 2: Based on clinical experience. The counselor has worked with many couples over the years and has noticed that a partner asking to meet with the counselor alone often subsequently discloses a secret in the absence of the other partner.

Hunch 3: Based on established client patterns. Wally has reported that in the past he has often used what the clinician thinks of as "geographic cures." When he got out of high school, he said he wanted to get away from the small town where he was born and "start fresh." He had previously reported that when his young son was having difficulty in school, Wally moved the family to another town "to give him a clean slate." Perhaps Wally is looking to move in order to make a change that he hopes will help him feel better.

Hunch 4: Based on knowledge of social conditions. The clinician has seen many reports that men in their sixties are very unlikely to find another job when they are laid off. She knows that there have been many plant and company closings in the surrounding area. She thinks that Wally may feel that his only chance of staying employed is to move.

Hunch 5: Based on the clinician's personal experience. The clinician comes from a traditional Polish working-class family and has noticed that in her community the men often don't talk about financial or work issues in front of their wives, in order to protect them. She has often heard the phrase, "We don't want to worry the women and children." Knowing that Wally is Polish, she thinks that his desire to meet alone may have to do with these traditional Polish working-class values.

Hunch 6: Based on reading between the lines. Wally has occasionally talked about his wife's involvement with the grandchildren. In previous conversations he has said things like: "She's always over there"; "Now that the babies take so much of her time . . ."; and "When she finally gets home . . ." The clinician has stored away all of these phrases, thinking they might indicate that Wally is feeling left out or jealous over the amount of time his wife is spending with the children and grandchildren.

EXERCISE 7.1 *Hunches*

Develop a number of hunches about the clients in the following vignettes. What is the basis of your hunch (theory, experience, knowledge about social conditions, etc.)?

Leah is a 13-year-old runaway living on the streets with a group of three other teens. They show up at the food kitchen occasionally, where a counselor has talked with Leah about the possibility of coming back into school and maybe into foster care. Leah actually seems interested in school. She tells the counselor: "I might like to finish school. I was good at it, but there's no way I'm living in another family. I've been on my own too long and I don't want to take orders from anybody. Besides, my friends need me. We do okay."

Arturo is a 34-year-old musician making his living playing in a small quartet that performs at functions like weddings and bar mitzvahs. He is seeing an employment counselor about career training: "I don't know, I guess I should get a real job. I'm 34 and it doesn't look like I'll make it as a classical musician. My wife says it's time for me to quit fooling around. I love what I do, but there's no future in it."

Huston, age 49, has just been released from jail, where he served 11 years for child sexual assault. He's meeting with his probation officer: "Man, I'm uptight about living outside. It's kind of scary after all these years. I have no family left; my only friends are the guys I met in the slammer."

Kimsoo, age 44, came to the United States to undertake religious studies toward becoming the first woman minister in her village back home. After being here for four years, she is experiencing a number of conflicts about returning to Korea: "I feel really torn. I always thought I wanted to be a minister, and my family and church are counting on me. But things here are so different than back home. Plus, I didn't expect to get involved with an American the way I have."

Intuitions, hunches, and feelings provide rich data for supervision and the enhancement of clinical listening and responding abilities. With experience, these processes can be used in sessions with clients as material for work. Clinicians can consciously develop and improve their hypothesis-building capacities in the following ways.

1. Value your intuitions, speculations, and sensory responses and make these explicit for further analysis.

2. Review your ideas and reactions with supervisors and consultants, exploring many possible alternative views of what these data might mean.

3. Attempt to predict from your hunches and guesses what may happen in ensuing sessions, so as to be able to test out your thinking against what actually transpires.

4. Keep revising your impressions in supervisory discussion, because people, events, and transactions keep changing.

Levels of Inference

When clinicians develop hunches, they are making inferences based on the information they have thus far. Michael Neitzel and Douglas Bernstein (1987) offer a nice discussion of the *levels of inference* clinicians may use when making hypotheses.

Clinicians who use low levels of inference stay close to the data and do not make major leaps away from known facts. For example, Helga complains of trouble sleeping through the night. A clinician using low levels of inference might suggest that something was worrying Helga. Clinicians who use moderate levels of inference often base their hunches on known correlations between one behavior and other behaviors. For example, a clinician using moderate levels of inference might infer that Helga is depressed, knowing that sleep disturbance is often correlated with depression. Clinicians using high levels of inference see the behavior as a sign of some deeper issue or meaning interpreted through the lens of a preferred theoretical model. Such clinicians might hypothesize that Helga was a victim of sexual abuse in her family and that it occurred at night, leaving her hypervigilant at night, which disturbs her sleep.

Neitzel and Bernstein further suggest that the level of inference is closely related to the clinician's theoretical orientation. Behavioral and humanistic therapists often use low or moderate levels of inference; psychodynamic theorists may use moderate to high levels. High levels of inference can be risky, as they are often based on intuition, personal experience, and speculation. The greater the speculation, the higher the level of inference. Clinicians need to be extremely careful about sharing hunches that are highly speculative in nature. Because of the power invested in professional pronouncements, clinicians can worry or mislead clients who trust the clinician's statements more than their own experience. Furthermore, speculations developed on the experience of a clinician in one culture only can seem way off base to the client from another culture.

E X E R C I S E 7.2 *Levels of Inference*

Go back to Exercise 7.1 and see if you can rate the level of inference in your hunches. Do you find that your hunches are most frequently based on low, moderate, or high levels of inference? Notice any pattern in your ratings. Discuss in small groups why becoming familiar with the level of inference you use matters.

Sharing Hunches

Because our hunches are only informed guesses, we must be careful how we present them to the client. Clinicians should *offer hunches tentatively,* sharing ideas provisionally, as questions or as a possibility rather than a certainty:

"Could it be that . . .?"

"Perhaps . . ."

"I wonder if . . ."

"Is there a chance that . . .?"

Clinicians need to *avoid the pitfall of assumed brilliance.* Some clients may have a need to have an authority tell them things and may agree with the clinician's hunches, subordinating their own judgment to that of the clinician.

On the other hand, clients might reject a clinician's hunch even if there is some truth in it. This can occur because clients are reacting against the clinician, or because they are not yet ready to make the connection that the clinician has made. It requires a great deal of skill to *know when to let go of a hunch and when to store it away.* Clinicians may come back to an issue later if they feel the client is readier to "hear" it or deal with it; or clinicians may conclude that they themselves were off base in their speculation.

During my third meeting with Fatima, I remember thinking that the trouble she was having with her roommate seemed to be like two sisters fighting over who was most loved. I had a hunch that her relationship with her

*roommate might be evoking some of the competitive feelings she might
have had with her sister. When I mentioned this to her, she said: "You
psychologists are all alike. Always trying to read something into things. I
can't believe you could actually be so stereotypic. I thought you were really
getting to know me. How could you be so wrong?" I felt stupid and naive. I
remember it took me a long time before I was willing to take a risk and
share a hunch again.*

*When I first broached the subject with him, Mustafa rejected the idea that
the reason he might not be applying for jobs as an electrician in Boston was
because he was fearful of entering a "white-dominated trade." He said he
just knew there weren't any jobs. A couple of weeks later he said he had been
thinking about it and that he now felt that some of his reluctance was about
being a Muslim among all those "Irish Catholic guys."*

Well-timed and sensitively shared hunches can help clients develop new
perspectives. Sharing hunches also models for clients the process of looking
for alternative meanings or possibilities in their thoughts, feelings, or actions.

There are a number of ways that clinicians can share their hypotheses.
They can directly share their hunch using an "I" statement. Often, however,
because we want clients to experience a sense of efficacy and to develop their
own voice, the clinician may share a hypothesis in such a way that the client
feels it came from him or her. In the following example, note the differential
responses of the client. With Clinician A, the client attributes the wisdom to
the clinician. With Clinician B, the client *assumes ownership* of the idea.

Examples

Carrie and Jana have been a couple for two years. They are often
fighting but seem to keep getting back together. The clinician, aware
of their family histories, has a hunch that they do not stay separated
because each of them is afraid of living on her own.

Clinician A: Looks to me like both of you may have some fears of
separating. (Clinician directly shares her hunch.)

Client: Yes, you are right, I think we might.

Clinician B: Sounds *like you're saying* that both she and you might be
afraid of separating. (Clinician B is also sharing a hunch, but
does it in such a way that the client feels that it came from her.)

Client: Yes, I do think so.

The clinician must always remember that the hunch could be wrong, and
that *sharing an inaccurate hunch is okay.* It may help clients clarify an issue or
clarify their own perspective as separate from the clinician's. When clinicians
offer a hunch in a tentative or provisional way, it encourages clients to correct

or amplify. Clinician tentativeness is expressed in tone and language. It is fine to share a hunch directly, as Clinician A does in the previous example; but she could also have shared it by saying, "Could it be that . . .?" or "Have you considered the possibility that . . .?" These questions make it easier for clients to think about whether the clinician's hunches are accurate.

Clinicians can decide how, when, with whom, and to what extent to share their hunches. Such decisions are often a matter of judging how quickly and comfortably clients can correct clinician statements when necessary, especially given the authority that both clients and clinicians tend to attribute to clinician insight and wisdom!

Excessive sharing of hunches by the clinician may become tiresome as well as stifling of the client's voice. Clinicians do not and *should not always share their hunches.* Keep in mind that we clinicians wait for more information with which to validate or invalidate our speculations, and that we put high developmental priority on providing opportunities for clients to author their own narratives. Before sharing any hunch, clinicians should ask themselves what effects sharing that hunch might have and be prepared to take responsibility for any negative fallout.

> *I remember being in supervision with a young psychology intern who was always sharing his "ideas about what's going on" with the client. He intended to be helpful and was often confused when his clients stopped coming to see him or complained that they felt he was judgmental.*

⦿⦿ CLIP 7.2
Sharing Hunches

EXERCISE 7.3 *Sharing Hunches*

Go back to Exercise 7.1 and attempt to frame a response in which you share your hunch with the client. Videotape your responses and play them back. What do you notice?

Encouraging Client Hypothesizing

Hunches often come from clients themselves, sometimes well before the clinician ever thinks of the material offered up in the hunch. Some clients are more "psychologically minded" than others: they do a great deal of speculating on the meanings and motivations in events and readily develop their own working hypotheses.

It is very important to be conscious of the ways in which this reflective capacity is nourished and developed. Clinicians can emphasize the importance of thinking about meanings and interrelationships and encourage clients to *develop their own working hypotheses* by frequently asking what clients think about things or how they understand situations. Clients can be helped to search out their own hunches if the clinician uses prompts such as:

"Let's stop for a moment and think about this."

"How could we understand this?"

"What's your take on this?" or "What are your thoughts about this?"

"What might be some different ways to think about this?"

Clinicians can reinforce clients' *constructive introspection* by responding positively.

"What an interesting idea."

"So you're trying to figure out where this might come from. Good work!"

"It's so important that you're coming up with these insights."

Another way to encourage clients to respect and develop their own hunches is through a purposeful use of silence—*silence for pondering.* After the client says something or shares a story, we intentionally leave a brief period of silence, assuming a pensive expression to indicate that we are thinking about implications, contemplating meanings. Here we model for clients the importance of taking time to think things out rather than responding glibly or rushing on. Sitting with the silence is a natural capacity in some clinicians, but it may have to be consciously developed by others so that clients can be left sufficient space to gather and plumb their own thoughts.

Related to purposeful use of reflective silence is *holding our smarts.* As clinicians we can come to value the sound of our own voices and wisdom too much, too readily offering our own hunches instead of gently urging clients to risk developing their own. Clinicians may pay lip service to the principle of empowerment by always asking the client to speak first; but when the client doesn't respond quickly enough, clinicians may too quickly come in with their own ideas or thoughts. Beginning practitioners often mistakenly define the helping process as the imparting of wisdom and worry excessively about not conveying enough to clients to appear competent and helpful. There is great merit in developing knowledge and ideas, and clinicians should develop their skills in hypothesis building. However, they must learn to refrain from sharing their own ideas whenever it would be more helpful to the client to exercise his or her own thinking.

A friend of mine who is a rock climber (and therapist) shared a quote with me from Rebuffat (1965) about guides that I think captures an aspect of clinical helping, too: "With the inevitable repetition of the same ascents, the work of the guide could become tedious, but the guide is not just a machine to climb slopes of ice and walls of rock, to know the weather and the route. He does not climb for himself: he opens the gates of his mountain for his companion. He knows that such and such a climb is interesting, that this particular area is as delicate as a piece of lacework, he knows at which turn there is, suddenly, a wonderful view. He says nothing, but his reward comes with the smile of his companion when he sees it."

Sometimes clients may not want to develop their own hunches, expecting the clinician to come up with explanations and answers. Uba (1994) notes that this is particularly true for Asian American clients, who may expect the clinician to figure out what is wrong and tell them what to do differently. As we noted, it may be tempting for clinicians to leap in, particularly if they feel that the client's journey is one they know well and can speculate on in helpful ways. While it may at times be helpful, and even necessary, for the clinician to share hunches and hypotheses, it is important that clients develop and utilize these skills themselves wherever possible. Clinicians should encourage clients to develop hunches and hypotheses, helping them to affirm their own voices, to recognize that they are the experts on their own stories. In this way, clients will develop skills that they will keep long after the clinical relationship comes to an end.

Making Observations about Stuck Patterns

Clinicians can help clients enlarge their perspective by making observations about stuck patterns of thinking, feeling, or behaving that seem to get in the way of the goals the client wishes to achieve. Sometimes the client is unaware of these patterns and the clinician needs to gently suggest the patterns in the tentative form of a hunch. For example, the client may be a woman who feels strongly that she will be judged harshly for speaking her mind and, as a result, does not speak up in most situations. The clinician may observe how the client's resultant silence has prevented her from moving up in her job in a company that rewards verbal initiatives. She might offer her observation in the form of a hunch: "I notice something interesting about you. Because you're afraid you'll be criticized, you remain silent and then, ironically, you often get criticized for not speaking up." If the client agrees with the hunch about a pattern holding her back, she might respond with comments such as, "I never realized I did that before" or "I never thought of it from that perspective."

Reflecting Discrepancies

As we listen to clients' stories, we often pay attention to discrepancies or inconsistencies. Among other things, *discrepancies* can manifest as inconsistencies between two statements, between thoughts and feelings, between intentions and actual behaviors, and between verbal and nonverbal communication. It is very human to be unaware of our discrepancies until they are brought to our attention, and they are often quite illuminating of struggles, ambivalences, or conflicts we are not quite ready to resolve. Clients are often unaware of their own contradictions or inconsistencies. Clinicians may point out discrepancies to clients to help them examine the several sides of an issue or reaction so that they can proceed in the work with new perspectives, with more information and clarity about themselves, their situation, and how the mind works when divided about things.

Clinicians try to note discrepancies as they arise. They may then choose to directly reflect the discrepancy; they may develop hunches based on observed inconsistencies; or they may wait to see if a pattern develops that would make for a more compelling hunch. Some clinicians call pointing out discrepancies *challenging* the client (Egan, 1994), and others call it *confronting* (Ivey, 1994; Kadushin, 1997; Okun, 1997). We believe that *reflecting discrepancies* can serve many functions, depending on the intent of the clinician and the impact on the client. The clinician may intend to clarify; the client may feel challenged or confronted.

The techniques that clinicians use to point out discrepancies are many and varied. Some common techniques are:

1. *Reflection of discrepancy.* Examples: "While you described your sadness, you were smiling" or "You've said that you like school, and you've said that you hate being a student."

2. *The "on the one hand . . . on the other hand" technique.* Example: "On the one hand, you say that you really like your job; on the other, you are always late for work."

3. *Name it directly.* Examples: "I sense an inconsistency here" or "I hear two things at once" or "You seem to be of two minds about this."

⚏ **CLIP 7.3**
Identifying Stuck Patterns

EXERCISE 7.4 *Helping Clients See Discrepancies*

Divide into groups of three. Using the following examples, role-play various ways of pointing out the discrepancy to the client. Note how it feels to be the client and how you respond to different ways of having discrepancies pointed out to you.

Salina, age 55, is talking to an EAP counselor because her boss has said she must: "I don't have a problem with drinking and I don't know why people say I do. Sure, I have a few. Who doesn't? They say it affects my work, but, hey, I give them a good morning's work. Sometimes I have a few drinks with lunch, but that's no big deal. My boyfriend says he doesn't like how I act in public. Half the stuff he accuses me of I don't remember. I'm just having a good time, so what's his beef?"

Marcel, age 30, a recent widower, says he wants to find a new mother for his young children. He's been going to every church singles event for the last six months. He is talking to his pastor: "I miss Gabrielle so much. It's only been seven months since she died. She was a rare find. I can't imagine anyone taking Gabrielle's place, but the kids really need a woman's touch."

Education or Information Sharing

In clinical work, *education* or *information sharing* refers to introducing new concepts or information the client may be unaware of as another means of widening possibilities or extending opportunity. Information can be liberating. The abused single mother who is afraid she will lose custody of her children if she seeks safety in a homeless shelter, the male teenager who is attracted to other males, and the lonely widower who has few social contacts can all benefit from information and resources.

Information sharing usually occurs in situations in which clients are unaware of resources or of their rights in a particular situation. Clinicians frequently provide information about transportation, respite care, funding sources, training opportunities, child care, and preventive health care services. In addition, clinicians may find that they need to inform clients about legal rights or protective services.

Information sharing may be accomplished in several ways.

Helping clients identify sources of information. The clinician can directly ask whether the client knows where to get the needed information. The questions the clinician asks about outside sources of information can help the client delineate what information is needed and how to go about getting it. Some clients are able to identify sources of information and obtain information for themselves. Clients' confidence and resourcefulness are often increased by successfully seeking out their own information, and success at this task can reinforce skills that will be useful in the process of locating other needed resources and networks. Elaine Pinderhughes (1989) notes that such empowerment work "shifts the client's perspective from that of self as powerless, to that of self as a member of a valued group using effective strategies to acquire the necessary resources to meet his or her goals" (p. 111).

> "Do you know where you can get information about TMJ (temporal mandibular joint disease)?"
>
> "How would you find out about legal rights of lesbian mothers?"
>
> "Do you know about self-help groups for anorexia in your area?"

Providing materials. Some clinicians, especially those who work in specialized services, have resources and materials readily available for use by clients. A clinician who works in a drug treatment program might have pamphlets about AIDS prevention. Someone who works in a hospital with people who have had spinal cord injury might have brochures from health care companies about home health equipment. Some clinicians have bulletin boards where they post information about mutual aid groups or other supportive services that they think might be of interest to their clients. As technology advances, clinicians should also be aware of information that is available via the Internet, and they may want to post information and resources on the Internet themselves.

Bibliotherapy is a form of intervention in which the clinician refers clients to specific readings, sometimes lending clients the books. Clinicians can also give clients audiotapes or videotapes for their use at home: for example, relaxation tapes or conference tapes on subjects that would be instructional and supportive for clients.

Directly imparting information. If clinicians have the expertise, they may at times choose to give clients information directly. The clinician working with a couple who has decided to adopt may directly share information about what to expect during the prescreening interview with the agency social worker, informing the couple that the interviewer often asks to see the room where the child would sleep. The clinician who is working with a client who is phobic about AIDS may reassure him that he can't get AIDS through kissing or hugging.

Clients can be very appreciative of the clinician's imparting of information, which can serve as a shortcut when people are especially busy and already stressed. However, when providing information, we are careful not to have clients see us as "the expert" or "the one with all the know-how." Harry Aponte (1994) has aptly observed that the mission of providers "is to serve, not to colonize" (p. 11). Giving direct information can tempt some clients to come back any time they have a question instead of exercising their own resourcefulness. Teaching them how to get needed answers gives them confidence and skills they can use forever. Finally, when providing information, clinicians should be careful that the client doesn't feel pushed toward or into a particular stance or service. For example, if the clinician gives a pregnant 13-year-old information about abortion but not about adoption, she and her parent or guardian may feel that the clinician has tried to influence her in a specific direction.

Accompanying clients in seeking information. Sometimes the clinician may want to accompany the client who is attempting to get information, offering to go with the client to lend support. At other times, the client may ask the clinician to come along. In some clinical settings, going with clients to obtain information and services is a valued, routine function; in others, it would be an exceptional occurrence. The clinician needs to think carefully about what the implications for the client and the working relationship would be of accompanying the client, or of going with one client but not with another.

> *I was working with a client who was dying from bone cancer. He was interested in getting information about dying at home. He asked if I would go with him to a meeting with the people from the local hospice because he was afraid he wouldn't be able to remember what was said and he wanted my help in processing the information and figuring out what to do. I was glad to go with him, and it gave me a chance to meet people in his potential helping network and learn more myself about what they could offer.*

Sharing information through self-disclosure. Through selective and judicious sharing of personal information, clinicians can sometimes provide clients with helpful information. For example, with a client about to undergo abdominal surgery and deciding how soon to return to work, the clinician might share that she had similar surgery and felt tired in the afternoons for over a month after surgery. Information sharing through self-disclosure is often based on learning from life experience and is meant to convey empathy as well as information.

When sharing information through self-disclosure, it is important to be brief and to avoid sounding either condescending or self-righteous. Before self-disclosing, always pay attention to where the client is and to the impact this sharing will have. Some clients will see the disclosure as informative; some may be pleased to know more about the clinician; others may find that the self-disclosure moves them away from their own issues. In the example given above, the client may find that she is now worrying over the clinician's health, subsequently asking more about the clinician's surgery instead of focusing on her concerns about her own surgery. One risk of sharing information through self-disclosure is that the client may feel pressured to act in the way that the clinician did; one benefit is that such sharing may strengthen the mutuality of the relationship. (We will discuss self-disclosure more fully in Chapter 9.)

OO **CLIP 7.4**
Sharing
Information

EXERCISE 7.5 *Sharing Information with Clients*

In small groups, come up with a number of issues around which you might feel comfortable sharing potentially useful information through self-disclosure. Role-play and videotape some scenarios, rotating the roles of client and clinician. Discuss the impact that your sharing information in this way has on the client. Try sharing the same information with the client using the other techniques suggested. Watch the role plays and notice the differential effects on your client of conveying the same information in different ways.

Introducing New Topics

Clinicians always attend to the whole "shape" of their contacts with clients. Attention is paid to what is being focused on across a series of contacts, not just within each interview. Is the focus too scattered or too limited? Are there repeating themes or "stuck" themes or themes that may be diverting from material not yet covered, thus limiting the client's and clinician's perspective?

Clients may work intensely on certain situations, relationships, or themes while never touching on others. Preoccupation with particular stressors or persistent problems is understandable, yet at times it can prove unproductive as subjects are discussed over and over without leading anywhere. At other times, clients and clinicians can unwittingly stay narrowly focused in order to avoid more painful or taboo areas. In any event, it sometimes falls to the clinician to raise new areas for exploration, to fill out the picture. Introducing new perspectives can help clients enlarge their perspective on self or context, especially when things have been omitted from a story because the client doesn't think they matter. Sometimes focusing on a new area will highlight the strengths of a client or situation.

> *Lonny and Carla fought like cats and dogs in the office. You name it, they argued about it. Then they would proclaim, "See? All we know how to do is fight." It seemed that there was nothing to hold them together. I realized that we'd been talking, and they'd been arguing, about everything—money, time, sex—but they never talked about their children. When I asked about the kids, their whole demeanor changed. They softened; they agreed with and appreciated each other as parents. The whole feeling in the room changed, and I felt the first glimmer of hope for this couple. Here was something about their "team" to build on.*

New topics need not be introduced abruptly. The clinician usually waits for an appropriate opening—even just a pause for breath—and then gently introduces a new topic.

"We haven't talked much about . . ."

"I'm curious to know more about . . ."

"I realize I don't know anything about . . ."

"We've talked a lot about . . . but not about . . ."

"While we're on that subject, . . ."

Changing the Perspective of Others: Working for Social Change

We have previously emphasized our belief that social forces, including the attitudes of others, account for much of our clients' distress. Far too many people are left feeling that *they are* problems, rather than that *they have* problems, which are often due to socioeconomic and political factors beyond their control. As clinicians, we recognize that in addition to helping clients gain new perspectives, sometimes the best intervention we can make is to work to change the attitudes and beliefs of others and work to change larger systems and institutions, especially those that limit opportunities for others.

> *I was a school counselor who was seeing a couple of high school students who identified as gay. As these two young men talked about their experiences, it became clear that a lot of the stress they felt was in response to the attitudes that some of their teachers seemed to have toward them. I realized that in order to help the students, I also had to work with the teachers. I offered an in-service for teachers in which I used a number of techniques including self-disclosure on the part of lesbian/gay/bisexual*

students about the extent of the pain they experienced in being either ignored or attacked. I shared information about sexual orientation development, and I had the teachers role-play scenarios in which they had to experience the plight of lesbian, gay, and bisexual students. Some of the teachers said that the workshop raised some issues that they had never thought about. The students later reported that they felt a little more sensitivity on the part of some of the faculty.

One of my classmates in social work school was in a wheelchair because of multiple sclerosis. She wanted us to perceive more fully how many barriers there are to mobility in the supposedly enlightened environment of a university. She had us each experience what it was like to be in a wheelchair for half a day. Because the entrance ramp was blocked by bicycles chained to it, I had to be carried into the building by strangers happening by. Then I had to try to make it across the street in the wheelchair with a stoplight that changed so fast that I couldn't get across. I asked for help from passersby, who would stare at me and walk right on by. Others offered help when I didn't want or ask for it. I returned to the meeting room exasperated and really full of ideas about what should happen differently for people in wheelchairs. We were all quite shocked that we'd never really appreciated what they go through. That one day really shifted my perspective about barriers to access.

Workshops, community trainings, and media presentations all help change the perspectives of others and may have an indirect effect on clients with whom we work. As we stated earlier, we believe that the clinician has a social and professional responsibility to work for social change on their clients' behalf. Even better are those occasions when we and clients can find appropriate ways to be present in the same political or social action campaigns and protests, affirming our common humanity and strengths.

EXERCISE 7.6 *Broadening the Views of Others*

In small groups, make a list of commonly held social attitudes or perspectives that you believe may have a negative impact on your clients. Choose one and design a public education campaign around it. What techniques will you use to help people alter or broaden their perspectives? Describe persons or institutions that you believe are likely to respond favorably or unfavorably to your efforts.

Conclusion

In this chapter, we have emphasized techniques that help clients develop new perspectives, yet often the work requires that the clinician develop new perspectives, too. In Chapter 1 we reviewed many ways in which theoretical and practice models had for many years misappropriated power and authority to providers, subordinating client knowledge and experience in the process, and medicalizing caregiving, according little place to cultural traditions of care or to natural helping networks. Today, client and clinician work together to try to create new ways of seeing things that allow the client more respect, flexibility, responsibility, and choice. This effort often requires that clinicians give up customary ways of seeing things in order to be open to evolving new visions with the client. Clients often take the lead in pointing out to clinicians and service agencies their unhelpful or undermining attitudes, policies, and behaviors.

As clinicians, we can broaden our own views using the same techniques that have proven useful to help clients develop new perspectives. Bystanding, brainstorming, observing and working out our own discrepancies, role playing the part of the other, gathering new information through continuing education, and looking for and changing stuck patterns in ourselves are all ways we can expand our perspective. Supervision, consultation, and continuing education are essential to this process; and, of course, interacting with clients can help us broaden and deepen our perspectives. Clients and their moving stories remain perhaps our best reminders that the "personal" is still so often the political and the systemic.

Suggested Readings

A basic premise of the cognitive therapies is that changing ways of thinking not only helps clients gain new perspectives but also helps clients feel and do things differently. Two classic works in cognitive therapy are:

Beck, Aaron, T. (1976). *Cognitive therapy and emotional disorders*. New York: International Universities Press.

Ellis, Albert. (1962). *Reason and emotion in psychotherapy*. New York: Lyle Stuart.

A useful guide to the multiple uses of videotaping in clinical work is:

Heilveil, Ira. (1983). *Video in mental health practice: An activities handbook*. New York: Springer.

An interesting book on metaphors is:

Kopp, Richard R. (1995). *Metaphor therapy: Using client-generated metaphors in psychotherapy*. New York: Brunner/Mazel.

CHAPTER 8

Changing Behaviors: Helping Clients Do Things Differently

Sometimes people come to see clinicians because they want to change patterns of behavior that are not working for them, or because they want to learn new skills and new behaviors. Clarinda wants to find new ways of handling her anger rather than yelling. Howard, diagnosed with obsessive compulsive disorder, wants to learn how to control his compulsive hand washing. Estrella wants to learn how to be more assertive at work. Pete wants to develop better study habits. Lincoln, who is mentally retarded, wants to learn the skills he needs to live on his own.

Sometimes clients come for practical information about how to do things. Bernice wants to know how to adopt a child as a single woman. Yves wants his boys to get green cards so they can help support the extended family. Lana wants a referral to the Reach to Recovery program in her area.

Clients may come to see a clinician because other people are concerned about their behaviors. Chet is referred by his teacher to the school guidance counselor because Chet calls out things in a disruptive way in class. Gilbert is sent by the court to see an alcohol counselor after being convicted for driving while intoxicated. Gladdie is taken to see a neighborhood clinic counselor by her children, who are concerned that she has scarcely left the house since the death of her husband.

Sometimes clients may not be coming to do things differently. Although not initially seeking to change behavior, the client comes to realize that connected to the presenting problem are behaviors that might be useful to change or new skills that might be beneficial to learn. Francesca comes complaining that she is depressed and unhappy. In talking with the psychologist, she discovers that if she did some things differently—for example, getting together with others even when she doesn't feel like it—she might begin to feel better. Selina comes to see a social worker about her boyfriend's abuse of her. In talking with the social worker, Selina realizes that her children have been affected by her boyfriend's violent behavior, and she then wants to learn how to talk to them about it. In due time she decides to end her relationship with her boyfriend and asks how to get a restraining order.

Clinicians often help clients focus on changing individual personal behaviors. However, it's also important to recognize that clients may work to change patterns of behavior in the larger society. Frederick came to see a pastoral counselor about his plan to volunteer to help reconstruct some of the southern black churches destroyed by arsonists and about his fears about personal safety. Shusei is taking a course on conflict resolution at the local mental health center because she wants to serve as a volunteer mediator in family court.

After Selina is successful in moving away from her relationship with her abusive boyfriend, she decides that she wants to help other women overcome what she refers to as "marianismo" (the female counterpart of "machismo"), which she believes contributes to Latina women's willingness to put up with violence from men. She sets up a local educational program and eventually becomes a national Latina spokesperson. Damien, who attended the Million Man March, now reports a heightened sense of belonging, power, and responsibility, which led to a new commitment to be actively involved in parenting his young son. Sometimes working on behavior change leads to social action, as it did for Selina. At other times, social action can lead to personal behavior change, as it did for Damien.

Ripples in a Stream

As clients change their behaviors, learn new skills, or accomplish practical tasks, many aspects of their lives are affected. Not only behavior but perspective, emotions and feeling states, self-concept, and achievement levels may all change, as all are interrelated. Sometimes people ask: "Does changing one's perceptions change one's behaviors, or vice versa?" "Does changing one's behavior change one's mood, or vice versa?" "Does insight change behavior, or vice versa?" We think that it does not matter so much which occurs first; what matters is that something occur, for we know that changes in any domain have a ripple effect on all others.

People often find that when they do things differently, they see and feel things differently. As clients learn to do things differently, their perspective about themselves—how they envision their potential and place—changes. Successful achievement and connection with others, even in small amounts, can often counteract hopelessness. By *achievement* we do not mean scaling life's Everests or winning important posts in government; rather, achievement is finally doing those things in daily life that the client had wished to do but that had formerly seemed impossible. Achievement could mean making one friend or speaking up for the first time.

As behaviors change, so do relationships. Doing things differently not only affects one's own behavior, it can also affect the behaviors of others with whom the client relates. Working for social change affects the individual's perspective, mood, self-concept, worldview, and activities but also affects large groups of others and, perhaps, society as a whole. Black men coming together in Washington, D.C., for the national 1996 Million Man March occasioned some much needed review and commentary throughout the larger society regarding persistent discrimination based on race, class, and gender, and it stimulated a number of organizations to stand up more forthrightly for societal change.

In Chapter 7 we discussed some techniques clinicians use to help clients see and feel things differently. In this chapter we will focus on techniques clinicians use to help clients *do* things differently, using many of the principles we have already discussed in previous chapters.

Exploring What the Client Is "Doing Right"

As we help clients learn new behaviors and skills, we note again how crucial it is to elicit client strengths, minor triumphs, and successful adaptive strategies and activities, no matter how small. There is a natural tendency in clinical work to focus on what clients want to do differently, especially when using a time-limited or problem-solving approach. However, we recognize the importance of *emphasizing what is working* for clients, what clients like, what they want to preserve and expand, as well as what they want to change. We find that it helps in work with clients to underscore the importance of what is working for them and how it came about—not by magic or fate but by hard work, persistence, and successful connection with others who care and help.

> *Chip was in training to be a firefighter and was talking about how anxious he felt when he had to go into a burning building. I knew that he had participated in the Gulf War and I asked him if he felt a similar fear then. He said he did. I asked what he did to enable him to get through it. Chip said that in the Gulf War he learned to pray when under fire. I asked if he could use this now. He was surprised, saying he didn't think counselors believed in things like praying. I said that I do and that I was glad if it comforts him. He said that he doesn't tell his buddies, but when he's in a bad fire and is afraid, he prays silently in his head for himself and the others involved.*

Similarly, the clinician will explore with clients what *problem-solving skills they have learned* from struggling, coping, and mastering things in the past. These problem-solving skills can potentially be used in present situations. Many people undervalue their former experiences because of past mistakes and failures that continue to haunt their thinking. When we see this happening, we emphasize with the client the transferability of skills and behaviors, underscoring as assets those effective behaviors and skills that are already in the client's repertoire.

> *Alphonse said that in struggling with his alcoholism, he learned how to relinquish battles over things he cannot change, and now he tries to focus effort on that which he can do something about. This helps him be more patient with his rather rigid supervisor, instead of butting heads with her all the time.*

> *Jobeth learned from raising three teens alone that she has more strength than she ever thought, and that if she just takes one thing at a time she can get through many challenges without being overwhelmed.*

> *Trish said she learned from the protective services worker how to count to ten and leave the room before hitting her children. Now she recognizes that counting to ten and cooling off in another room are also good ways of avoiding angry confrontations with her landlady.*

Helping Clients Own Their Part in Things

Now and then most of us manifest the human tendency to perceive that the causes of our difficulties lie in others or in forces outside of our control. Many people go about their daily lives unaware of their motivations, of particular triggers of happy or sad feelings, of others' effects on them, or of possible ways their histories might be shaping what they say and do. It will be important for clients' learning to do things differently that they be able to assume responsibility for their own behaviors that may be contributing to problems and learn to credit themselves for behaviors that result in successful change.

Identifying Behaviors to Change and New Skills to Learn

To help clients do things differently, the clinician helps them identify behaviors, relationships, and tasks they wish to work on or new skills they need or want to learn. A number of guidelines facilitate this process.

1. Clinicians try to help clients be as *concrete and specific* as possible in describing what they want to do differently. As noted earlier, the clearer the clinician's and client's view of desired objectives and possible strategies for attaining them, the more likely they are to accomplish them. It helps to develop clear images or metaphors of what the change will look like so that clinician and client will know when they've achieved it.

2. Clinicians help the client identify in which *contexts* the behavior occurs. Clients are encouraged to examine when, with whom, and under what circumstances the targeted behaviors occur. An awareness of the circumstances in which the behavior occurs can help the clinician and client think about appropriate interventions. Behavior is never separate from its context.

   Jason was referred to the psychologist for his aggressive behavior with younger children at the residential treatment center. Upon exploration, the psychologist discovered that this behavior was pretty much limited to the residential program and that Jason did not seem to have this difficulty with younger children at school.

3. The clinician helps the client identify *precipitating events and "triggers,"* or easily pushed "buttons," that seem to set off a habitual behavior pattern or sequence. For example, every time Paul's wife asks him if he has stopped for a drink after work, he gets angry and slams the door, goes to the basement workshop, and stays there fuming until after everyone is in bed. Annmarie noticed that she was most likely to be short-tempered with her children when one of them says something about missing their father.

   Sometimes these triggers and sequences are so deeply imbedded and out of awareness that the clinician must patiently retrace with the client circumstances or interactions that precede unhappy moods, behaviors, or preoccupations that the client can't explain. The clinician has to do some detective work with the client in order to discover and understand the precipitants of the behavior. Bringing into awareness those factors that were previously split off from conscious memory is referred to by psychodynamic clinicians as *insight development.* Insight can help clients understand and change their behaviors as well as their moods and feeling states.

Example

   Client: I've been acting very short-tempered all week. On Wednesday I was in a particularly foul mood.

   Clinician: Were there any particular things that happened that day?

   Client: No.

   Clinician: What were your thoughts or feelings on waking?

   Client: Nothing special.

   Clinician: How about events or people the evening before?

   Client: Nope; watched TV, went to bed seemingly okay.

   Clinician: Anything on TV that distressed you?

   Client: No . . . cop shows, news.

Clinician: Was there anything about this day of the week or date that had any significance for you?

Client: (Hesitates.) There *were* a lot of ads on TV for Father's Day . . .

Clinician: Hmmmm. Father's Day is coming up. Might you be missing your father at this time?

Client: I never think about him . . . (then she begins to cry) My mother always told me that it was best if we just got on with our lives: "There's no sense crying over spilt milk." I guess I felt that she was so hurt about my father's death that I shouldn't even miss him, as that would hurt her, too.

---

4. The clinician and client work together to identify the *consequences* of the current behavior: what things reinforce or encourage the behavior, as well as those things that serve as disincentives (reasons the client wants to change the behavior). They also explore the effects of the behavior on others, as the reactions of other people in the client's life are likely to impact the planned work and may serve as encouragers or discouragers of change.

   Ricardo was referred to the teen shelter counselor because he kept running away. I kept looking to find out what was happening right before he would run away—to see if there was something that triggered his behavior. It took a while for me to ask what the consequences were of his running away. He told me that when he runs away, it is the only time his parents talk to each other anymore. He said, "Sometimes they even come to get me together."

5. The client and the clinician attempt to identify *exceptions* to stated problematic behaviors or behavioral sequences. The clinician listens for "I've always" and "I never" statements, then gently challenges them and searches for exceptions that represent client strengths. For example, regular visits with the clinician may be used as an exception to the avowal "I can never make and keep a relationship." It will be important for clients to try to build up more "exceptions" like these in their daily lives, to act as encouragements. Clinician and client can also explore the possibility that there are contexts in which unwanted behavior does not occur with the same frequency or intensity.

⏻⏻ CLIP 8.1
Identifying
Exceptions

Example

Client: I never seem to be able to finish things on time. Everybody says that about me, too. I just can't meet deadlines.

Clinician: I could swear you told me when we first met that you had done okay in boot camp—and in fact met your girlfriend at squad leader camp. Did I get that wrong? You must have been doing okay to be chosen as a squad leader.

Client: But that's different. That was the army. If you screw up there, you lose pay, time off, like that. You can't be late with stuff there.

Clinician: Since you say you are invariably late, how come you weren't late with stuff then?

Client: Hmmm . . . let me think a minute. Well . . . there were rules and codes that you followed; it was real plain what you had to do and what would happen if you didn't. It was not confusing at all.

Clinician: So then it helped to have things spelled out clearly, have a specified timetable, and be shown how.

Client: I didn't think about it like that. I just followed the rules and did okay. As a matter of fact, I hated to leave the service, but the pay was so low I couldn't support a family on it.

Clinician: I wonder if there are other jobs we could think of where there would be those kinds of codes or instructions that would make it clearer and easier to meet deadlines.

---

6. It is often useful to ask clients to think about what *specific skills or behavioral sequences* they would need to learn in order to do things differently. The desired goals can be broken up into simpler component skill and behavioral parts so that they seem more ordinary, sensible, and achievable. If the client doesn't know what steps or skills would be required, the clinician can help identify specific behavioral sequences that may be necessary, checking out the client's comfort level with the suggested steps and fine-tuning them as they go along. For example, the social worker who is working to help Lincoln live on his own might need to elucidate the specific behaviors he needs to learn to achieve his goal: get up on time, attend to his personal care, be able to do his own shopping, master the bus fares and routes, and so on. Note that here we are using partializing and prioritizing skills again.

7. Doing things differently can be hard. Before attempting to make a change, it is often helpful to identify the *resources* available to do this difficult work. The client's preexisting skills can be resources, as can other people who may support the client in making the change. If the client has few resources or is under a great deal of stress, it may not be a good time to attempt to make a change. The clinician tries to help the client develop resources that will provide support and backup as the client attempts to do things differently. Helping clients improve their situation—for example, getting a good permanent housing situation—may be necessary before clients can effect other kinds of behavior change.

8. As clients talk about how they wish to do things differently, the clinician must *assess how realistic* the hopes are. An old joke captures the spirit of this exploration very well:

Patient: Doctor, will I be able to play the flute after my hand surgery?

Doctor: Only if you were able to play it before.

The clinician constantly engages in reality checks: (a) the client's *capacity* to change, (b) the client's *motivation* to change, and (c) the *opportunity and resources* to make the desired behavioral change. Each of these factors may change over time, so the clinician and client must periodically reexamine their behavioral goals. Sometimes both the client and the clinician have to let go—at least temporarily—of overly ambitious expectations and goals.

EXERCISE 8.1 *Identifying Behaviors to Change*

Think of three problematic behaviors that you would like to change in yourself. Be as concrete and specific as possible. In what contexts does each behavior occur? Note any precipitants or triggers that set off the unwanted behaviors. What are the current consequences of each behavior? What reinforces each behavior, and what makes you want to change it? What specific skills or behavioral sequences would you need to learn in order to change the behavior? What resources do you have for making the change? After looking at all three behaviors, choose one that you believe would be realistic for you to actually work on this week. We will come back to this behavior in a later exercise.

Normalizing Ambivalence

People may feel anxious and ambivalent about change. This anxiety is understandable given that there is no change without loss. Artists ask, "Will my art be ruined by therapy?" Clients ask, "Will the worker take my kids away when she hears how I really behave sometimes?" Clinical interns ask, "Will I lose my spontaneity and humanness if I take on the discipline of my supervisors?"

It is wise to expect and actually predict that some ambivalence is likely to arise as the work proceeds. *Ambivalence* involves feeling two opposing ideas, feelings, or impulses simultaneously: "I want/don't want to change"; "I do/don't trust this clinical social worker"; "I will be able to attain my goals/I am pretty hopeless." Each swing of the pendulum may give rise to the other direction. The clinician and client should talk about the ambivalence when it manifests itself, for it will almost always show up in behaviors like lateness to meetings, abrupt endings, and struggles with the clinician that are difficult to fathom.

Often people do not adequately anticipate the sense of loss they will experience in giving up old ways, even though at times it feels exciting to contemplate or experience the change. The clinician can help by noting that sometimes behaviors are like old friends, and they have to be mourned before moving on to the new. It helps both clinicians and clients to normalize conflicted feelings about giving up the familiar for the unfamiliar, which means giving up some control over our lives as we open them up to others' scrutiny, feedback, and potential influence.

Techniques for Helping People Change What They Do

There are numerous techniques available to help clients do things differently. Many of the techniques discussed in the last chapter to help clients see things differently will result in clients feeling and doing things differently as well. The following are some additional techniques to help clients do things differently.

Setting Priorities

As we said in Chapter 6, when talking about goals for clinical work, it is important to help clients prioritize the many things that they would like to do differently. The counselor helps clients set the tasks that they will work on in a reasonable and realistic sequence, and gives clients some impetus to continue moving forward with the work to change behavior.

Step by Step

In Chapter 6 we discussed breaking goals down into their component objectives. Often those specific objectives require new behaviors and specific skills. These, too, can be broken down into smaller, more readily achievable steps and their component parts—the process of *partializing*. When working for behavior change, clinicians and clients can move slowly through a series of steps, sequenced from the easier to the more difficult.

> *Taletha, a shy teen, wanted to work with her school counselor on how to make friends because she was lonely and doubted that anyone would pick her as a friend. She didn't talk to the other girls at school. When she was in a group of girls, she said she felt really self-conscious. She couldn't imagine what to say and thought that the other girls all thought she was stupid. This made her even more anxious and less willing to talk. Therefore, she never went out with the team after games.*
>
> *The counselor suggested they think about starting small by working toward making one friend. They detailed the things Taletha would have to*

do to make a friend. As they worked together, the counselor noted and commented that Taletha often looked down and away instead of at her while they talked, and she muffled or fumbled her words when nervous. Taletha agreed to practice a number of times making eye contact and exchanging comments with the counselor to improve her confidence in her social skills.

The counselor went to one of the high school basketball games and noticed that Taletha was quite a good player. When she was on the court, she seemed confident and she certainly was able to make eye contact with her opponents—often staring them down as she drove into them.

Taletha identified "a candidate for friendship" and spelled out the steps of approach: volunteer for the same team in gym, begin to make eye contact and exchange greetings, ask for help with a basketball technique, and so on.

The counselor, borrowing from the way Taletha said she "psyched herself up" for a game, taught Taletha some techniques that she could use to counter her negative self-talk by "pumping herself up."

In reviewing the work the counselor did with Taletha, it is obvious that the counselor attempted to break the large task of establishing new friends into small, more easily achievable component parts. Behavioral therapists refer to the process of breaking a task into its component parts and then rewarding successive approximations (small steps) to the desired behavior as *shaping.*

CLIP 8.2
Partializing
Behavior

EXERCISE 8.2 *Component Parts*

Using the following chart, continue the process with Taletha of breaking down behaviors into their component parts. Are there other components that you would want to work on with her? Would you do anything differently from the counselor in the scenario?

Desired behavior	Component parts	Subcomponents
Make new friends	Improve self-esteem	Positive self-talk; talk about things she felt good about
	Approach one student	Practice eye contact; make small talk
	Go out with the team	Babysit to earn spending money; convince mother it's safe to go

---

EXERCISE 8.3 *Identifying New Skills and Their Components*

What new skills or behaviors would you have to learn to change the behavior you identified in Exercise 8.1? Break the new behaviors or skills down into smaller component parts. Prioritize the behaviors or skills you would focus on first.

Modeling

One good way for clients to learn new skills or to change behaviors is to watch other people acting in a desired way. *Modeling* is based on the principle that people will learn new behaviors, attitudes, values, or feelings by observing others (Bandura, 1976). People are more likely to imitate the behavior of the model if they feel that the model is similar to themselves or is a respected authority figure or celebrity. TV commercials and advertising campaigns are often based on using a model's influence to get people to behave in certain ways. People are also more likely to imitate the behavior of the model if they see the model being successful or reinforced for the behavior. The behavior must also seem desirable to the client.

Clients need to be encouraged to find their own style or way of being, rather than just imitating the model's behavior. Students in a workshop on nonviolent conflict resolution might watch a tape in which they observe other students demonstrating the technique. Yet each student must be encouraged to not just parrot what they've seen but to modify it so it fits with their own style. As you continue to observe clinical mentors and models, you will find that you, too, will need to slightly modify the behaviors you observe so that you can truly "own" them as your own and internalize the behaviors.

E X E R C I S E 8.4 *Learning from Models*

Think of a behavior that you have learned from someone else's modeling. Who was the model? What did you see him or her do? What were the consequences of the model's behavior? What made that behavior desirable to you? How did you modify the behavior you observed in order to make it your own? What reinforced the changes you made to be more like the model?

Clinicians are important models whether or not they intend to be. If the client wants to learn how to be more direct, it is helpful if the clinician models that directness in the relationship itself. Another way that clinicians can model is by sharing their own experiences with a particular way of doing things. As we noted before, however, it is important that clinicians be judicious in self-disclosure. They must always remember the power and authority inherent in the clinical role. Clients may feel that they have to behave exactly as the clinician did, believing that the clinician knows best. It is important for the client and clinician to acknowledge that there might be many other models or ways of handling a particular situation.

Clients can find other models by joining groups or workshops with others who share a common interest in learning similar skills. Self-help groups are based on the premise of mutual aid, in which participants can model caring and emphasize potentials while providing support and close attention to each other. AA meetings, Widow to Widow programs, and religious groups all provide opportunities for clients to observe and practice new behaviors in response to modeling from others who engage or inspire them (Gitterman & Shulman, 1994).

Books, films, videos, and Internet offerings can help clients learn new ways to be and do. Suggesting that a client read about someone with whom he or she can identify may provide a model for behavioral change as well as offer specific information about steps that can be taken toward desired change. For example, a young mother can profit from a book or TV show about a woman similar to herself who details how she mastered adversity and went on to establish her own day care center or Neighborhood Crime Watch group.

Rehearsing New Behaviors or Skills

Behavioral rehearsal allows the client to practice new behaviors or skills in the safety of the clinical relationship. Behavioral rehearsal usually takes some of the anticipatory anxiety out of future events. It also gives clients a chance to master behavioral skills by identifying the ones needed, trying them out with the clinician's feedback and encouragement, managing feelings and doubts as they arise, and then proceeding to try them out in the actual situation with more ease and confidence than would have been possible without the rehearsal. *Assertiveness training* is a very popular form of behavioral rehearsal often carried out in groups. Groups afford the benefit of a diversity of models with many different styles of self-affirmation in arenas of shared concern, as well as the opportunity to give and receive aid.

In another form of rehearsal, the clinician and client can *role-play* scenarios or interactions in which the client can practice the new behavior. Clinician and client can work collaboratively here. They may exchange roles in the scenario, allowing the clinician to model the desired behavior, or the clinician might play "the other" with whom the client attempts the new behavior. Both clinician and client provide feedback to each other, practicing and fine-tuning potential interactions.

If possible, it can be helpful to *videotape* the role play and have the client watch and comment. Taping allows clients to observe and critique themselves—commenting on both what works and what doesn't. Such self-observation can contribute to the building of self-awareness and insight. This work comports with the major premise of our book: that interns and clients learn new behaviors most easily when they can (1) see the behaviors enacted by an experienced other, (2) rehearse them, (3) practice them in real-life settings, (4) observe themselves enacting the behaviors, and (5) share their experiences with others for further discussion and reinforcement in order to fine-tune their behaviors.

In *imaginal rehearsal,* clients rehearse new behaviors in imagery, pretending that they are acting in desired ways. Many of us rehearse things mentally, to prepare for anticipated events or situations. Carrying around positive images of having worked out a good plan of action can help clients build confidence as a side benefit of rehearsing new behaviors.

Eventually the goal is to have the client try the behavior in real life—*in vivo*. While behavior rehearsal might happen in the clinical setting, it eventually moves outside to "the real world." Clients can be encouraged to try the new behavior gradually, starting out in small ways or safe settings. The client may practice the new behavior in a group therapy setting or try out a new behavior with people with whom it is easier to take risks. Clinicians should remember that the behaviors "mastered" in a clinical setting are usually harder to execute in the real world, where many complications can arise and reinforcement may be poor or nonexistent. For example, the woman who learns to be more assertive and to express her opinions may find that, even though this behavior is reinforced in school settings, it is frowned upon and even punished in her family.

> *I was working with a client who was very shy. She said that she often felt uninvolved or like she was standing outside of the conversation when she was in social situations. We talked about what specific things she could do that might help her feel more a part of the conversation. She decided that she could reflect back what the person just said and ask questions as a way to begin to engage. We practiced these skills in the office for a while, with me playing a friend. She said that she would like to try these skills at the next big party. I suggested that she try it one night at dinner with her partner so that she could practice in a safe environment and get some feedback.*

EXERCISE 8.5 *Behavioral Rehearsal*

You have been engaging in behavioral rehearsals throughout this class as you have practiced interviewing skills in role plays with your fellow students. What kinds of feedback have been most useful to you? What experience has been less useful, and why?

EXERCISE 8.6 *Practicing New Behaviors*

Think of a situation in which you would like to try out a new behavior. It might be the behavior you identified in Exercise 8.1 or a different one. In groups of three, identify a behavior that you would like to practice. Using role plays, rehearse the new behavior, getting and giving feedback from others.

Use of Reinforcement

People tend to act in ways that have been reinforced. *Reinforcers* are consequences or events that occur after a behavior and increase the probability of the behavior occurring again in the future. Clinicians can make use of this knowledge by exploring with clients how they are reinforced for current behaviors, as well as what might be desirable reinforcement for new behaviors (Pryor, 1984). Allysa reports that smoking has always made her feel calmer and that this effect was what was reinforcing her smoking. Nick always got attention from the teacher when he would clown around. (Although the teacher was yelling at Nick, he liked the attention.) Carol said that she would go out and buy a new CD if she lost 10 pounds.

What is reinforcing to one person may not be reinforcing to another. Telling a child that if she is good she can have a lollipop works only if the child likes lollipops. Therefore, when working with a client and using reinforcement, the clinician must remember that to be effective, reinforcers must be valued by clients and established by them.

> *I was working as a counselor in an alternative school program for "acting-out" adolescent youth. One of the students, Damar, refused to sit at the table when the teacher requested that he do so. I decided that I would try to get him to change his disruptive behavior using a reinforcement program. I knew that the student had to determine what would be the best reinforcer. When I sat down with Damar and asked what reward he would want for complying with the teacher's request, he said "Sex or drugs." Well, needless to say, these were not things we could use as reinforcers. We eventually negotiated that he would be reinforced by being able to sit in "the teacher's chair"—one with wheels. Eventually, Damar wheeled himself closer and closer to the table and stayed there.*

One specific method for using reinforcement is the *contingency contract*. Contingency contracts are clearly articulated agreements that say to a client, "If you do this, then you will get that" or "If you do this, you will lose that." Contingency contracts are frequently used in halfway houses, group homes, school settings, and involuntary detention centers.

> *In working with Steven and his family about his temper outbursts at home, the human service worker helped them decide what kinds of rewards Steven would get for specified behaviors. They also set up a list of privileges he would have to give up if he engaged in certain identified problematic behaviors.*

> *I have my own sort of contingency contract. I tell myself that for every ten papers I grade I can get a reward—a cookie and a cup of tea.*

Residential settings often employ *token economies*, a specific kind of contingency contract. In a token economy, the client actually earns tokens or points for desired behaviors. These can be used to "buy" a desired reinforcer in designated amounts. For example, a teen may trade tokens for a trip to see a movie or a baseball game.

Teaching clients about reinforcement and helping them establish their own reinforcements are useful ways of helping clients learn how to do things differently.

Homework

Homework is a term often used to describe specific behavioral assignments, such as keeping a behavioral log, practicing meditation, going to a meeting, trying to express feelings more directly, recording times when one has self-defeating ideas, and the like. Any work that the client plans to carry out between sessions can also be called homework. Homework can be assigned by the clinician or can be mutually developed by client and clinician together.

Homework may involve other people. A sister may agree to accompany a woman who has agoraphobia to the supermarket, to encourage her and help her use her calming techniques when she feels panicky. The parents of a 10-year-old might be involved in reinforcing his desired behavior of studying for one hour after school each night. A friend may role-play a prospective employer in a behavioral rehearsal for a job interview.

Behavior change affects others, whether they are involved in homework or not. The clinician and client need to identify those people in the client's life who may be affected by the change in the client. It is helpful if these stakeholders support the anticipated behavioral changes. The clinician may meet with these significant others to offer them reinforcement and support in helping the client change. Sometimes other people or larger systems are obstructing the work. In that event, the clinician may need to shift the work to engaging those people and systems and trying to agree on goals and roles.

> *Archie was a 48-year-old man with mental retardation whose aging parents called the agency because they were worried about what would happen to Archie when they died. I began to meet with Archie and attempted to teach him some skills that he would need for living in a group home: doing his laundry, making his bed, cooking his own meals. One week I suggested that Archie practice making his bed each day for the next week and that he tell me how well he did. When I questioned him the next week, he said he didn't make his bed at all. He said that his mother would come in each morning and remake it for him, telling him that he wasn't able to learn how.*
>
> *I decided to meet with Archie's parents and encourage them to let Archie do things for himself—even if they weren't done perfectly. Otherwise he would never learn how to be independent. His parents were afraid of losing the role they had played with him for many years; their care of him was their main activity. I helped them redefine their role as teaching him new things. As Archie and I continued our work, I would occasionally meet with his parents to support them in their roles as Archie's teachers.*

Using Influence to Help Clients Do Things Differently

Clinicians can help clients do things differently by directly using their *influence* to try to help clients move toward desired behaviors. Because of the power inherent in the professional role, this kind of professional activity obviously increases pressure on clients to behave in given ways, and many clinicians don't like to exert influence for that reason.

Sometimes, however, clinicians choose to use the power of their role because it is part of a theoretical orientation in which being directive is a legitimized role. Sometimes they make use of their *influence* because they believe that clients or their dependents will be adversely affected if certain behaviors recur or certain actions aren't taken. Sometimes clinicians put their weight behind behaviors or actions they think will significantly improve the client's life.

The use of direct influence is affected by culture. The culturally responsive clinician must recognize that some clients may expect and prefer that the clinician tell them what is wrong and what to do about it. Some Native Americans and Asians who are used to following the orders of traditional healers may prefer that the clinician use advice giving and directives. Clinical approaches that are based on Western concepts of client autonomy, independence, and self-discovery may not be useful. We agree with Doman Lum (1996), that for some clients "nondirective techniques are meaningless." At the same time, we believe that clinicians must carefully understand the power dynamics of working with clients, particularly those who have been oppressed and marginalized and who may feel compelled to go along with whatever the clinician suggests.

The following techniques demonstrate a variety of ways in which clinicians use influence to promote behavior.

Offering suggestions. At times the clinician may give suggestions to clients about how to behave in a particular situation. Advice giving is usually avoided unless people and situations are very "stuck" because it presents the clinician as the knower and the client as the recipient—something we try assiduously to avoid. As we have stated previously, we believe it is important for clients to feel responsible for their own behaviors. Hence, the clinician frequently gives advice in a tentative way, asking clients what they think about the suggestion.

> "Perhaps if you tried (state suggestion). Do you think that might be helpful?"

> "I have a suggestion (state suggestion). Let's see what you think about it."

> "I was wondering if you could (state suggestion). Might that work?"

Giving directives. At times the clinician may directly tell a client what he or she needs to do. For example, the milieu therapist may tell Justin that he must keep his pants zipped. The psychologist on the inpatient service may tell Doris that she cannot hit other patients. The social worker may tell a mother that she must attend a jobs skill training program if she is to continue receiving public assistance. Allen Ivey (1994) notes that when giving directives the clinician must be clear and concise and check out whether the directive was understood, as well as determine what impact it has on the client. In giving directives, the clinician is particularly careful to convey respect and caring for the client. Using directives too frequently can backfire and leave clients feeling either blamed or controlled—although, as noted, some clients may see the clinician who uses directives as caring and the clinician who does not as neither caring nor helpful.

Accompanying clients. Clinicians might accompany clients to meetings or to agencies that are important to client well-being. They may go with a client to a crucial legal hearing if their presence would facilitate testimony. They may accompany a client to appeal what seems an unfair rejection of application for benefits, when verbal appeals by phone have failed for reasons that are not clear. Clinicians might go with a shy immigrant mother to register her children for nursery school or arrange to give a teen client a ride to his first Alateen meeting. (However, as we mentioned in Chapter 2, the clinician needs to pay careful attention to personal safety issues when accompanying clients in the community.)

Accompanying clients may have many results. Clients can feel incredibly supported by the presence of the clinician. In addition, accompanying a client may help the client follow through with an intended behavior; it is hard to wiggle out of something with the clinician right there. When accompanying a client, it is important that the clinician check in with the client. The clinician might ask, "How is it to have me here?" The clinician might also check in again during the next scheduled meeting: "Looking back, was having me go with you the right decision?"

Representing the client. Barry Cournoyer (1996) discusses the skill of representing the client with others, using clinician authority to broker services that the client has not been able to obtain alone. For example, the clinician may ask for a meeting with officials from the housing authority to try to convey a client's desperate situation in order to help the client get priority housing.

Calling on authorities to enforce a behavior change. At times the clinician will have to involve others in helping the client change his or her behavior. For example, the mother who is abusing her child may not be able to stop without some outside intervention. Clinicians are required by law to report cases of suspected abuse or neglect of children, older people, or people with disabilities.

> *I'll never forget the first time I had to file a 51A (a report of suspected child abuse). I was working with Kathy, a young mother who had a 2-year-old daughter. I had observed how the daughter cringed if the mother made any moves toward her. I also knew that the mother was under a great deal of stress and said that at times she was so annoyed with her "selfish" daughter. I informed Kathy that I knew she didn't want to hurt her child and that she was trying to be a really good parent, but it was difficult with so many pressures on her. I told her that I was going to try to get her some help by*

calling in the Department of Social Services. I hoped that they would do an evaluation and help her get the resources she needed to take care of her child and to avoid hurting her. Kathy was angry at me and asked if DSS would take her daughter away from her. I said that I hoped they wouldn't, but that if they did, I hoped that she would be able to get her back real soon.

They didn't remove her daughter, but they did offer her some respite care, and she became eligible for job training. I was really scared about what this would do to my relationship with Kathy but I think she really felt my caring and the fact that DSS didn't remove her child made it easier. We continued our work together. I am not sure what would have happened if they had taken her daughter away, but I would hope that we still could have found a way to continue our work.

Warning the client that the relationship will be terminated unless the client meets certain conditions. Sometimes there are behavioral conditions that must be met in order for the clinical relationship to continue. Some teen residences require that the members be sober in order to continue living in the house. A clinician may say that she will terminate the clinical relationship if a client does not follow through on an agreed-upon behavior change. An outpatient clinic may have a policy that clients who cut themselves will not be allowed to continue as outpatients. A social worker may insist that she will not continue to meet with a client individually unless the client attends the group therapy session every day.

As harsh as these requirements may seem, they may serve as an impetus for change, modeling structure, seriousness of purpose, and succeeding where other methods have failed. Such strategies are controversial, however. Some clinicians worry that such terminations would leave the client stranded without crucial structure and support. Others would say that clinicians are acting out their frustration or anger with the client, often simply reenacting unresolved power struggles from the clinician's and client's earlier lives. These kinds of warnings and terminations should never be carried out without considerable conversation with clients beforehand, and only under the most thorough supervision.

CLIP 8.3
Using Influence

EXERCISE 8.7 *When All Else Fails*

Are there any circumstances under which you would terminate a clinical relationship with a client? Make a list and discuss the pros and cons of this strategy with your fellow students in class.

Addressing Behavioral Resistance

The tendency to feel resistance or ambivalence about changing often manifests itself in both clinicians and clients as clinical work on changing behaviors proceeds. A client will start to work on a behavior targeted for change—say a habit like binge eating about which she was to keep a journal—and will suddenly "forget" either her journal, the correct time of the appointment, or the appointment itself. She might say that these things happened "because" of the bus coming late or the need to take work home so that there was no time to write in the journal. In another instance, a clinician might not show up for supervision saying that he had so much on his mind that he forgot. Some clinicians refer to these behaviors as forms of *resistance.*

Holding on to some autonomy or to old familiar ways that feel more under our control are expected and natural self-protective strategies when we are not certain what change will bring or how safe we will be when change has taken place. Sometimes clients need to take a breather or a rest from the work of behavior change. At other times, the clinician may inadvertently push the work too fast or too deeply, stirring up more anxiety than the client can tolerate. This anxiety may be verbalized, but it can emerge in behaviors instead. Cancellation, lateness, forgetting, getting off track, becoming defensive about the return of old nonproductive patterns—all can signal discomfort, a need for a breather, or reluctance to proceed because one fears losing more than one will gain by changing behaviors, contexts, or relationships.

CLIP 8.4
Addressing
Resistance

At times the clinician will directly address behavioral resistance by attending to behaviors that are undermining stated mutual agreements. This process may involve simply sharing the hunch that perhaps the client is feeling divided about proceeding for reasons that need airing and sorting through together. It may involve reaching out by phone or visit to someone who has canceled or dropped out, in order to process what has happened. The technique is used to get things on the table unambiguously so as to clarify and ventilate attitudes or conflicts that are stalling further work together.

Validating, Commending, and Celebrating Accomplishments

It should be obvious that the clinician should recognize, validate, and celebrate the client's achievements of changing old behaviors and learning new skills. Validation can be an important social reinforcer, encouraging the client to continue the work. In some settings, there are specific rituals to recognize client achievements. In AA groups, for example, clients are given a pin for one year of sobriety. In halfway houses, clients might be "promoted" to a new level based on their upholding their part of a contingency contract. A clinician might share a cake and coffee to celebrate a client's success in getting a job after years on welfare.

EXERCISE 8.8 *Changing Your Own Behavior*

Go back to the behavior you chose to work on this week. What techniques would you use to change that behavior? With two colleagues in class, work on changing your behavior. Keep a record of what techniques you used and how effective they were. Did you encounter any resistance in yourself as you tried to change? Continue to work on changing the behavior using different techniques until you are successful. Plan a way to celebrate your success.

Conclusion

You may have noticed that we believe that clinicians can learn the skills of clinical interviewing in much the same way that clients learn new behaviors. We believe in helping students understand new ideas and learn new behaviors by clearly identifying what is to be mastered and breaking it down into steps, utilizing specific skills. These steps and skills are most readily learned from clear, consistent, and encouraging models with whom there can be good-natured exchange in the process of rehearsing new behaviors. Interviewing skills are best learned in relationship with others. Self-observation through videotapes and feedback from others can help refine skills. We believe that learning through connection, collegial exchanges, shared risks, and mutual aid are all reinforcements for new learning.

Suggested Readings

Following are examples of the number of excellent resources on behavioral change.

Bandura, Albert. (1977). Self-efficacy: Toward a unifying theory of behavior change. *Psychological Review, 84,* 191–215.

Hutchins, David, & Cole, Claire. (1992). *Helping relationships and strategies.* Pacific Grove, CA: Brooks/Cole.

McCrady, Barbara. (1991). Behavior therapy. In Raymond J. Corsini (Ed.), *Five therapists and one client* (pp. 141–193). Itasca, IL:F.E. Peacock.

Prochaska, James O., Norcross, John C., & DiClemente, Carlo, C. (1994). *Changing for good.* New York: Morrow.

Pryor, Karen. (1984). *Don't shoot the dog! How to improve yourself and others through behavioral training.* New York: Bantam Books.

Watson, David L., & Tharp, Roland G. (1993). *Self-directed behavior: Self-modification for personal adjustment.* Pacific Grove, CA: Brooks/Cole.

A good resource on an empowerment perspective is:

Gutierrez, Lorraine. (1990). Working with women of color: An empowerment perspective. *Social Work, 35,* 149–153.

CHAPTER 9

The Clinical Relationship: Issues and Dynamics

A Unique Relationship

A client once said to me, "This is the strangest relationship I've ever known. I trust, love, and reveal myself deeply to someone I barely know."

A clinical relationship can be one of the most important and memorable relationships in a person's life, for both client and clinician. Its power and meaning for people are evidenced by its widespread appearance in the popular culture as the subject of numerous jokes and cartoons and as a topic in novels and films. Many people come to count on the professional clinical relationship as a source of support, reflection, information, and activity for meaningful change. The qualities of nonjudgmental acceptance, confidentiality, client-centeredness, and purposefulness render the clinical relationship a unique experience in most people's lives. It feels almost too good to be true, and for most people, it takes some getting used to.

The clinical relationship not only provides a context *in* which change can occur, it is often the means *by* which change occurs. The clinical relationship can be used as an interpersonal laboratory in which developments and issues arising within the relationship can be worked on in vivo to bring about change.

Using clinical skills in the relationship requires not only knowledge of common human dynamics and interaction patterns but also great self-awareness on the part of the clinician. Clients' lives and stories are precious. Our responsibility for their protection and safety in clinical work includes a responsibility to observe and adjust our own thoughts, feelings, behaviors, and intentions so that we stay client-centered and purposeful in our professional use of self. This ongoing self-observation is aimed at minimizing the effects of the clinician's unresolved issues, personal biases, and blind spots on the clinical relationship.

We believe that the development of awareness, knowledge, and skills about the relationship itself is one of the most difficult aspects of clinical education. Beginning clinicians often think that, because they are nice people or have had a lot of good relationships, the relational aspect of work with clients will come easily. New learners are routinely surprised to discover how complicated the relationship can become in the course of purposeful work together. While the clinician and the client enter into a relationship to work on a task or accomplish designated goals, almost inevitably they will also attend to the process of their relationship as they work together.

Most newcomers to clinical work are unaccustomed to the degree of attention to process that is required in clinical interviewing: the noticing and retaining of detail and nuance; the reflecting on meanings; the repeated self-exploration and adjustment in response to client needs; and the complex art of interweaving purposeful self-restraint and self-expression. The beginning clinician takes on the enormous task of learning how to attend to self, other(s), and the process of the relationship, while simultaneously focusing on the purpose and goals that gave rise to the relationship in the first place. There is, in short, much to learn. In previous chapters, we have focused on many of the skills the clinician uses in the interviewing process. This chapter discusses some of the special features of the clinical relationship and elucidates skills useful in addressing these issues in the relationship process.

Relationship Dynamics: The "Real" and the "Symbolic"

It is important that the clinician attend to his or her reactions to the client, as these reactions often provide important information for further consideration. In addition, clinicians should pay careful attention to clients' reactions to them. The reactions of the client and the clinician to each other are dynamic and interactive. Some theorists attempt to distinguish between the "real," in-the-moment encounter between the two people, and the "symbolic relationship"—what has been referred to in the psychodynamic literature as the transference or countertransference relationship. The following discussion of the psychodynamic concepts of transference and countertransference may be helpful in understanding some traditional psychodynamic formulations about the importance and use of the clinical relationship.

Transference

In psychodynamic theory, *transference* has been defined as the unconscious process by which early unresolved relational dynamics or conflicts are unwittingly "transferred" to the current relationship with the clinician, then acted out or expressed as though appropriate in the moment. It is crucial to remember that transference is an unconscious process and that when individuals are caught up in transference they are unaware of its influence on their thoughts, feelings, and behaviors in the present moment. Remembering this helps the clinician be more understanding, patient, and less reactive to what would otherwise seem to be irrational or unwarranted behaviors in their clients, themselves, or others.

Psychodynamic theorists describe both positive and negative transference as expected features of helping relationships. Both positive and negative transference can mobilize unresolved developmental issues for both clients and clinicians regarding dependence, competence, authority, closeness, trust, and both tender and sexual feelings. In *positive transference,* the client idealizes the clinician and may experience him or her as incomparably brilliant, caring, and helpful. Such idealizations, when not extreme, are thought to fuel the early stages of most human attachments and to sustain relationships through times of hardship and disappointment.

> *My supervisor told me that a teen client of mine seemed to be viewing me as a "kindly grandfather," even though I was a 26-year-old woman. She noted from an earlier process recording how the boy had fished and hunted with his grandfather, the only positive figure in his grade school years. Now he is frequently asking me to do things with him, things he used to love doing with his granddad.*

Psychodynamic clinicians believe that positive transference helps sustain the working alliance in spite of mistakes and disagreements. Clients may be unconsciously expressing in the clinical relationship unsatisfied longings for a wise, caring, and safe helper from whom to gain soothing and strength for the work at hand. Unfortunately, positive transference also lends itself to exploitation by unprincipled practitioners, as it tends to blind clients to their clinicians' manipulations, and its halo effect can make clinicians seem far more caring and wise than they actually are.

In *negative transference,* the client is thought to unconsciously express or act out in the moment old, unhappy, "stuck" scenarios with the clinician as though the clinician were actually the exploiter, the abandoner, the molester, or the punisher who has harmed the client in the past. Clients may misinterpret what the clinician says or does, may mishear words, or may mistake benign clinician behaviors as uncaring, exploitative, intentionally mean, or belittling. The inherent messages are frequently "You don't really care" or "You hurt me just like X did"—charges that reflect the antithesis of clinical purpose. Negative transference can be hard to tolerate, especially when one is doing one's utmost to be available, supportive, and helpful while under attack. It can drive a wedge between the two unless the clinician is conscientious in getting continuing supervision to assist in the management of reactions and of clinical process with the client.

At times the clinician's manner or style may inadvertently approximate that of someone harmful to the client in the past. Furthermore, clients may even seem as though they are actually trying to get the clinician to harm them—for example, by flirting with or asking the clinician to socialize with them, by offering gifts or bribes, by menacing the clinician, or by openly violating laws the clinician is mandated to uphold.

Countertransference

Freud coined the word *countertransference* to describe the clinician's unconscious reactions to the client. Clinicians today are asked to routinely scrutinize their process for countertransference, as psychodynamic practitioners expect it to occur in situations that replicate unresolved scenarios in the clinician's past. For example, a normally accepting clinician might begin to loathe and dread a particularly critical client. On reflection, she comes to see that, because of her own early experience of criticism from her perfectionistic father, she is taking the client's criticism personally and is resenting the client for it, as though at this moment she were back in the room with her own critical father. This realization helps her relax with the client and explore his criticisms more empathically.

Beyond Transference

Feminist therapist Laura Brown (1994) suggests that the symbolic relationship between clinician and client is more than and different from transference as it is typically described:

> The therapist is not simply defined as a neutral screen upon which internal reality is projected by a client; thus, the client's end of the symbolic exchange is not simply a distortion of the therapist based upon the client's prior experiences. Nor are all the passionate responses of therapist to client and client to therapist defined as necessarily derived from disruptive or disturbed elements in each person's past. Instead, the symbolic relationship in feminist therapy consists of lively and interactive responses to the changing meanings of the various factors that carry symbolic significance to either participant in the therapeutic encounter. While individual past experiences lend significance to the relationship in feminist therapy, the present and its signifiers are considered equally important in shaping and forming the symbolic layers of interaction. In addition, the participants' collective pasts and their positions as members of communities that may have met, touched, and even clashed apart from their individual experiences will inform how they symbolically experience one another. (p. 98)

Lillian Comas-Diaz and Frederick Jacobsen (1991) speak of *ethnocultural transference*—in which previous inter- or intraethnic cultural experiences are unconsciously transposed onto the clinical relationship. Such a reaction might manifest in a number of ways: a client might be overly compliant or demonstrate mistrust and suspiciousness regarding the clinician. Similarly, a clinician might overexplore cultural issues to the detriment of meeting client needs; might deny differences, failing to spot them as salient in the moment; or might communicate pity, guilt, or aggression around ethnocultural issues.

We agree that the clinical relationship is multilayered, complex, and interactive. The clinician must attempt to understand the relationship as both "real" and "symbolic" and as evolving over time.

Reflecting on Self in the Relationship

We have found the following questions helpful in reflecting on possible symbolic reactions with clients.

> Why am I reacting with this particular client in a way that is unusual for me?
>
> What buttons might this client be pushing in me?
>
> What buttons in the client might I be pushing?
>
> What do critical (seductive, bossy, self-centered, demanding, etc.) people stir up in me?
>
> Are my reactions to this client (or client story) being displaced from another life experience?
>
> Can I identify a pattern of reacting to certain types of people in characteristic ways that are not purposeful or helpful to the client?
>
> Do I think of some clients all the time, and some, almost never?
>
> Am I favoring some clients over others?
>
> Am I regularly reveiwing my work with all my clients or with only some?
>
> Is personal reflection enough to change my reactions, or do I need supervision or personal therapy to assist with professionalizing my responses with clients?

It is essential to engage in regular personal reflection and conscientious work in supervision to better understand the dynamics of the clinician-client relationship. Because relationship dynamics have been a central focus of psychodynamic therapy, that focus is often misunderstood by beginners to be the "real meat" of all clinical work. Not only do many of today's time-sensitive working agreements preclude such a focus, but working with the symbolic requires regular process supervision by a highly skilled and thoughtful clinical mentor accomplished in this complex work. By no means should beginning practitioners simply launch impulsively into speculation with clients on possible past/present links underlying behaviors in session. After reviewing written or taped process recordings over time, supervisors will help the clinician decide if it would be useful to undertake any work with clients on symbolic relationship issues and, if so, how to undertake such work with proper timing and sensitivity.

Relationship as Foreground or Background

At times the relationship serves as background for clinical work, providing a safety net or holding environment for the work of sustainment or change. At other times the relationship becomes the foreground, the focus of the work itself. A number of factors determine how the relationship is defined and the extent to which it is purposefully made the foreground or background of the work.

1. The clinician's *theoretical orientation* usually suggests what kind of relational activity, style, intensity, and focus constitute an effective and purposeful use of relationship. Psychodynamic theory, for example, emphasizes the importance of directly addressing the dynamics of the relationship, asserting that in the clinical relationship the client reenacts unconscious feelings about significant others in his or her past (transference). The clinician focuses on interpretation of clinician-client dynamics in order to help the client "work through the transference." Behaviorally oriented clinicians may see clinician-client interaction chiefly as providing information about the client's repertoire of behaviors. They may directly use the relationship as a means for rehearsing interpersonal skills or modeling the management of future scenarios. Almost all theorists suggest directly focusing on the clinical relationship when problems arise, such as when there is direct conflict or when the client cancels without explanation.

2. *Ethnocultural norms* for relationships—and relationships with professionals—are important influences on how and when the clinical relationship will be foreground or background. There may be no equivalent for client-clinician relationships in many cultures, so that at the beginning, and periodically thereafter, a respectful negotiation of relational roles and expectations may be necessary. For example, in some cultures, the "social worker" is an agent of the state who provides food, money, and housing only. A "counselor" might be expected to be a wise person who listens to problems and then unilaterally pronounces advice or solutions. Negative comments by the client on the helping process might be conceived of as unthinkable. Focusing on the relationship itself might feel rude or inappropriate. Again, it is important that clinicians know how their clients frame the "help-seeking" process, as well as the relationship and its importance or unimportance. We have noted that sharing food and more personal talk are important elements of building rapport with many clients, and in that sense they are very much "foreground" relationship considerations, even though the relationship and its dynamics per se will rarely be an explicit focus of the work.

3. The use and management of the relationship are affected by the *context of the setting, clinical goals, role of the clinician,* and *time parameters.* The clinical relationship may be a less direct focus of attention in settings or roles in which clinicians see many people briefly—for crisis intervention,

the giving of practical information, problem solving, or the mobilizing of resources. The dynamics of the clinical relationship are more frequently a focus of discussion in those settings in which the clinician's primary purpose is to provide longer-term counseling or therapy.

4. The *stage of the relationship* or of the interview process affects decisions about use of the relationship. In initial or brief encounters, the clinician's primary relational tasks are to be warm, attentive, empathically attuned, responsive, and focused with the client on mutually determined goals for the meetings. As trust and safe experience accrue, the clinician may focus with greater frequency on the relationship itself to provide feedback, conflict resolution, self-disclosure, and intentional relational skill rehearsal. Later, as the work together draws to a close, developments in the relationship can be used as familiar examples of what happens within relationships and of how awareness and skills can be learned with caring others through thoughtful interchange and feedback.

5. *Factors in the client and the clinician* also affect the use of the relationship in clinical work. Clients' cognitive and emotional capacities, their relationship histories, and their comfort with intimacy all affect the degree to which relationship dynamics can be productively addressed. Factors in the clinician that can influence the use of relationship include education and skill, openness to insight and client feedback, and willingness to adjust self to the needs of clients. While we have affirmed our belief in client and clinician as "co-evolvers of the story," we also believe that the clinician remains ethically and practically responsible for knowing when, how, and to what extent to make direct use of the relationship in the clinical interview.

Directly Addressing the Relationship Process

The clinician may directly address the relationship process for a number of reasons:

1. To provide the client with necessary information about what to expect in the clinical relationship at the beginning of work.

    ### Example
    A clinician at the college counseling center clarifies with the client the roles, responsibilities, and conditions of the working relationship: what the client can expect from the clinician and the setting and what is expected of the client. The clinician discusses confidentiality and its limits so that the client will know under what circumstances the clinician might have to report information disclosed. She explains informed consent procedures and invites the client's comments, reactions, or questions about the nature of their relationship.

2. To help clients accomplish designated tasks.

Example

A clinician who, as an intake worker, sees a woman once to evaluate her eligibility for food stamps might not normally focus direct attention on the relationship dynamics. However, if the client's style of angry demandingness with the clinician is so disruptive that it might derail the application process at the food stamp office, the clinician shares her own reaction to the behavior and inquires briefly into possible outside sources of the anger to determine if other kinds of intervention are indicated. If not, she alerts the client to the probable effect that the client's anger may have on staff at the food stamp office. She then very briefly explores other ways the client might express her needs and get them met.

3. To help clients develop relational competencies—the skills necessary to develop and maintain relationships with others.

Example

A clinician working in a group home with clients who are focusing on loneliness or failed relationships makes reference to ways that the clinician experiences the clients. The clinician then helps the clients explore their reactions to him with the aim of enhancing clients' interpersonal awareness and feedback skills.

4. If there are problems or issues in the relationship that need to be addressed.

Examples

A social worker who feels that there is some unaccustomed strain or uneasiness in the room directly talks about her observation with the client.

A counselor who notices that the talkative parolee suddenly has nothing to say this week wonders aloud about whether the silence has anything to do with the relationship between them.

After announcing a planned vacation, the psychologist spends some time talking with the client about how she feels about this interruption in their work together.

The milieu therapist suggests that the resident and clinician should talk about why things don't seem to be moving in their work together.

A rehab counselor on an inpatient psychiatric service interrupts his explanation of a job application process when he feels that the client's anger and frustration are making him feel unsafe.

A hospital social worker is seen by his client at the Gay Pride March. In the next session, he explores with the client her reactions to seeing him in the march and her discovery that he is gay. They talk about how this knowledge may affect their working relationship.

The drug counselor whose client has given her an expensive present for Christmas discusses with her client the meaning of the present in their relationship and their work together.

5. At the end of the relationship for purposes of summarizing the work and affirming gains.

Example

At the end of their six months of working together, an employee assistance counselor invites the employee to reflect with him on the nature of their work together. He talks with her about his perceptions of her, requests that she share with him her perspective on their work, and they talk about how they have both been affected by their work together. They talk about the outcomes of the work and evaluate their accomplishments.

In addressing the relationship process, the clinician may use the skills of (1) examining the moment, (2) processing the overall process, and (3) exploring indirect or parallel references to the relationship.

Examining the Moment

At times the clinician will *examine the moment*—address what is happening in the clinician-client relationship at a given moment in time. This me-and-you-in-the here-and-now work usually aims at gaining greater understanding of dynamics, of highlighting a repeating dynamic, or of working through tensions or feelings apparent at that moment in the interview. Egan (1994) refers to this skill as *immediacy*. Examining the moment can be particularly useful when something unexpected happens, when some outside event impinges on the relationship, or when the clinician notices something out of the ordinary.

Working with what is happening at the moment, the clinician has a choice of focus. He or she can *focus on the client:* "I notice this or that about you right now." This centering on client experience or behavior is a way of building the client's self-awareness and modeling the safe, direct expression of feelings.

Example

Clinician: Althea, let's stop a minute. I noticed that, just now, when I asked you about your son, you crossed your arms and started to kick your leg. What was going on for you just then?

Client: I guess I felt like you didn't believe what I just told you.

Clinician: Can you help me see what I did or said to leave you feeling that way?

When examining the moment, there may be *focus on the relationship* itself: "I'm noticing this or that right now about the relationship between us." Such focus models noting and responding to the nuances of communication and builds skills in tending to a relationship. This is particularly important if there appear to be unexplored feelings and issues that might undermine the relationship.

Example

Clinician: Things feel so tense here today.

Client: (Silence.)

Clinician: This doesn't feel like our usual way of working together. What do you make of it?

Client: I have something to tell you, but I don't know how.

Attention can also *focus on the clinician's own feelings and reactions:* "I'm noticing this or that about myself in relation to you right now." Sometimes this focus is used to model comfortably revealing oneself or to model expectable reactions to what is being discussed.

Example

Clinician: You weren't looking at me when you told me the story of being in the hospital with Jeremy, so I wanted you to know that your account brought tears to my eyes.

Client: I'm sorry to make you cry. Nobody likes to hear about the death of a child.

Clinician: Please don't apologize. It's so sad, but I'm very glad that you are talking with me about it, and I'm moved by your story and your bravery.

At other times the clinician will share reactions to demonstrate the client's impact on the clinician. When this *direct feedback* to the client relates to the negative effects of the client's behavior on the clinician, it has to be undertaken very cautiously. The clinician must carefully monitor his or her own responses and discuss them with a supervisor before disclosing them to the client. In an emergency situation, however, the use of self-disclosure might be necessary to maintain safety in the moment. It is important, therefore, that all clinicians discuss with their supervisors how they would handle a situation in which they felt unsafe, in case such a situation arises.

Example

> *Clinician:* You're scaring me with this shouting and threatening, Knox, and I can't listen and react well when I'm scared. Please sit down with me and try to calm down now so we can keep talking about what's happened.

Examining the moment can be used not only to help the client explore what is currently happening in the relationship, but also as a source of feedback that may have implications for other areas in the client's life.

Example

> *Client:* When will I ever have a boyfriend? I feel so-o-o-o awful. Everyone else has had a lover but me. I feel like I just crawl across the ground while everyone else is up and running. It's not fair. My life is awful. (Whining)
>
> *Clinician:* Sounds like you feel really disappointed that this hasn't happened for you. (Clinician thinks to herself: "She is bright, healthy, financially okay—her life could be so much worse, especially compared to the woman I just saw who is poor and dying of cancer, with two young kids and nobody to take care of them.")
>
> *Client:* Yeah, when Lenora (best friend) got raped, I went to visit her in the hospital and I thought, "Look, she's got her friends and family here, her boyfriend sent her flowers, she's got everything . . . it's not fair.
>
> *Clinician:* Might you have been feeling a little jealous of all she seemed to have?
>
> *Client:* Yeah . . . she even had sex! (referring to the rape)
>
> *Clinician:* (Feeling appalled by the client's response, the clinician decides to share her reaction in order to help the client understand something about the effects of her behavior.) Just now when you were talking about how awful you felt about not having a lover, I found myself thinking: "Gee . . . this situation is not all that bad." I was startled by my thinking that . . . it's just not the way I usually respond when a person is hurting. Your pain is very real, so I had to ask myself why I'm having thoughts like that. Then I thought, "Well, maybe it's the way she described her situation so dramatically: 'It's so-o-o-o awful, I crawl across the ground'." When you said that you were jealous of your girlfriend who had been raped, I think I found it hard to be

supportive of you. I know that you must feel bad about what happened to her and I am sure that you recognize how awful it was for her. It was hard to hear your pain without reacting to the way you phrased it.

Client: Hmmmm . . .

Clinician: I've a hunch you could be feeling that no one appreciates how bad *you* feel. People saw your friend's pain and gathered around her . . . even I took her part in my thoughts. No one seems to hear you.

Client: No one seems to care—everyone acts like I don't have anything to complain about.

Clinician: I wonder if sometimes other people might be responding to you as I did. Instead of giving you their care and support, they seem to minimize your pain—perhaps because of the way you express it . . . ?

While it is the clinician's responsibility to monitor what is happening in the relationship and make use of important moments, the client also is likely to comment occasionally on what is going on in the moment. Such *noticing by the client* gives the clinician the opportunity to reinforce the client's ability to tend to relationships—an important skill in all relationships and one for which clients may receive little validation or thanks.

Examples

Client A: Can we stop a minute? I just wanted to tell you how nervous I felt when you just said that you will be out of town next week.

Clinician: I'm glad you stopped us to talk about this. Please say more about what happened for you when I said that.

Client B: You look uptight. Do you need a minute?

Clinician: I'm sorry to take your time with this . . . I guess I *am* worried. When I came in the front door, my cat had dripped blood in the entryway, and I have her on my mind a little. I just cleaned up before you rang the bell.

Client B: Do you need to take five minutes to go check on the cat? I have my crossword puzzle from traveling on the bus.

Clinician: Thanks, I'll just be a minute. Let's make up the time on the other end if that's okay.

Client B: It's okay, I have a cat and I would be just as worried if she were sick.

CLIP 9.1
Examining
the Moment

It is the fortunate clinician who has a client who is willing to share with the clinician when a statement or behavior of the clinician has a negative impact on him or her. The clinician needs to appreciate the strength of the client in making such direct feedback.

Example

> *Client:* I don't know how to tell you this, but I feel really uncomfortable when you walk me to the door. I get the feeling that you're afraid I won't leave.
>
> *Clinician:* I had no idea you felt like that. Thanks for telling me. Let's talk some more about it.

EXERCISE 9.1 *Examining the Moment*

In small groups, practice the skill of examining the moment with clients in the following scenarios. Think of as many ways to express yourselves as you can.

> *Jermaine, an excellent 19-year-old college basketball player, has come to see the campus counselor to mull over whether to graduate or to drop out now and join a pro team. As you comment on how hard the decision is and review potential options, he begins to glaze over and stare out the window.*

> *Cookie, a depressed, often silent 14-year-old, comes into the session looking unusually bright and animated, although not saying anything.*

> *Edgar, an 80-year-old man seeking to have his wife arrested for physically abusing him, frowns and huffs as you explain that there needs to be a home investigation before further action can be taken.*

When you have completed the exercise, talk together in a large group about the usefulness and the complications of examining the moment.

Processing the Overall Process

At times, clinicians *process the process*—discuss the overall course of the relationship with clients. The clinician may do this to point out a theme or pattern, whether positive or negative, in the relationship and to trace its development backward over the course of the work so far. The clinician may sum up in broad strokes developments or achievements of note.

Example

> *Clinician:* You know, Van, it's amazing how you've hung in with this relationship in spite of all your fears of people taking control of

you. We had our moments back there when you thought I was
trying to make you join that group.

Client: Yeah, I just did not want to be in any group, and you kept
pushing it on me. A few times I thought of quitting.

Clinician: Yes, and it was important—so different for you—that you
could say you'd rather see me alone because you needed the
privacy.

Client: I thought you'd be mad.

The clinician also invites the client to process the process with an *invitation to examine process,* such as "Could we look at how things have been going
in the relationship these last six weeks?" The client may be able to respond to
such an invitation easily, may require more time or support, or may not be
able to make process observations. The clinician supports all reasonable
client efforts to make process comments, as it is important for clients to
develop the skill of observing and commenting on relational processes.

The clinician can help the client *anticipate possible problems in other
relationships* in the future if the relational behavior exhibited in the clinical
relationship is enacted with others.

⊙⊙ **CLIP 9.2**
Processing
the Process

Example

Clinician: During our work together, I have noticed how quickly you
interrupt me if you feel that I am going to say something
appreciative toward you. You will often stop me before I can give
you a compliment, or you denigrate what you have done. For
example, last week when I said that you were very generous to
have volunteered to work overtime over the Jewish holidays,
you said, "Anyone would have done the same thing."

Client: Yeah, I get embarrassed when someone tells me I do
something well.

Clinician: I can imagine that other people notice your discomfort and
then don't tell you about their positive perceptions of you. One
of the results is that you often feel that you don't get much
feedback.

Client: I just get so embarrassed.

Clinician: That might be a problem in the new job you're taking,
since you have to have quarterly reviews with your supervisor.
Any thoughts about that?

The clinician can use overall process comments to *strengthen client
awareness regarding the process of relationship building.*

Example

> *Clinician:* One of the things I appreciate most about you is the way that you have of stepping back and looking at what is going on in our relationship. You've often helped to focus our attention on things that we should be talking about . . . things that sometimes I hadn't thought about. I think that that must be what makes your friends appreciate you so much.

EXERCISE 9.2 *Processing the Process*

In small groups, practice the skill of processing the process with the clients in the following vignettes.

> *Olandra always pressures for advice, but then responds with "Yes, but . . ."
> to everything the clinician suggests.*

> *Kenny has been skipping every second or third session, saying he "just forgot."*

> *Jerri has been great at going out and trying things, no matter how hard, and keeps at it, even though feeling discouraged at times.*

Exploring Indirect References to the Relationship

The clinician always listens for *parallel patterns or themes* in the client's comments. We have mentioned how sometimes after clients lose someone to death, they may find themselves losing keys, gloves, and so on. In *exploring indirect references* to the relationship, the clinician wonders whether the client may be responding to issues or feelings arising in the clinical relationship.

Example

> *Client:* I am so tired of people asking me questions. My mother-in-law keeps asking me how I'm doing and I'm sick of her nosing around in my business

> *Clinician:* Is that how you feel with me sometimes?

> *Client:* Well, now that you mention it . . . I know that I am here to talk about how I feel about my sister's accusations of sexual abuse by my father, but sometimes I just want to forget about it. When I see you each week, it is a constant reminder.

> *Clinician:* So at times it feels like I'm pushing you to think about things you would rather forget?

Client: I guess I would be worrying about it anyway, but it's easier to think that if I weren't seeing you and you weren't asking me questions, I wouldn't think about it at all.

In the preceding example, the clinician addresses a reference to something outside the relationship (reactions to questions by her mother-in-law) to see whether it paralleled anything that might be going on in the clinical relationship (reactions to the clinician's questions). Conversely, a clinician can explore things going on inside the clinical relationship that may relate to relationships or events outside of the clinical relationship.

Example

Clinician: You'd rather not have to think about it at all.

Client: I find myself getting mad at you.

Clinician: It feels like I'm making you do something you don't want to do.

Client: I don't want to be mad at my father . . . that's really what I'm feeling . . . How could he do that—how could he force her?

In this example, the clinician intentionally chose her words, recognizing that they parallel how the client may feel about her father "making" her sister do things she "didn't want to do." This kind of attention to parallel themes requires very careful monitoring and is part of the attention paid to relationship issues.

Cautions about Addressing the Relationship Process

There can be complications in examining the moment, processing the process, or reflecting on indirect references to the relationship. No matter how useful it feels to clinicians, focusing on the relationship displaces other topics or work at hand. The clinician has to compare the expected benefit with the cost of such a focus: will the time the discussion takes truly forward the agreed-upon work? Furthermore, being noticed in such detail may prove too intense for some clients (just as it does for some clinicians) who are more comfortable simply focusing on agreed-upon goals or tasks.

Examining what is happening in the moment, in the process, and in indirect references to the relationship is a continuing part of the clinician's thinking. However, it does not have to be made manifest with clients for "good clinical work" to happen. In fact, a problem can arise when clinicians overvalue focusing on the moment, processing the process, or examining indirect references to the relationship so frequently that the exchange risks becoming a "Woody Allen type" parody of clinical conversation. The clinical relationship should never be the center of the universe.

Addressing Issues of Difference, Power, and Influence
Addressing Client/Clinician Differences

In Chapter 1, we talked about color, class, gender, cultural, sexual orientation, physical ability, and other differences and their implications for the clinical relationship. These differences are often fraught with concerns about power, voice, and the right to determine one's own fate as often as possible. Very often it is appropriate to put issues of difference on the table right away, to demonstrate the clinician's awareness of widespread concerns about such differences and willingness to tackle difficult subjects. At other times the clinician may wait until remarks or behaviors suggest that discussion of differences is indicated. The clinician may address these issues in a number of ways.

Examining the moment.   The clinician may use the skill of examining the moment to directly address differences between client and clinician. This is most easily done when the subject comes up, often in responses to the clinician's naiveté or lack of knowledge.

Example: Catholic Clinician, Jewish Client

Client: My sister suggested that I join a *havurah.*

Clinician: A hurrah?

Client: No, a *havurah.*

Clinician: Tell me more about that.

Client: (Client explains the *havurah.*)

Clinician: What was it like for you that I didn't know about a *havurah?*

Client: I wouldn't expect you to know.

Clinician: You know, this helps me remember that we haven't talked about what it means for you to see someone who isn't Jewish—that's such an important part of your identity.

Sometimes clinicians raise the issue of difference to open channels of communication when the client has signaled a reaction to difference. Taking time out to examine things in the moment often strengthens the alliance, and signals to the client that everything is valid grist for the mill of examination and sorting through. Clinicians need to develop both understanding and composure, as clients' behaviors and statements around differences can sometimes make it hard to remain empathic and nonjudgmental.

Example: Black Clinician, White Client

Clinician: I noticed that when you walked in and saw me, your jaw dropped.

Client: Uh . . . I was surprised you were a man. I thought with the name "Lacy," you would be a woman.

Clinician: Some of my white clients have told me that initially they reacted to my being a person of color. They say they worried I couldn't help them the way a white person could.

Client: People actually said that to you? Didn't that hurt your feelings?

Clinician: As a matter of fact, I think it's really important that people be able to speak their minds here so that we can talk about things and try to work them out together. Counseling doesn't work too well if people sit on things they feel strongly about.

Client: Well . . . to tell you the truth, you're the first black professional I ever got help from. I don't know how it will be.

Clinician: How what will be?

Client: How it will be to tell my friends at the mill that I have a black psychologist.

Clinician: How do you imagine them reacting?

Commenting on a client's indirect reference to the relationship. Clients often lack experience in confronting differences and realizing that differences have an impact on relationships of all kinds, including the clinical one. They may address differences only obliquely, but this gives the attentive clinician an opportunity to make the latent manifest.

Example: Battered Woman with Male Clinician

Client: You'll never again find me anywhere near a man for long.

Clinician: Since I'm a man, let's take a minute to see how it is for you to be talking with me. Sometimes clients feel they have to take whoever they get as a counselor, but that's not true here. I want to make sure you're in the best situation for you.

Client: I do hold back. You'd hate me if you knew what was on my mind half the time.

Clinician: I am so glad you let me know about holding back, although I'm not surprised, given what guys have done to you. I'd like to hear more about what you've been thinking, if you feel okay telling me.

Client: I've thought of asking for a woman to talk to.

Clinician: What are your thoughts about that?

Example: White Clinician, Caribbean Client

Client: I hate those white folk at work who keep saying that they wish they could have dreads like mine.

Clinician: What do you hate?

Client: The way they pick some stupid part of me like my hair to talk about. I feel like their pet sometimes.

Clinician: Do those feelings ever come up between you and me?

Clinician introduces the difference into the conversation. If the client does not offer, the clinician will often bring the subject up, since clients may fear the consequences of broaching differences with a clinician. This is especially true if the clinician is a member of a group that the client thinks of as powerful and potentially harmful, or about whom the client has strong antipathies or feelings.

Example: Straight Clinician, Lesbian Client

Clinician: Darcy, we have never talked about the fact that I'm straight and you're lesbian.

Client: It never seemed to come up since I was just talking about work and stuff.

Clinician: A lesbian woman might feel that her sexual orientation does affect how people react to her at work. I was wondering if you had any thoughts about that.

It is essential that the clinician explore the relational and political implications of differences, as they are often intertwined with power and privilege issues that need to be recognized and discussed. For example, Lillian Comas-Diaz and Beverly Greene (1994) describe a "hierarchical transference," related to the clients' histories of subordination, that many poor, female clients of color may manifest in response to clinician authority. They might manifest powerlessness and helplessness in the relationship—feelings that need to be noted and worked through as an empowering aspect of relational work.

OO CLIP 9.3
Addressing
Indirect
References

Clinician Power and Influence

Closely related to client/clinician differences are issues of power and influence. Clinicians do have real power and are not simply benign, caring others. From the standpoint of reality, a professional whose assessments, reports, or testimony will contribute to life-affecting custody determinations or judicial proceedings has real power, to which clients may respond with anxiety, uncertainty, and defensiveness. At times, this clinician power needs to be addressed directly.

Sometimes the client brings up the subject of the clinician's power, directly or indirectly. In such instances it is important that the clinician attend to the underlying messages and intensity of affect attached to the client's communications.

Examples

"You could get my kids back for me if you really wanted to—just like that!"

"You people think you know everything and can make other people do anything you want with your psychological tricks."

"I don't like you to look in my eyes; it makes me feel like you're trying to read my mind."

"*You* can go on vacation whenever you feel like it, but I have to get the approval of the whole team, my parents, the school. Would *you* like it?"

"You're the doctor—you tell me!"

"I liked you because I could tell right away that you knew what I was feeling without me really having to tell you."

"Well, I suppose you are going to go right out of here and report me." So go ahead, I'm not afraid of inquisitioners."

The clinician responds to such statements with empathy, acknowledging a power differential in the clinical relationship and perhaps asking the client what it is like to think of the clinician as having more power. For some people, to see the clinician as powerful could be unpleasant; for others, it could be reassuring. The clinician explores both sides of the client's reactions, as well as past experiences with people who may have exploited power over the client.

Examples

Client: You could get me my kids back if you wanted to.

Clinician: What's it like to think I have that kind of power and am not using it for you?

Client: I feel mad about it sometimes.

Clinician: I would feel mad, too, if I thought somebody could help me but wasn't. When you're mad with me about it, what thoughts come to mind?

Client: I picture you talking secretly to my family worker and telling her I'm not fit to have my own kids.

Clinician: Oh . . . this helps me begin to understand why you seem so tense with me sometimes . . .

Client: So go on and report me, I'm not afraid of inquisitioners.

Clinician: Am I sounding like an inquisitioner?

Client: You got that right.

Clinician: That's not what I ever meant to sound like . . . you've had so much meddling in your affairs over the years. Can you help me do a better job here? Can you show me how I sounded?

Client: You said three weeks ago that you have to report any intended crimes, and today I said I felt like knocking Max's block off.

Clinician: It could be hard to trust me if you're worried I'm going to think of the angry things you say here as crimes. Where did you get the idea that your angry thoughts are crimes?

In addition to real authority invested in certain clinical roles, clinicians often have symbolic power—the power, expertise, and influence attributed to them by clients. At times the clinician elects to address such issues directly, as when the client attributes any good things that occur in the work to the clinician's brilliance rather than to the client's efforts.

Example

Client: Thanks to you I can now get my kids back, get some child care, and go get that high school equivalency offered at the school up the street.

Clinician: Thanks to me? Mostly what I did was encourage and cheerlead. You're the one who did the hard work every day of the last year and a half. You went to the meetings, you worked with the homebuilders, you met with the protective worker and got counseling with Esteban.

Clients may also blame all their misfortunes on the clinician's interventions or mere presence in their lives. This premise, too, can be addressed as it arises in client statements, such as, "My last worker had real good luck getting me jobs; you must not have the kind of connections she did."

As we discussed in Chapter 7, sometimes clinicians assert or address the use of their power or influence with the client in order to set limits or to move work forward in a particular way. When clinicians intentionally choose to use direct influence, it is important that they attend to the resulting effects on the client and on the relationship.

Example

> *Clinician:* Last week, I said that you had to go to five AA meetings a week in order for us to continue working together. I wanted to check in with you first thing today to see how that sat with you.

EXERCISE 9.3 *Power*

In your journal, record your answers to the following questions.

Have you seen a professional use power over a client?

What were the circumstances?

What were the effects?

Have you ever used the power of your professional role with a client?

What were the circumstances?

What were the effects?

Client Power and Influence

One of the goals of the clinical relationship is to help clients feel and experience their own power in the world. Since the clinical relationship acts as a microcosm of human experience in the world, clinicians can help clients experience and assert more power by recognizing, examining, and increasing the client's power in the clinical relationship itself.

Clients actually have a lot of different kinds of power in the relationship. They can approve or disapprove of clinician responses, activities, and ideas. They can continue or drop out whenever they wish, even if mandated (they can elect to take the consequences rather than see a clinician, and many do). They can pay or refuse to pay for the relationship, and they can keep clinicians and agencies waiting for payment by not filling out or mailing in necessary forms. They can complain to agency heads and boards, local and state elected officials, and through letters to newspapers or appearances in the media. They can say complimentary or disparaging things about the clinician to other clients and professionals without speaking directly to the clinician, and they can sue the clinician for perceived damages if they feel harmed by the care given.

Clinicians can be awed by clients who have socially perceived status and power, particularly the rich and famous—the VIPs. Rules and limits can be stretched in ways that do not help such clients cope with ordinary frustrations. In addition, clinicians can fail to be as searching in their exploration or as frank in their feedback as they might with non-VIPs. Often, only senior personnel are allowed to interact with "important" clients, so beginning clinicians rarely have an opportunity to learn about how to deal with the entitlement or very real vulnerabilities of these clients. Confidentiality can also be violated when clinicians cannot resist boasting of a famous person who was seen at their agency.

> *A wealthy elderly man came into rehab for physical therapy for serious injuries from a fall while intoxicated. His wife would sneak bottles of liquor into him in her knitting bag. He would come to afternoon physical therapy sessions somewhat high. The wife was a very impressive person.*
> *Her brother had donated a lot of money to the hospital and no one wanted to confront her about bringing in liquor.*

But all clients, regardless of social status, have very real power in the clinical relationship. Just as clients may be deeply affected by their interactions with clinicians, so, too, are clinicians often deeply moved and changed by interactions with clients. Just as clinicians may help clients "see things differently" and "do things differently," so do clients affect how clinicians perceive things, feel things, and act. Our ways of viewing and experiencing the world can be radically changed by our experience with clients, and almost every clinician's empathy, listening skills, and capacity to respond quickly have been improved by client feedback. While clinical supervision often focuses on the things clinicians are doing helpfully, it probably equally often focuses on verbal or nonverbal signals from clients that the clinician missed, detoured around, or dismissed some content as less important than other content.

While the clinician brings clinical skills and expertise to the relationship, the client brings his or her own self-knowledge and expertise. Although the roles in the clinical relationship are not equal, the clinical relationship is an *egalitarian relationship* in that there is equal respect and value, even though there are differences in roles. The goal is to help the client achieve more power, both in the relationship and in the world (Brown, 1994).

Overvaluing the Power and Influence of the Clinical Relationship

As clinicians, we can put so much stock in our persons, skills, and theories that we overvalue the clinical relationship and what it can achieve. We can even begin to believe that events and realities in the client's life should be subordinate to the clinical work and relationship. A client's tardiness or sudden absences may automatically be interpreted as related to the client-clinician relationship dynamics, when we know that children really do get sick at the last minute and buses actually do run late sometimes. We try to avoid putting clients in the position of feeling guilty about their behaviors in the relationship because this relationship, while meaningful, is only one of the important forces in their busy lives. The more connections they have with others, the more this is likely to be true.

> *A psychiatrist told my friend that if her parents who lived in England should die suddenly, she should plan not to spend more than a few days in England or it would interfere with the "level of caring" in their work together.*

> *My client, a really poor single mom, called to say she needed to miss a week because it was three days until her next check, and if she spent the money for carfare, she wouldn't be able to buy peanut butter and jelly to keep the kids fed the next few days. My supervisor told me that "anybody can afford one dollar for the train." Later I came to know better.*

Beginning clinicians can also undervalue the power and meaning of their relationships with clients. They may rebuff praise when it would be good for the client to give it or minimize the importance of what they say with clients or the importance of clients' latenesses or absences. They may skim over learning, as though clinical education were just more courses to be gotten through. Striking some balance, it is probably fair to say that this unique relationship is very important to many people but not the "be all and end all" that some professionals wish it were.

Conclusion

The clinical relationship provides not only the context in which change can occur but also the means by which change occurs. The clinical relationship, as a real human relationship, provides the client with the opportunity to develop relational competencies, including how to tend and discuss process in a relationship, how to resolve interactional problems when they arise, and how to increase respect and mutuality in a relationship with another.

While each of the parties in the relationship has preferences as to how much relational focus there should be in their work together, it is the clinician who is charged with a fiduciary, or trusteeship, responsibility for ensuring that the relationship is safe, effective, and appropriately centered on the client's needs. In Chapter 10, we will address how the clinician deals with the disclosure of personal information and other specific boundary issues in the relationship.

Suggested Readings

An excellent discussion of the clinical relationship and issues of power and influence can be found in chapter 4, "The Relationship in Feminist Therapy," of:

Brown, Laura. (1994). *Subversive dialogues: Theory in feminist therapy*. New York: Basic Books.

Other excellent resources include:

Comas-Diaz, Lillian, & Greene, Beverly. (Eds.). (1994). *Women of color: Integrating ethnic and gender identities in psychotherapy*. New York: Guilford.

Comas-Diaz, Lillian, & Jacobsen, Frederick, M. (1995). The therapist of color and the white patient dyad: Contradictions and recognitions. *Cultural Diversity and Mental Health, 1,* 93–106.

Mirkin, Marsha. (Ed.). (1994). *Women in context: Toward a feminist reconstruction of psychotherapy with women*. New York: Guilford.

Murphy, Bianca C. (1994). Difference and diversity: Gay and lesbian couples. *Journal of Gay and Lesbian Social Services, 1*(2), 5–31.

Pedersen, Paul. (Ed.). (1988). *A handbook for developing multicultural awareness*. Alexandria, VA: American Association for Counseling and Development.

CHAPTER 10

The Clinical Relationship: Addressing Self-Disclosure and Other Boundary Issues

Professional boundaries refer to the lines of demarcation between clinician and client as they come together in a work-focused relationship. Theoretical models may describe in some detail what they construe to be the ideal arrangements, behaviors, and operating procedures in a professional clinical relationship. Professions, agencies, institutions, and individual states have *standards of practice* or *ethics and regulatory codes* defining the dimensions of a professional relationship and describing the behaviors and practices that are and are not permitted between professional and client. (See the Appendix for how to obtain the ethical codes for counseling, social work, psychology, and marriage and family therapy.)

Traditionally observed boundaries in the clinical relationship have included the following understandings. The relationship remains centered on the client's work needs, not the clinician's needs. The contract itself acts as a quasi-boundary around the conversation, suggesting focus and direction for the work and minimizing drift. Clinical work is usually further structured by specific time constraints on the number and length of meetings. Planned contacts outside the office should be for the express purpose of forwarding contracted clinical work, not to develop other forms of relationship. The clinical relationship, while friendly in tone, is to be maintained as a working one, not as a friendship and not as a prelude to a friendship. Sexual contact between clients and clinicians is strictly prohibited. Unavoidable outside contacts are discussed in the session to resolve potential complicating effects on the clinical relationship and on other people.

In the last chapter we explored some of the situations in which the relationship becomes foreground, and we elucidated some skills useful in addressing these issues in the relationship process. There are boundary issues that frequently arise in the clinical interviewing relationship that also might require that the clinical relationship become foreground. In this chapter we will focus on boundary issues including (1) disclosure of personal information about the clinician, (2) confidentiality issues, (3) limits on conversation, (4) out-of-office contacts, (5) requests for more time, (6) gift giving and receiving, (7) sexual attractions, and (8) limit setting.

Disclosure of Personal Information About the Clinician

At times the client may obtain information about the clinician, which can happen in the following ways.

1. The clinician may choose to share some personal information with the client.

2. The client can receive information about the clinician from others or can unwittingly discover something about the clinician.

3. The client may ask the clinician personal questions.

The disclosure or nondisclosure of personal information about the clinician should always be carefully explored, first in supervision and then later with the client if disclosure occurs.

Self-Disclosure

Self-disclosure refers to the clinician's sharing of demographic information or personal experience with the client. We have already discussed many of the ways that self-disclosure can be used as part of other skills. To recapitulate:

1. *Information sharing.* In Chapter 7 we used as an example the clinician working with a client who is about to undergo abdominal surgery and isn't sure when she will be able to return to work. The clinician who had also had abdominal surgery shared the information that she was tired for about six weeks.

2. *Modeling.* In Chapter 8 we talked about how the clinician can help the client do things differently by modeling, one form of which is through self-disclosure: "When I was studying for the licensing exam, I found that one thing that worked for me was to put aside 2 hours every morning before everyone else got up."

3. *Empathy building.* In Chapter 4 we discussed how a judicious self-disclosure could help the client feel joined and understood: "I imagine how shocked and sad you must be feeling. I remember so clearly that feeling of pain after my divorce and thinking that it would never go away."

4. *Examining the moment.* As discussed in Chapter 9 in addressing what is happening in the relationship at the moment, the clinician can reveal what he or she is thinking as a form of feedback: "As you were talking about how you had to take care of your brother, I found that I was feeling sad—you were such a little girl and there was no one taking care of *you*."

Self-disclosure can be particularly important when working with members of minority groups. Many lesbian, gay, and bisexual clients have expressed their gratitude for having clinicians who were "out" to them and provided healthy models of affirming their lesbian, gay, or bisexual identity. Elaine Pinderhughes (1989) affirms the importance of shared personal information in rapport building with many clients of color. La Fromboise, Coleman, and Hernandez (1991) note that clinicians may find it necessary to use self-disclosure and demonstrate their cultural sensitivity before they ask their Native American clients personal questions. Many Asians believe that it is improper to talk with strangers (Weijun Zhang, cited in Ivey, 1994, pp. 282–283) and that they should discuss their problems only with family members. Thus, the clinician is often assigned an honorary kinship role and is referred to as aunt, uncle, or elder brother or sister (Lum, 1996). All of these situations require that clinicians be flexible in disclosing personal information about themselves to their clients.

Whenever and for whatever reasons clinicians consider using self-disclosure, they should ask themselves the following questions *before* using self-disclosure.

Why am I considering self-disclosure around this issue?

Why am I using self-disclosure at this moment in time?

Is it in the client's best interest?

Is there any way I could accomplish the same goal without using self-disclosure?

What are the potential effects on the client of my self-disclosure?

How might this help our relationship? What possible negative effects might it have?

Am I sure that I am not doing this to meet my own needs at the expense of the client?

How will I feel if the client tells other people what I have disclosed?

Clinicians should evaluate the effects of self-disclosure and should directly check in with the client about the information revealed. They also should personally reflect on the following questions *after* self-disclosure.

How did the client make sense of what I have shared?

Did the client have feelings about or reactions to what I disclosed?

How do I notice the self-disclosure affecting the relationship?

Did it have the intended effect?

Have I asked the client what it was like for him or her to have me share that information?

If I had to do it over, would I disclose in the same way, or at all?

E X E R C I S E 10.1

How do you feel about revealing personal information about yourself? What kinds of questions would you feel comfortable answering for clients? Age? Relationship status? Family history? Training and degrees? In small groups, discuss the pros and cons of sharing personal information, and discuss the differences between offering the information and being asked questions. In what ways do you think this kind of sharing is similar or different for clients? How do clients come to "know" clinicians without actually hearing much specific information about them?

Disclosure by Others

Sometimes clients may learn something about the clinician because it is revealed accidentally or by others.

Examples

A client may see a clinician attending an AA meeting.

A client may learn that a clinician has breast cancer when he learns that she will be speaking as a breast cancer survivor at a public hearing on funding for cancer research.

A client may discover that her daughter is working in the same law firm as the clinician's gay male partner and that they are considering adopting a child.

As with intentional self-disclosure, the clinician must evaluate what effects the information might have on the client and then directly address these effects with the client. In addition, the clinician might explore what it was like for the client to learn the information indirectly or from someone else.

Example 1

Clinician: Todd, we haven't talked about what it was like for you to learn that I was a member of AA.

Example 2

Client: My friend Ginger told me that you will be talking at the breast cancer rally.

Clinician: Yes . . . and . . . ?

Client: Well . . .

Clinician: Do you know what I will be talking about? (To determine if the client has the information that the clinician has had breast cancer already.)

Client: No.

Clinician: (Clinician decides that she had better tell the client directly.) I have had breast cancer, and I will be speaking at the rally about the need for more funding.

Client: Oh.

Clinician: What's it like for you to learn that about me?

Client: I'm glad you're an activist.

Clinician: And, what's it like for you to hear I have had breast cancer?

Client: I guess it scares me. I didn't know you were sick.

Clinician: (Deciding to share more information to alleviate the client's fear.) I had a very small tumor removed two years ago. My prognosis is excellent.

Client: I'm glad to hear that.

Clinician: (Letting client know it's okay to talk about it.) Given your history of people who have left you by dying, I expect this might raise some strong feelings for you. I want you to feel comfortable talking to me about those feelings as they come up for you. For example, it's important for us to get back to your saying that you're scared.

Example 3

Clinician: I just found out that your daughter Carrie is working at the same law firm as my partner, Len.

Client: Yeah. That's weird, huh?

Clinician: That kind of puts you in an interesting position. You may be finding out things about me that I haven't told you and that you haven't asked.

Client: Yeah.

Clinician: I hope that you will feel comfortable talking to me about anything that comes up for you. I am confident that we can handle it together.

Client: Well, now that you mention it, Carrie said that she was going to a baby shower for Len.

Clinician: Yes, Len and I are adopting a son. What was it like for you to find out this information from someone else?

Client: It's so weird because I think I know you so well, and yet here is this important thing that is happening in your life and you hadn't told me.

Responding to Personal Questions

Sometimes clients will ask personal questions: How old are you? Are you married? Have you ever had an abortion? Whether the clinician chooses to answer depends on a number of factors, including theoretical orientation, personal comfort in sharing information, agency preferences or policies, and anticipated effects on the client. Feminist therapists for example, often use judicious self-disclosure to reduce unequal power in the relationship. Clinicians need to think carefully about the effects of both answering and not answering client questions. Not answering is a traditional psychodynamic strategy designed so that the client might project any anxieties, frustrations, or fantasies onto the "blank screen" of the clinician, indicating earlier unconscious issues that might need to be recognized and explored. Many nonpsychodynamic clinicians do not respond to personal questions in order to encourage the client to search for other possible meanings or motivations.

Disclosures are always a subject for continuing review. Sometimes clients will say they are glad or relieved to hear things, but later on they will share more complex reactions of which they were not initially aware. Similarly, a clinician may feel that disclosure feels right and comfortable at times and at other times may feel overexposed.

Some clinicians may decide that they do not want to answer a client's direct question. It takes skill and finesse not to answer a direct question without leaving the client feeling embarrassed and rejected. We have found that it is often helpful to reflect what the underlying purpose of the question might be and to address that. It is also possible simply to explain why you're not answering.

Example 1

Client: (During a first interview.) I was wondering how old you are.

Clinician A: Maybe you're wondering if I have enough experience to work with you on the issues you've mentioned

Clinician B: I am wondering what reasons you might have for asking me my age. (To stimulate exploration by client of meanings behind the question.)

Example 2

Client: I don't know much about you. Are you married? Lesbian? Where do you live? Do you have kids?

Clinician: It's natural that you would want to know a lot of the "facts" of my life. Therapy is this weird relationship that in some ways is quite imbalanced. I know a lot about you and the facts of your life, while you know very little about mine. However, I do think that in one sense you know me quite well. Over the last four weeks you have gotten a sense of me in a very real and genuine way, even though some of those facts might be missing. Do you know what I mean?

Example 3

Client: Last week when you told me you were pregnant, you asked me if I had any reactions. I didn't then, but now I do have a question.

Clinician: Okay . . .

Client: Are you going to put the baby in child care?

Clinician: Could you also be wondering if I will still be working with you, or putting you in someone else's care?

Client: Hmmm . . . I never thought of that. Maybe I am.

◉◉ CLIP 10.1
Information about the Clinician

Sometimes the clinician will choose not to answer the question but will want to explore the client's fantasies about the clinician. These fantasies may provide useful information about the way the client sees and experiences things.

Example

Client: (Office is in clinician's home.) Do you live here by yourself or what? I didn't mean to pry . . . just curious about it.

Clinician: What thoughts have you had about it?

Client: Not many. Just wondered.

Clinician: I'm interested in what you imagined.

EXERCISE 10.2

In teams of three or four, role-play a client and clinician. Have the client ask the clinician personal questions. In the role of the clinician, practice different ways of responding. Note how you feel when the client asks you a question. If possible, videotape the role plays. As you watch them, note both your verbal and nonverbal behavior in response to the client's questions. Discuss with your team what you have observed.

Confidentiality

We have already mentioned that, at the beginning of the relationship, the clinician discusses with the client confidentiality and its limitations. We will again address confidentiality issues when we talk about out-of-office contacts in a later section of this chapter. Here we explore some situations in which confidentiality needs to be addressed as a boundary issue in the clinical relationship and as an issue with both ethical and legal consequences. Whenever confidentiality issues arise, the clinician directly addresses them and their impact on the relationship.

⊙⊙ **CLIP 10.2**
Confidentiality as a Boundary Issue

Example 1

> *Clinician:* Delma, I wanted to let you know that I have just received a request from your insurance company to fill out a form about our work together.
>
> *Client:* Yeah, I remember you said you might have to do that.
>
> *Clinician:* Let me tell you what they are asking and what I will say. (The clinician goes on to describe what information is requested and what information he will provide.) Do you have any questions about it?
>
> *Client:* No, I think that's okay.
>
> *Clinician:* If you have any concerns about it, please let me know.
>
> *Client:* Well, will you tell them what I told you about my brother? (Client had disclosed that brother was a drug addict.)
>
> *Clinician:* I don't have to reveal that information at all.
>
> *Client:* Good, I was worried he might get fired.

Example 2

> *Client:* I just saw someone from my church in your waiting room.
>
> *Clinician:* What was that like for you?
>
> *Client:* I don't want her to know that I'm coming to this agency.
>
> *Clinician:* Tell me what you're worried about.
>
> *Client:* I don't want her to know my business.

> *Clinician:* What do you think she might think about your being here?
>
> *Client:* (Responds with her fears.)
>
> *Clinician:* (Clinician explores the client's concerns and then reaffirms the confidentiality.) It's true she will know that you are here and she may have her fantasies about why, but no one here will say anything about what you and I talk about.

Limits on Clinical Conversations

We have noted previously that there are boundaries (confidentiality, time) *around* the entire clinician-client conversation. In addition, there are boundaries *within* the conversation, including (1) the focus, which structures, concentrates, and clarifies the conversation; and (2) any existing proscriptions against certain topics of conversation in particular settings.

The Focused Conversation

The clinician helps the client stay focused on the topic at hand so as to avoid getting sidetracked by other issues the client may raise. For example, if a client has contracted with an employment counselor specifically to work on job skills but the client continually brings up concerns about his relationship with his son, the clinician may either (1) explore the issue in more detail to see if there is a possible connection between the client's concerns and the issue they have contracted to work on; or (2) help the client *refocus* on the task at hand but consider talking with a family specialist about parent-child concerns. Unless the ongoing agreement is to talk about anything that arises for the client, the clinician usually tries to help the client stay focused in order to make the most of their time together.

Example

> *Clinician:* Luis, I know you're worried about your relationship with your son, but we had agreed that your need to work is so urgent that right now our main job is to help you figure out how to get ready for this next interview. I hear your worries about Luisito, though, and I'd be glad to get you hooked up with one our family life counselors, to talk about your relationship with your boy. I feel that it's important today to stay on course with our work.

The Proscribed Conversation

Sometimes the agency setting proscribes certain areas of conversation. The social worker at a Catholic family agency may be prohibited from discussing abortion as one of the options for an adult woman who is facing an unwanted pregnancy. The high school counselor may be told that because of a vote by the school board, she is not permitted to discuss issues of sexual orientation with any of the students.

E X E R C I S E 10.3

Do you believe that an agency has a right to restrict the topic of conversation between a clinician and client? Under what circumstances? How would you handle a situation if the agency you worked for proscribed an arena of clinical conversation?

When clinicians are prohibited from discussing certain issues, they must clearly articulate the limits to the client and offer a referral to an appropriate professional if the client would like to discuss that topic further.

Examples

Clinician A: Nancy, this is a Catholic family agency and I am not permitted to talk with you about abortion as an option for handling this pregnancy. If you want to consider that, I can refer you to a counselor at Family Planning who can explore that alternative with you.

Clinician B: Thomas, it sounds like you are thinking you might be gay. That isn't something that I, as a school counselor in our town, can talk about with you. There is, though, a youth worker in town who has had lots of experience talking with kids about sexual orientation issues. I can refer you to him if you'd like.

E X E R C I S E 10.4

In teams of four, role-play the following scenarios in which you are prohibited from discussing certain topics with clients. Discuss the ethical issues such a prohibition might raise for you. How would you handle a situation in which you disagreed with the stated policy of the agency for which you worked? In your discussion, remember the ethical principle of upholding contractual agreements with employer agencies, as well as working for the best interests of your client. Record your reactions in your journal, and prepare to disuss them in class.

As a high school guidance counselor in a Catholic school, you are forbidden to join students who have asked you to march with them in the local Gay Pride March.

> *A 27-year-old mother who is receiving welfare assistance asks you if you think it is okay that she is working two nights a week as a waitress and not reporting the income to the government. She says that she couldn't pay for food and heat if she didn't have this little extra income.*
>
> *A managed care plan prohibits you from discussing with your clients your view that their son needs to be in a day treatment program, which the plan has rejected as too costly.*

Out-of-Office Contacts

Not all clinicians see their clients in offices. However, we use the phrase "out-of-office contact" to refer to those times when the clinician sees clients in settings outside of their normal meeting place.

Planned Contact Outside of the Office

Contact outside of the normal meeting place may be a planned part of the work together. Planned out-of-office contacts include home, hospital, and institutional visits. These places may be the normal settings for meetings—the hospital social worker will routinely see her clients in their hospital rooms—or they may constitute an out of the ordinary event, as when the counselor who usually meets with a client at the clinic suggests a home visit. The clinician might also accompany someone to an AA meeting, go with someone to the Welfare office, or drive a client to the battered women's shelter. These types of activities are clearly related to easing the way for the client to get needed services.

Some clinicians may attend commitment or marriage ceremonies, christenings, graduations, healing services, or funerals. Sometimes they provide a supportive presence for lonely or isolated people. At other times they may join with family and friends to help celebrate or honor an occasion that marks special achievements related to the aims of clinical contact.

EXERCISE 10.5

In your journal, record your thoughts about whether or not you might attend a client's wedding. Under what circumstances, if any, would you do so? What factors would go into your decision? What might be the advantages of your attendance? The disadvantages? Discuss your responses in class. What watchwords might guide your behaviors while there (for example, "Remember, this is work")?

In all the situations in Exercise 10.5, the clinician bases the decision on whether to see the client outside of the normal meeting place by thinking about whether or not it furthers the work they are doing together. There will be times when clients ask clinicians to see them in other situations. Clinicians usually don't enter into activities and relationships with clients outside of the office unless there are compelling professional reasons to do so. Though a friendly tone may characterize the working relationship, the clinical relationship isn't a friendship. Putting some boundaries around the relationship clarifies its work purpose and focus and removes from the client the onus of trying to guess how far the relationship can be taken or what motivates the clinician's attention and caring.

> I remember when I was working at the group home, I went with the residents to see a movie as part of their recreational activity. For me it was work; for them it was fun. One of the residents asked me if I would go to the movies with him the next week when he was out on a pass. I had to explain the difference that when I went with the group it was part of my role as a resident counselor. I wasn't just going out with the group as a friend.

When a client asks a clinician to be seen in a setting other than their normal meeting place, the clinician needs to carefully consider the request and discuss it with a supervisor. If the decision is not to go, the clinician should support the client while clearly articulating the reason for the refusal.

Example

A clinician has helped the client cope with depression so serious that she had lost a job as an accountant as a result of it. Over the last six months, they had discussed the client's desire to open her own accounting office. She had been discussing how excited she was about having a party to celebrate her "return to the real world."

Client: I want to ask you if you would come to my office warming.

Clinician: How were you picturing it would be with me there?

Client: You've been so important to my improvement. I guess I want you to see what I've made of myself.

Clinician: It's really a celebration for you of overcoming your depression as well as of opening the office.

Client: That's why I want you there.

Clinician: It's nice that you want to include me. I, too, share your excitement in being able to go back to work—and to set up your own office at that. You have every right to feel proud.

Client: I know. Thanks, I do feel proud.

Clinician: Unfortunately, I won't be able to come. I don't usually see clients outside of the office. I find that that doesn't work for me. Maybe we could celebrate your success here. I will, however, be thinking about you that day. Would you like to bring in pictures of your office?

Client: Yeah, I'd like to bring in pictures of the party, too.

Clinician: Great.

When meeting purposefully with clients outside the customary meeting place, it is important to be careful that roles are clear and boundaries, though flexible, are still well defined.

Example

The client is a teenager who dropped out of high school. He has met with the youth worker regularly over the last three years. They have worked together to help him get back into an alternative school program, and after many difficulties the client is going to graduate.

Client: So—you gonna come to my graduation?

Clinician: I'd be happy to be there.

Client: We're gonna have one big party after.

Clinician: Well, I'll be at the ceremony, but I won't be coming to the party.

Client: Why not, man?

Clinician: We've spent a lot of time working together to get to this day. I am delighted that you did it and I want to be there to celebrate your success, so I'll be at the school. But, I'm your counselor, and counselors don't usually go to parties with their clients.

Client: Why not?

Clinician: Well, that's one of the rules about this relationship. It's part of what makes it different from other relationships that you have in your life. I stay a little more detached, and that may be one of the things that helps us work together so well.

Client: Huh, this sure is one strange relationship.

Clinician: Yeah, but we've used it well.

Client: So what are you gonna do, stay in the back of the auditorium?

Clinician: Well, how should we handle this? I'd be happy to meet your mom and your aunt or anyone else right after the ceremony if you want to introduce me, but you don't need to.

Client: Yeah, I want you to meet them.

Clinician: Well, let's talk about how we can do that and what it'll be like.

Clinicians must always think about the implications of their presence for clients and directly address the topic with them. This is particularly true when there is a change in setting, but we believe it is always important to explore the client's reactions to the clinician's encounters with other people or places in the client's life. The clinician might ask questions such as:

How was it for you, my coming to your home last week?

How was it for you when I met your sister?

What was it like for you when I went with you to the hospice?

Now that you're seeing me in the clinic instead of in the shelter, how does it feel?

E X E R C I S E   10.6   *Outside Contact*

Outside contact can be complicated, as clinicians sometimes have flexible interviewing strategies, such as talking with a client at a coffee shop where conditions are less formal, or having a meal with a family in their home. What, then, would be the difference if clinicians and clients went to the movies, if it gives the clients good feelings about themselves? Record your response in your journal, then discuss this topic in class.

Unplanned Contact

There are other times when the clinician and client do see each other outside of their normal meeting place. A clinician may see a client at a party, on the street, or in the bank. These unplanned contacts are not part of the work together, but they should be briefly addressed in the relationship.

Clinician: Bumping into you at the market was the first time we've seen each other outside the office.

Client: Yeah . . . I didn't know what to say.

Clinician: I thought we handled it well by just saying "hi." Have you had any other thoughts about it?

Client: No. Now I know that if we bump into each other again, we can just say "hi" and move on.

Clinician: That would be fine. We can also talk in our session about anything that comes up for you if we meet.

Sometimes the clinician may know in advance that outside contact may occur. It is helpful to ask clients in advance how they would like to handle expected contact.

I routinely discuss with clients how we want to handle the situation if we see each other outside the office. Some clients would like me to say "Hi, how are you?" and move on. Others would prefer that I ignore them so they are not in the position of having to explain to friends who I am or how they know me.

Clinicians must put clients' needs first and try to avoid specific situations if they know clients will be there and might be uncomfortable in the clinician's presence. Some clinicians believe they should avoid any contact with clients outside the office, even if the client would be okay with it; this is often because of clinicians' theoretical perspectives or their wishes to keep their work and private lives separate.

A couple of times, I have had to leave a small party or even a restaurant because I knew a client was there and that she would feel uncomfortable seeing me dancing, talking, or socializing with others.

I live in a very small town and I have to be careful about what dinner invitations I accept. Twice in the past year I have been invited to a dinner where a client of mine would have been present. I have learned to ask the host who is coming and if a client is, I find an excuse not to attend.

Sometimes clinicians cannot avoid interacting with their clients outside of the clinical relationship.

I live in a village of 1750 people and bump into my clients everywhere—market, gas station, beauty shop, gym. There's one Catholic church and we attend it pretty often at the same time. I have to be extremely careful in protecting confidentiality, but there is no way I could not have contact outside. Once people see I don't tell their stuff, we relax about it.

Remember that, without the client's permission, the clinician cannot reveal anything about the nature of his or her relationship with the client. If you bump into someone you have worked with and a friend asks who it is or how you know him or her, you have to find a way to answer that doesn't disclose the relationship with you. We have used the following responses.

"I know her from town."

"Just someone I know."

"We've known each other for a while."

"I know her through work."

These vague responses can feel awkward, but it is crucial to maintain client confidentiality.

I've told people I know that if we're walking along and I suddenly turn my back on them and don't introduce them, just walk ahead and I'll catch up. In one funny instance a charming teen client of mine saw me walking in the square, followed me, and jumped out of the bushes, doing a little song and dance. My friend and I laughed, and I just said, "Go ahead and I'll catch up in a minute." My client said, "He's cute . . . is that your main squeeze?" I just laughed and asked what she was up to in the square, she caught me up briefly, and let me go on. What can you do? A clinician's friends learn not to ask when things like this happen.

🔘 **CLIP 10.3**
Out-of-Office
Contacts

Addressing Requests for More Clinical Time

Clients will sometimes ask for more time than has previously been agreed to. They may ask for extra meetings, phone calls, or extensions of the length of regularly scheduled meetings. Clients who request more time may be upset, anxious, in need of anchoring contact or assessment, or may even be testing the clinician's caring by pushing on the limits of the relationship. The clinician's response should be flexible, and it will depend on a number of factors.

1. The *clinician's practice framework* shapes the response. For example, clinicians using a brief treatment framework might confine all contact to the given sessions and encourage clients to hold material until the next session. Crisis intervention specialists might be available 24 hours a day for a given number of weeks or months. Many clinicians use a combination of variable personal availability and local emergency resources to provide a ready response to reasonable client requests for more time.

2. Clinician decisions about offering extra time will also depend on the *agency's rules and procedures* regarding coverage for clients' needs. For example, some have emergency services that they prefer clients use outside scheduled appointments; others do not wish staff to take client calls at home.

3. The *clinician's assessment* of the client's agenda, capacities, needs, and availability of other supports will influence clinician response to requests for more time. Clinicians will carefully assess how requests for more time do or do not seem to complement the agreed-upon goals for client functioning and growth. Extending time to some clients is a necessary lifeline in crisis, but for others it can be an invitation to exploit the clinician or to undercut their own new strengths. Only with some experience with each other can the client and clinician determine what is truly in the best interest of the client's functioning, and decisions may vary from time to time. The degree of seriousness of an emergency arising in the client's situation will also determine response.

4. The clinician's response will also depend on the *amount of time and energy* the clinician can reasonably devote to requests for extra time, particularly after hours and between sessions that are booked one after another. Clinicians sometimes develop "calling times"—specific times for telephoning during the day or evening—whose limits clients are asked to respect so that clinicians can renew themselves.

Whether or not the clinician agrees to requests for extra time or phone contact, he or she must carefully address the meaning for the particular client of both the request and the clinician's response. Any change in the originally agreed-upon contract needs to be carefully considered. Upholding reasonable conditions and limits may help clients get the work done more efficiently, and for clients with poor boundaries and time sense, it may assist in the internalization of structure.

Time constraints are one of the unusual aspects of the clinical relationship, and one that differentiates it from many other types of relationships with which clients are familiar. Holding with set times leaves the clinician time for work with many clients; it also helps structure work so that clinician and client are less likely to exhaust themselves with too much data, analysis, or emotional intensity. But this clinical sense of time may be at variance with that of clients. As Tafoya (1989) noted, "Many native languages do not measure time in standard units. The Sioux language has no translatable equivalents for words like *late, waiting,* or *time.* The term 'Indian time,' often interpreted as being late, in fact refers to doing something when 'it [the time] is right' " (cited in La Fromboise, Berman, & Sohi, 1994, p. 33)

Changing the rules suddenly, while perhaps necessary in serious emergencies, can be confusing for clients. For example, regularly extending the session for extra time and then suddenly ending on time may leave clients feeling that they've lost something special or have done something wrong.

Example 1

Client: Could you see me every other day? I'm so panicky . . . I don't think I can make it through the days.

Clinician: I can hear how rough things feel to you just now and I'd like to hear more. I am not going to be able to see you more often, but let's see if we can find other supports for you.

Example 2

Client: Can I have your number in case I get depressed over the weekend?

Clinician: What kinds of things are you worried about? (After the clinician explores in depth what the client's concerns are and ways the client might handle it—like calling friends, going out, positive self-talk—he might say the following.) Yolanda, I don't accept calls at home, but if you feel it's an emergency and you feel you need to talk to one of our staff, we have on-call workers you can reach by phone, 24 hours a day. If you want, I will tell them that you might call.

Clients may not ask for additional contact in advance. They may just call the clinician or appear at the agency for unscheduled meetings.

Example

Client: I got your number from the phone book and I hope it's okay that I'm calling. I couldn't wait until our next appointment to tell you that Gordon said I shouldn't call him at work anymore. I'm so mad and I just didn't feel like waiting until Tuesday to tell you.

Clinician: I am sorry to hear that you are having such a hard time, but it's pretty late. I don't usually take calls at home, but I want to make sure you're okay.

Client: I'm fine. I just wanted to tell you.

Clinician: Okay. We can talk more about what happened on Tuesday.

If clinicians agree to see a client for extra sessions or to receive calls at home, at some point they must clarify any limits on this service. They should also clarify who will be available to the client when the clinician is not available or during any clinician absences.

Examples

Clinician A: Pietro, I can talk with you for 10 minutes on Wednesday morning, but we have to stop on the dot at 11:00. Can you do that?

Clinician B: Francis, we can have an extra half-hour meeting this week, but we won't be able to do that on a regular basis.

Like everything else the clinician does, providing extra time or contact should be carefully considered. Extra contact can be justified as appropriate support for clients under unusual stress, but it can also undermine client resourcefulness if the client does not attempt to seek other sources of support. In addition, the clinician can feel helpful and even "heroic" providing extra contact at certain times but at others may feel resentful, thus sending clients mixed messages about what is okay to ask for.

Gift Giving and Receiving

Sometimes clients give clinicians gifts. These gifts may represent messages about the relationship, and sometimes it can be useful to explore what clients were thinking and feeling when they thought of giving the clinician a gift, how they picked the gift they did, and how they pictured the clinician reacting when the gift was presented. It's not unusual for clients to give clinicians gifts they wish they could have for themselves. Someone who has been taught throughout life to do for others in order to earn love may profit more from discussing a small gift and being asked to keep it for herself, than from the clinician's keeping the gift. On the other hand, some people may try to control the clinician by showering him or her with gifts, and others may be uncomfortable either giving or receiving presents.

The acceptance of a small gift (Hanukah card, flowers in thanks for special help) is often appropriate and respectful of the client's need to honor the relationship and its meaning. In such circumstances, the clinician thanks the client for thoughtfulness and responds with courtesy—tasting an edible treat only if the client will share it; putting the flowers in water. The use or placement of the gift should not make other clients feel they are expected to give gifts as well. A clinician may accept small tokens from some clients and not from others, and all responses should be carefully thought out and based on the client's specific needs.

Sometimes clinicians don't accept gifts. Regarding them as symbolic messages of dynamics in the clinical relationship, the clinician may talk about the meanings and intentions behind gifts, rather than accepting them. In these instances, the refusal has to be couched in a respectful and plausible discussion of the clinician's reasons for declining the gift.

> *A client gave me "an Easter present" of a gold crucifix right when she was the maddest at me. I said she seemed to be mad (she was glowering and seething), so I wondered why she would want to give me something. She asked whether I was going to give it back, and I said that, to me, the important thing was to understand what she was mad about. She said she wasn't mad. Then she looked at the crucifix, then at me, and said, "I guess I was picturing you on the cross in a lot of pain, so you could finally feel like I do." I wondered if she was feeling that I didn't appreciate her pain, and she said she didn't think I did.*

Clinicians try not to accept expensive gifts so as not to get caught up in anything seductive or anything that compromises clinical judgment by making the clinician feel somehow beholden. Yet sometimes the clinician can reinforce a client's faltering sense of self-worth by simply accepting the gift and appreciating the client's thoughtfulness.

> *When I was leaving the agency, a client brought me a gift. She was poor and I didn't want to take a gift from her. I said that I knew she appreciated our work together and that I would always remember her. I wasn't sure if I should take the gift, but because she begged me to take it in thanks for our work, I decided that I should at least open it. It was a pen with my name on it, and so I decided that I couldn't give it back to her. I told her that I would always remember her for the specialness of herself—even without the gift.*

It is important to think about the client's culture and what the consequences may be of not accepting a gift. In many cultures, a gift is always given to thank another person for services rendered or to show respect for another. Rejecting such a gift might be taken as evidence of extreme disrespect for another's way of being. However, repeated gifts should be explored, and it is best not to treat as irrelevant regular "surprises" like coffee or donuts, as the client may unwittingly be repeating the relational pattern that was reinforced throughout her life—that of serving, feeding, or pleasing powerful others. It can be more helpful to clients in the long run to note and suggest such possibilities, as the first step toward freeing them from patterns in which they are locked.

> An Irish client of mine, the caretaking oldest of 11 children, always killed herself at the holidays baking cakes and cookies for others. She had even been in a convent where she baked for the pleasure of others. This was a woman who asked for nothing and who got scarcely anything from others— something we were working to improve. Lo and behold, at Christmas she brought me a huge pudding that she'd stayed up all night to make. She mentioned that after our meeting, she was going home to bake some more of these for cousins. When I refused the pudding for the sake of helping her to see her self-abnegating pattern, she burst into tears and got very mad with me. These were unpleasant, yet very important, feelings to get on the table. She was able to grasp the point I was trying to make with her, and the next Christmas, she sent me a note of relief and gratitude that she wasn't baking for people anymore and felt great about it.

Supervisors can help beginning clinicians frame a variety of responses to gifts deemed inappropriate. Often, simple statements can be effective.

Examples of Clinician Responses

"I appreciate your thoughtfulness in bringing me this coffee, but I want this to be a place where you can finally get for yourself, and give to just you."

"I get plenty from the work with you without your having to bring me anything else."

"I like to think of this as a relationship where you can finally take instead of give for a change. Could you stand that kind of switch, do you think? It would be interesting to see what happened."

"Staff aren't allowed to accept gifts, but if you feel you want to say thanks for the work we do here, donations to the Tiny Tots program can be left with the secretary."

E X E R C I S E 10.7

In groups of three or four, make up some scenarios in which a client might bring a gift to the clinician. Role-play different ways of handling the situation, and if possible, videotape them. Under what conditions did you feel comfortable accepting a gift?

Under what conditions did you think it would be unwise? How did you address the issues with the client? What did you learn from watching each other and from watching the video?

Sometimes the clinician gives the client a gift. Usually such a gift is given at the end of the relationship, as a memento or symbol of the work together. For example, a clinician may give a client who was beginning to feel her own strength a magic wand representing the client's power; or a book of nature poetry to a client who uses nature as a comfort during times of loss. The gifts that clinicians give to clients need not be concrete. They could be the sharing of a blessing (such as the Irish blessing: "May the wind be always at your back . . . "); a memory of something strong or soothing (watching the sunset at water's edge); or a picture in the mind's eye of a significant scene from the client's life (imagining being held by a beloved parent).

Sometimes a gift serves as a symbol—something that the client can keep with him or her as a symbol of the connection between the client and the clinician.

> *When I was to be away for surgery, a client who'd had a lot of losses in her life gave me a soothing tape to play during the post-op period. She said she knew she couldn't visit me in the hospital, but she wanted to "be there," to do something to help me as I had helped her. When she later left for a six-week trip to Asia, I in turn gave her a tape of soothing music to play, saying I would be thinking of her, wishing her a safe journey, and picturing her having a great, relaxing time with her friends.*

Sexual Attraction

Sexual attractions can occur in the intimacy of the clinical relationship. A client can be attracted to a clinician, and a clinician can be attracted to a client. However, sexual interaction between client and clinician is strictly forbidden by the ethical codes of all of the helping professions, and it is a criminal offense in a number of states.

Briefly stated, when a clinician feels sexual attraction toward a client, the clinician does not bring it up with the client but, instead, discusses it with a supervisor. When the client is sexually attracted to the clinician, the clinician should, if possible, consult with a supervisor before addressing the issue in the relationship.

Clinicians may respond to a client's sexual attraction in any one of a number of ways or combination of ways. How and why the clinician chooses a particular response is beyond the scope of this chapter. As we have said before, the issue is complex and depends on a number of factors, including the clinician's theoretical orientation, the clinician's understanding of the client and what the sexual attraction may represent, the type of work the client and clinician are engaged in, and the way in which the client broaches the issue (as a concern or subject for study versus as a quip or a seductive invitation). Following are some relevant principles of practice, briefly stated.

1. The clinician can explore the client's sexual attraction and fantasies about him or her. Some clinicians believe that this exploration will provide useful information about the client's dynamics and is therefore appropriate for their work together. They would therefore employ the skills of *exploration and elaboration* to obtain more information about the attraction the client has expressed

2. The clinician can *reassure* the client about the commonness of the experience of tender and sexual feelings arising in situations of intense personal sharing. Clients often report feeling attraction to clinicians because of the intimacy of the clinical relationship, and they may feel frightened or confused by these feelings, especially if they have experienced sexual abuse at the hands of intimates or have come from strict religious backgrounds that expected sexual feelings to be suppressed.

3. The clinician can *refocus* the conversation on the contracted work. Sometimes clients may raise sexual feelings as a distraction from the work at hand if that work is too difficult for them at the moment.

4. Whether the clinician explores the issue in more detail, reassures the client about the commonness of the experience, or refocuses the conversation back to the topic, we believe that it is always important to *let the client know that we would never act on sexual feelings.*

5. It is important that the clinician carefully *record the discussion* of sexual feelings in their notes for use in supervision and to document clinician responses in case of any later misinterpretation by the client or others.

6. No beginning clinician should respond to a client's expression of sexual attraction without previously *discussing the issue thoroughly in supervision.* Since clinicians cannot predict when a client may express sexual attraction, it is wise to have a general conversation with a supervisor about how to handle sexual attractions, should they arise.

Example

Client: I had a weird dream about you last night. We were having sex. It's so embarrassing.

Clinician: I am glad that you told me about it. Counseling is an intimate experience in which lots of feelings can arise, including sexual ones. Would you feel comfortable telling me more about the dream, and let's see if we can understand this better?

---

7. The clinician can use *examining the moment* to directly address sexual behaviors on the part of the client.

Example

Clinician: Lauren, I notice that right now you are leaning forward in what might be perceived to be a seductive way. You have raised your dress over your knees and unbuttoned the top two buttons of your blouse. Let's talk about it.

Client: (Straightens out skirt and sits back.) I wasn't aware of it. But I have to admit, I do find you sexy.

Clinician: One of the things that sometimes happens when people share deeply in a professional relationship like ours is that they can feel sexually attracted to their worker. This is even more true in a situation like yours where, when you were growing up, closeness often led to sex. I want to be clear that we would never act on that attraction, but it seems important to talk about it some more.

Client: Wow, so I'm just like a textbook "patient" . . .

Clinician: Did I leave you feeling that way?

Client: I wasn't asking you for a date. I just said I thought you are sexy. No big deal.

Clinician: This isn't easy to talk about, I know, but it could help us understand how you get into sexual relationships with people without really knowing them, and then get hurt. It might help us see if you could be inadvertently contributing to that in ways we could work to change.

Client: Do you mean that maybe I come on to people without being aware of it?

Clinician: Do you think that could be so?

In the preceding example, the clinician explored feelings appearing in the moment of the work as they may relate to other experiences in the client's life. He also reassured her about the commonness of the experience. He affirmed safe boundaries that would allow them to talk about feelings without acting on them. It is this very capacity to feel, examine, and discuss things *without acting* that is a goal of both good clinical learning and sound clinical practice. On rare occasions the client may become sexually assertive, gazing at the clinician's breasts or genitals while talking; rubbing against the clinician provocatively on entering or exiting the room; or attempting other forms of physical contact such as "surprise" kisses or hugs. These behaviors can arise in clients who have grown up in an atmosphere of inappropriate sexualized intimacy and violence. They may also occur in some clients who doubt their attractiveness and urgently need it validated, albeit they are expressing these needs inappropriately. Paradoxically, some clients who fear closeness may actually cross boundaries in order to distance the clinician, whose repulsion they fully anticipate. For other clients, sexualized encounters may be a cultural or gender norm on which the client is acting at the moment.

Following supervisory review of the behavior, the clinician may be helped to directly address it and its inappropriateness to the professional relationship. As with most of the other boundary issues we have discussed, the clinician can follow up by exploring the meaning of the behavior from the client's own perspective and experience.

Examples

Clinician A: I've noticed that when we talk you often seem to be staring at my breasts. This makes me uncomfortable and I wonder if you could try making eye contact with me, or looking someplace else instead. Am I the first woman to mention this?

Clinician B: Birch, when you leave the room, you always lay your hand on my back as you go out. I'd rather you not do that, but I'm also interested in what that's about for you?

Directly addressing sexualized behaviors can help clients begin to establish boundaries appropriate to the context of clinical working environments. At the same time, clinicians must be professional in their own dress, manner, and tone so that they do not elicit the very behaviors they then confront.

EXERCISE 10.8
In small groups, take turns role-playing a client either talking about or manifesting sexual attraction. Practice how you would respond to the client without acting. Talk with your team about how to do that in a way that is neither demeaning nor encouraging of the client's fantasies or behaviors.

Limit Setting

Beginning clinicians may mistakenly feel that the principles of acceptance and nonjudgmentalism prevent our ever acting in ways that limit the client's freedom or cause unpleasant feelings. They may ask whether setting limits on client behaviors with the clinician is a clinician-centered rather than a client-centered activity. We believe that it is both. Clinicians cannot work productively in an atmosphere that threatens their fundamental sense of comfort and well-being, and clients can usually read rather accurately a clinician's negative reactions to things they do. All relationships have to have agreements and guidelines that all of the participants can agree to and that respect differential needs and preferences. Because the clinician acts as a model, letting someone persist in upsetting or offensive behaviors gives a confusing double message about what the clinician thinks is appropriate in relationships, and it models the kind of denial many clients have already had too much of.

In this chapter, we have given numerous examples of the clinician's setting limits with clients about such things as time, topics of conversation, privacy of the clinician, and sexual behaviors in order to maintain clear and comfortable boundaries in the clinical relationship. When setting limits, the clinician unfailingly conveys respect and caring for the client.

Conclusion

We believe that the process of establishing, tending, and maintaining the clinical relationship contributes fundamentally to helping clients change. This relationship not only provides a context in which change can occur, it is often the means by which change occurs, in the client and in the clinician as well. Learning to care about, tend, and more authentically participate in a relationship builds skills that will benefit both participants in their future connections and work with others. Ironically, the relationship itself can become so important that, while it is often a reinforcer of change efforts, it can also inhibit change. It can feel so rare and so good that the participants may unwittingly slow down change in order to postpone losing this very special relationship when work is completed and the relationship ends.

In the next chapter we review the major principles and techniques of the ending phase of work, including relational issues that can arise when terminating work together.

Suggested Readings

There are a number of excellent readings on sexual attractions and the prohibitions against any form of dual relationships in clinical work, such as:

Borys, Debra, & Pope, Ken. (1989). Dual relationships between therapist and client: A national study of psychologists, psychiatrists, and social workers. *Professional Psychology Research and Practice, 30*(5), 283–293.

Bridges, Nancy. (1994). Meaning and management of attraction: Neglected aspects of psychotherapy training and practice. *Journal of Psychotherapy, 31,* 424–433.

Kagle, Jill D., & Giebelhausen, Pam N. (1994). Dual relationships and professional boundaries. *Social Work, 39*(2), 213–220.

A useful reading on self-disclosure is:

Brown, Laura S., & Walker, Lenore E. A. (1990). Feminist therapy perspectives on self-disclosre. In George Stricker & Martin Fisher (Eds.), *Self-disclosure in the therapeutic relationship* (pp. 135–155). New York: Plenum.

CHAPTER 11

Endings and Transitions

Inevitably, clinical work comes to an end. As often as possible, endings are planned and are a natural part of a stated contract. For example, the clinician and client in an employee assistance program may agree to meet for a fixed number of sessions, or a social worker in a halfway house may agree to meet with a client only as long as the client is attending other specified programs. But endings can also happen in an unplanned way. They may be the result of unanticipated circumstances, as when the client has to move away, the clinician becomes too ill to work, the client discontinues the relationship, or the agency closes. Endings may be initiated by the client or the clinician.

Endings may seem to be a natural and timely closure to the work together, or they may seem precipitous. Regardless of the reason, a formal process of ending is undertaken to assist the client in summarizing and integrating the relational and task work with the clinician, as well as in planning for the future. This formal termination process may be quite brief or may be carried out over a number of sessions.

Termination, the word traditionally used in clinical work to describe the process of ending, is a term conceived in a much earlier era of practice heavily influenced by psychoanalytic theory of therapy. Traditional psychoanalytic theory anticipated so thorough and productive a therapeutic restructuring of client dynamics, defenses, and character that work could be terminated with the expectation of little future need for further work. However, we believe that termination represents a *transitioning process* by which clients moving to other systems of support and problem solving (family, mutual aid groups) often take the work and the relationship away with them as sustaining inner resources available for use in the future. But we also recognize that termination may not be the last time that the clinician sees the client. Clients with few resources, complex problems, or new objectives for work together sometimes return to see the same clinician with whom they ostensibly "terminated" or finished up. Therefore, although clinicians often use words such as *termination, endings,* and *transitions,* we believe that the process is often one of finishing work "for now." If we think of life and circumstances as forever fluid and dynamic, then the idea of *cycles of work* at different points in the life cycle makes perfect sense in the lives of many people.

Even Before We End: Foreshadowing

It is important to give both clinicians and clients as much lead time as possible to discuss ending and allow for the processing and digestion of the transition from this special form of caring and collaboration. Thus, whether or not there is a specified plan for ending, the clinician occasionally foreshadows the ending during the working relationship. This is particularly true in work with clients whose many prior relational losses make separations or endings hard to deal with.

An agreed-upon, planned ending is the nicest way to wrap up work together, as it provides many opportunities to review, compare expectations with realities, look ahead, and both regret and celebrate concluding this cycle of work. When there is a projected date for an ending, the clinician will foreshadow by occasionally noting the date so that client and clinician can be alert to it and plan the focus and pace of the discussion accordingly.

Examples

Clinician A: Before we begin work today, I wanted to review with you that it's the end of March, just seven weeks before my placement ends and I leave here to continue my education.

Clinician B: We said we would finish up after Christmas, and since Christmas is just three weeks away, I thought it might be good today to look at where we are and whether that still seems to be a good idea. If so, let's figure out how we can plan ahead for it so it doesn't just suddenly happen without us getting ready for it—especially here at the holidays.

Clinician C: This is our fifth of eight sessions; what would you like to accomplish by the time our meeting ends today?

When the contract is somewhat more open and continuing over time, clinicians may periodically review goals, accomplishments, and remaining issues and more frequently mention "when our work together is finished" to help clients keep the relationship and work in perspective. Here time is well used as both boundary and incentive for efficient use of work.

◯◯ CLIP 11.1
Foreshadowing the Ending

Initiating Endings and Transitions

Whatever the reason for or nature of the ending, there are several skills the clinician can use to ease the process of change for the client, maximize gains to date, and forward the transition to other supportive connections and activities. Because the skills used to end the work are much the same as those also used in transitions and breaks, we shall begin by elaborating ending skills and then demonstrate how these skills can be adapted for planned and unplanned transitions and interruptions in the work.

E X E R C I S E 11.1 *When Clinicians Should Initiate Endings*

Before reading more about endings, pause to identify some of your ideas about them. In your journal, describe the circumstances in which you feel the clinician should initiate the ending of the clinical relationship.

Clinician-Initiated Endings

Sometimes the clinician initiates the process of ending. This may be appropriate in a number of situations. For example, the clinician may initiate ending because the client and clinician have *accomplished their goals* and it is simply time to end their work together. The beginning clinician always first consults with his or her supervisor as to the appropriateness of ending before raising the subject with the client.

Where possible, it seems best to initiate conversation about ending early on in a given session, so that the client does not feel that the clinician wants to end the relationship because of something the client has just revealed or done. When the clinician suggests the possibility of ending for now, it is important to leave room for the client's responses and, in the absence of any immediate ones, to keep an eye out for nonverbals and indirect themes.

The following are several useful ways in which the clinician can introduce the topic of termination when the goals of the relationship have been met.

Examples

> *Clinician A:* Anna, things have gone so well for a while now. I thought today we might think about the possibility of our bringing our work together to a close.

> *Clinician B:* Miguel, you've been wondering when our work will be through. Should we decide on a date, far enough away to give you a few more weeks to reestablish yourself back in the community?

> *Clinician C:* By spring, Brian, I expect you'll be ready to try things without seeing me every week. I'd like us to keep things as they are for now, to support you through the holidays, but we might plan on ending our work together in March.

The clinician may also initiate ending the relationship because he or she feels that although the client could still use some assistance, the clinician is *unable to help.* This could be because the clinician does not have the expertise necessary to work with the client on a specific issue or to use a specific method.

> *I was working with a woman at the family planning clinic. We were meeting about birth control methods and STD prevention. She disclosed that she had been sexually abused. I knew that this would be an important topic for her to explore, but I certainly wasn't trained to work with it. I referred her to a more knowledgeable mental health counselor at the clinic.*

When the clinician feels that she or he can no longer work with a client because the client's issues are beyond the clinician's expertise, the clinician must carefully make a *referral.* This can be difficult, as the client may feel rejected or reluctant to see another clinician. Using the prior example, the clinician might proceed in the following way.

Example

Clinician: Serafina, I was thinking about what you told me at our last meeting about what happened to you in your family.

Client: Yeah.

Clinician: I think that having been sexually abused must have been an awful experience that you haven't gotten much help for.

Client: You're the first one I told about it.

Clinician: I appreciate your confidence in me.

Client: Yeah, I couldn't believe that I told you.

Clinician: What does it feel like to have told me?

Client: It felt okay . . . but I've been thinking about it a lot.

Clinician: You know, I think it would be really good if you could talk about what happened to you with a colleague of mine who has a lot of experience helping women who have been abused.

Client: I couldn't imagine talking to anyone but you. Can't you help me with it?

Clinician: Serafina, I really want to help you but I haven't had any experience working with women who have been sexually abused. I think the best thing I could do for you would be

to help you talk to Brenda. She is a wonderful counselor whom
I like a lot.

Client: Do you mean I can't see you anymore?

Clinician: Well, we were finishing up our work about birth control
and safe sex practices, so we would be stopping anyway. I know
it can be hard to think about saying good-bye to someone with
whom you've shared so much.

Client: Yeah. I always hate good-byes.

Clinician: What I would like to do is to set up a meeting for you with
Brenda and I would meet with you for a last meeting after you've
seen her to find out how it goes and to say good-bye.

EXERCISE 11.2 *Thinking about Termination*

In your journal, record your reactions to the preceding scenario. How do you think
the client feels? How do you think the clinician feels? What would you have done
differently?

EXERCISE 11.3 *Referral Role Plays*

Role-play a scenario in which you refer a client to another person or agency because
you are unable to help the client with the issues he or she has uncovered. Videotape
the role play. Watch the video with your team and then debrief: discuss what it felt
like to be the clinician and what it felt like to be the client.

Clinicians may need to initiate the end of the relationship if they feel that
a client is *not making use of the relationship.* This is a very complex and difficult
issue, and such an ending should be undertaken only after careful review
with a supervisor.

Example

Clinician: Leo, we've been meeting for a while about your problems
finding a job, and we don't seem to have accomplished much
lately. I am not sure that our continued meeting would be helpful
to you.

Client: Well, I like meeting.

Clinician: I don't think it is a good use of your time and money. I have
the feeling that you aren't sure that you really do want to work
on getting a job.

Client: Yeah, I do.

Clinician: Well, I've noticed that you haven't followed through on
any of the assignments we've agreed might help. We've explored

this a lot, and I'm still not sure why that is. However, I think that we should stop meeting for a while. If you feel that you are ready to practice job-hunting skills again, I'll be happy to see you again.

Client-Initiated Endings

Clients, too, can initiate endings for a variety of reasons. They may feel that the goals of the relationship have been met, that they are ready to try things on their own or to transition to another kind of work. Clients may also suggest ending if they feel that the clinician is getting ready to end the relationship and it is important for them to be the first to leave. In addition, clients can end work because they are at odds with the clinician or agency, because the issue being addressed in the work makes them feel uncomfortable, or because they feel they are not being helped. The clinician may or may not agree with the client's decision and must *carefully explore* the situation with the client to make sure that the client isn't initiating ending because of discontent with the clinician or clinical process. The clinician attempts to explore the issue while at the same time respecting a client's right to decide.

> *I remember a client who came in quite angry one week and said that he was leaving our counseling sessions. He said I hadn't helped him and he decided that he was through. My first instinct was to say, "Okay." I felt like I didn't want to seem defensive by pushing him as to why he wanted to go, and I worried that maybe I hadn't helped him. But then I remembered my supervisor saying, "You have to explore it." So I did, and kept saying to myself, "Don't be defensive . . . keep the focus on him . . . try to be empathic . . . this is a learning opportunity." It worked. He really felt I listened, and then he said he was mad at me for something I had said that had pushed his buttons. We explored those buttons and continued our work. I was glad I hadn't given in to my first instinct to say, "Fine, bye."*

Sometimes it becomes clear that the client wants to end and will do so, even if this goes against the clinician's best judgment. In such situations, after carefully exploring the issues, we believe the clinician should help the client end well, putting as positive a spin as possible on the work and the decision to leave. This avoids contributing to the client's potential feelings of failure or guilt. In addition, the clinician tries to keep the door open for future work or referrals.

Example

> *Clinician:* Well, it sounds as if you're really feeling that this is the time to stop. You've used the relationship well (summarizes way client has used it). While you may want to do some more work

later, this feels to you like it is enough for now. I'd be happy to help you or make a referral if you decide that you want to do more work on this in the future.

There are times when the clinician is concerned that the client is self-sabotaging, or playing out an old pattern of breaking off relationships just when they are working. The clinician may want to raise the possibility that such dynamics may be at work. The client may disagree, but at least the clinician has left the client with something to think about. The clinician may not feel good about this sort of ending, but it is important to recognize that decisions still rest with the client, and sometimes clients can learn things through the process of ending that they cannot learn within the relationship.

Example

> *Clinician:* Wayne, I'm worried that you may be doing with me what you've described doing so many times before: that whenever you get close to somebody, you take off.
>
> *Client:* What's it to you?
>
> *Clinician:* If at some point you don't let someone in and keep them in, I worry you're going to be lonely for the rest of your life. You've already told me how much that hurts.
>
> *Client:* I have to see on my own how it goes.

Outside Forces May Precipitate Ending

Clients or counselors may also initiate ending because of external circumstances. Insurance limits may necessitate an ending. Clients may no longer be able to afford the care being offered. A significant other may insist that the client end the relationship. Unexpected events can result in a client or clinician having to move away or change jobs (Penn, 1990). Participants can become too ill to attend meetings, and an agency might close with very little notice.

When an agency is closing, restructuring, or discontinuing some service, both clinician and client may feel displaced and upset. At times the clinician's anger or fears may seep into the clinical work with clients, escalating their own worries and feelings of loss. Clinicians need to find other places to work out their own distress so that their work remains centered on the client's experience and not on the clinician's. Supervisors can indicate any instances in which it might be useful to share clinicians' own reactions to changes in the agency.

I was working in a methadone clinic in a hospital where there was some talk of a merger with a larger teaching hospital. The clients picked up on it somehow. There were lots of rumors that the clinic would be closed. I remember Lorenzo saying, "Shit, man, I'm just gonna go back to using when they close this place." We had to spend lots of time reassuring them that we weren't closing.

I know that closing an agency is tough on the staff as well as on the clients, but I was shocked to hear that some of the staff just started not showing up and using their sick time right before the agency closed. I felt so bad for the clients. It wasn't their fault but they were the ones who were losing out. They didn't even get to say good-bye to some of the staff.

In situations where external circumstances necessitate the transition or ending, the client and clinician may both feel that things are beyond their control. This is especially true if their work isn't completed or if it is at a crucial point. Some people are barely fazed by ending this kind of relationship, but others—clinicians included—may need to grieve the loss of the relationship, at the same time appreciating all that they have been able to accomplish in whatever time they have had. In a classic work on endings, Hilliard Levinson (1977) describes the grief process that some clients and clinicians go through around endings, particularly those endings that were not expected. The following clinical vignette illustrates such a grief process following extensive, longer-term work:

Nonie and I had worked together for a couple of years on maintaining her at home in spite of a history of episodes of bipolar disorder. She was in her early thirties, had a child by someone she had had a fling with at the mental hospital, and was being supported by Rehabilitation funds to go back and finish college. Right at the point when she was trying to enter school and worrying about being accepted by her peers, I was offered a job that I could not resist at another agency. It meant moving from a mental health to a medical setting, where I would not be allowed to see my current clients. I loved Nonie, and we had been through so much together with her getting in jams and then out again. It gets to you to have to step away, for your own personal advancement, from someone you care about and have worked with so intensively, and who is counting on you to be there with them.

We did some work on ending well in advance of my leaving, but Nonie went off her meds, as I feared, and landed back in the hospital just when I left the agency. I felt terrible, and poured this out fairly regularly in supervision. I was helped to see that Nonie had probably gotten herself readmitted to have familiar people around to help her with her sadness. The staff at the hospital confirmed that this was what she was absorbed with in their meetings with her. As life would have it, a month after I left, I was shopping in the area market when I wheeled my cart around an aisle and literally ran smack into Nonie. I was so happy to see her again, but she burst into tears and could not stop crying. We sort of went off into an empty corner and did more talking about moving on to her new worker at the clinic, someone I knew would be great with her. Over the next six months she called me twice at home to ask me to please see her, and I just continued gently to underscore her strengths and encourage her back to her new worker. She did follow through as hoped.

Initiating Ending Too Soon or Too Late

Sometimes either a client or a clinician may suggest ending the relationship too soon. Clinicians might be tempted to prematurely end the clinical relationship with a client who is constantly hostile, demanding, critical, or "manipulative." *Client abandonment* is a term applied to the unethical and thinly disguised process of "dumping" or deserting clients who are still in obvious need of service but whom the clinician finds difficult to work with. A clinician who is frustrated with a difficult or angry client might be all too willing to initiate an end to the relationship and may try to justify this termination with impressive clinical formulations. Clinicians can be subject to licensing board investigation and civil suits for client abandonment.

Clients who are feeling anxious about the work might suggest ending just when things are "getting hot" or when they are on the verge of making a significant change. They, too, may use compelling language to justify their leaving.

> *Lorinda was a woman who came to the women's center for counseling about her relationship with an abusive husband. She was beginning to talk about the possibility of leaving him and had even asked me to look into some shelters for women who were victims of domestic violence. Lorinda and I had been meeting for about three weeks when she announced that she thought she needed to stop coming because she couldn't get a baby-sitter for her 1-year-old child and there was "Just no way I can keep coming." We talked about the difficulty she was facing (it was true that she had no sitter), but as we explored it in more detail, Lorinda said that perhaps she didn't want to come because she was scared she was on the verge of making a major change in her life.*

On the reverse side, both clinician and client may enjoy the work and the relationship and may want to hold on to the relationship for longer than necessary. Sometimes the clinician may continue to see a client for financial reasons because of the income the client provides or because the client is an "easy" client—someone the clinician likes and enjoys working with. Some clinicians find the work of ending so painful that they repeatedly delay putting words on an approaching ending, thus foreshortening important reflection and conversation that could greatly benefit the client. Moreover, clinicians and clients may not want to give up the caring warmth and wonderful experience of having someone who is there to listen in such a relationship-centered way. It is no favor to clients to delay the modeling and development of a necessary life skill: that of bringing a relationship to a conclusion with the knowledge that there will be other important relationships and that important aspects of this one can be stored forever in the hearts and minds of the participants if they wish.

> *I had seen Simcha off and on for several years for various problems around leaving home, getting established in a career, and partnering in a big city full of risks for young adults. We had become as comfortable in our work together as two old shoes, and clearly enjoyed each other. When it finally felt right not to come anymore, Simcha said laughingly that there must be some ethical rule that a social worker can't say no if a client wants to pay to come and be with the worker because it just feels so good, period.*

Sometimes clients can feel dependent on professionals, as though they would be unable to make it alone. Others may have suffered serial losses and may understandably resist experiencing another one. For some clients, contact with the clinician is perhaps the most interesting experience they have all week. Isolated individuals refusing referrals to other groups and activities outside their homes may even tell the clinician that when he or she stops home visiting, they will have little other human contact, which makes ending very painful. Periodic conversations with clinical supervisors can help ensure that clinicians and clients end relationships in a compassionate but timely manner.

The Tasks of Endings and Transitions

E X E R C I S E   11.4   *Your Own Experiences with Endings*

In your journal, discuss a time in the past when you ended a relationship. It might have been the ending of your own work with a clinician or the day you graduated from school or a friend moved very far away. Record the circumstances of the ending and things you experienced or said during the ending process. What thoughts and feelings come to mind now, looking back?

The tasks and skills involved in ending are many, and you may have noted some of them as you recorded your part in the endings you wrote about in Exercise 11.4. Although we will discuss the skills of ending in a particular order, they often overlap and ebb and flow. The work around endings can occur purposefully over a number of sessions, weeks, months—even in one meeting, if that meeting is all we have.

Announcing the Process: "Now We Are Ending"

Whether at the end of an interview or at the end of the work, the responsibility for verbally marking the ending time rests with the clinician. We have already noted that the clinician is responsible for marking the end of a session, and may say as the end approaches, "We have to be finishing shortly, so let's take a moment to review what we've said today, where we are, and what's ahead." In parallel fashion and using many of the same skills, the clinician has to say at a designated point in the work that, because the work and relationship are ending soon, it is time to acknowledge the ending and to do some work together specifically around that ending. The subject of ending is gently yet confidently broached as a natural and inevitable part of life and work.

Clients with serious cognitive limitations may not be able to grasp the meaning of the concept of ending or understand the nuances of a discussion focused on ending. Sometimes the best that the clinician can do is to employ a calendar or chart and mark off sessions so that there is a visual indicator of time moving ahead and, finally, running out. Often a loved one close to the client and skilled in communication with him or her can accompany the client and translate the clinician's intent and tasks to be done.

As time and ability permit, the clinician will note with the client that there are beneficial steps to be taken during ending time: dealing with reactions, reviewing accomplishments and remaining issues, planning ahead, and making any necessary arrangements to ease the way for the client. Sometimes this introduction of *focused ending work* is an occasion for relief and excitement; at other times the client may react with shock or dismay.

Example

Clinician: Well, Roland, we are coming to the end of our work together.

Client: I can't believe how quickly the time has gone.

Clinician: Me either.

Client: So we're "terminating." What does a person do when they are finishing?

Clinician: Well, I think it's a good time to remember where you were when we first met, to think about what we have done and where you are now in relation to the issues you came in with. It's also a time to think about how you may handle things in the future. We get to see if there are any loose ends that we want to talk about before you leave, and, finally, we say good-bye.

Acknowledging and Exploring Reactions to Ending: "How Does It Feel?"

Clients who see a dentist or an internist a number of times do not usually "work through" the ending of their work together. Even after a lengthy hospital stay, the staff do not usually ask, "How do you feel about our discharging you?" or "Did you have feelings about the people who assisted you while you were here?" A formal termination process is a phenomenon particular to clinical relationships, and many clients may not be used to focusing so intensely on ending a professional relationship. In addition, both clients and clinicians may be surprised at the intensity of their emotional reactions to ending—the more so if the contacts were initially mandated by others or laden with other complexities. For many clients, the ending phase of work is a great opportunity to celebrate their achievements and honor a valued relationship, then to move on (Fortune, 1987). At the same time, many clients, especially those who are loss-sensitive or isolated, may feel sad and apprehensive as they imagine ending work with the clinician.

The clinician may help by *normalizing feelings* and reactions related to endings and helping clients express these feelings as the process of ending unfolds. Some clients take endings in stride and have few reactions beyond mild regret at ending contact with someone they respect. For other clients, feelings may be overwhelming or intolerable, especially when they have unresolved losses from the past that can get stirred up by the present ending. Some clients attempt to avoid endings by describing urgent new crises or dilemmas, often of their own creation (such as impulsive sex leading to pregnancy). They may displace their feelings about ending the clinical relationship onto these crises—often crises of loss of some kind—rather than expressing feelings that are directly about ending the work (Levinson, 1977).

Some clients may threaten to harm themselves or others in response to the clinician's leaving, sending up an unmistakable "cry for help." Clinicians are alert to these possibilities, particularly in clients who may have had a history of harming themselves or others before undertaking clinical work. Many people use the term *regression under stress* to describe the familiar phenomenon of outgrown behaviors returning under pressure because they are familiar, almost knee-jerk outlets for distress that cannot at the moment be expressed verbally. Clinicians wisely discuss with supervisors a range of potential interventions they can make if emergencies arise during ending work. Sometimes action takes the simpler form of losing things: schedule books, keys to the house or car, important papers, and so on. Clinicians can suggest possible parallel reactions here by using familiar skills of examining the moment, processing the process, or directly addressing indirect references to the ending process. If clients can be helped to see connections between their unusual behaviors during ending and certain unexamined feelings underlying them, then in the future they may be able to recognize their customary distress signals sooner and perhaps speak out, rather than act out, their feelings.

Example

Clinician: Roland, have you noticed that you have started to lose things a lot lately? Last week you said you lost your car keys and today you lost your gloves.

Client: Yeah, I'm scattered.

> *Clinician:* Do you think it could have anything to do with losing our
> relationship soon? Sometimes it's easier to have feelings about
> lost things than about lost people.

Some clients may miss a session or two at this time, perhaps to abbreviate
or draw out the process of ending, to avoid pain of reflecting on loss, or
perhaps even to register protest. In such instances, it is often helpful to reach
out by phone or letter, suggesting a possible link between the missed sessions
and the process of ending. Here the clinician can gently ask the client to try to
come back in so that things can be discussed together rather than thought
about alone (the way that so many clients have learned to deal with unhappy
events).

> *Gary had suffered from a serious form of schizophrenia, but over a three-year
> period, he let me in so that we developed very good talks about his hopes
> for the future. It came time for me to make a change, and I moved to another
> town. I could not get Gary to come in to talk with me about this. Instead,
> he took off for Florida on his motorcycle and sent me a note on a restaurant
> napkin to say, "Hi there." In response, I sent a letter to his parents' home,
> telling him what my last day would be and hoping to see him. He just
> appeared in the waiting room that day, in motorcycle leather and helmet,
> and when we sat together to say good-bye, he pulled his helmet visor down
> over his face and talked with me through it. I could see the tears running
> down his cheeks behind the visor but did not comment, as I knew how hard
> this was for him. He was able to say that when you lose friends, it is sad.
> At the end, we hugged each other good-bye and wished each other well.
> For a time I could see him sitting on his bike outside the agency, loudly
> racing his motor. I was sorry to end with him, and he saw it in me as I saw
> it in him.*

Reactions to ending provide an important opportunity for clinician and
client to attend to the client's way of dealing with change and, time
permitting, to explore unresolved feelings from past losses, educating the
client as to how these feelings may be emerging in current reactions to
ending. Clients who can appreciate human reactions to loss and change and
the possibility of taking good experiences with them in memory are helped
to cope better with loss and change. They can learn to anticipate common
reactions to future changes and develop in advance good alternatives for
managing their reactions with a minimum of harm to self or others.

Remembering: "Where Were You When We Began?"

Client and clinician review goals and accomplishments in relation to where
the client's issues and circumstances were when the work began: "Let's go
back and look at where you were when we first met." Some clients remember
very accurately, and others not so well. In some situations, it can be useful
to bring in process notes from early encounters and review these together, to

refresh the client's memory of what they described as their situation and what feelings they had when they first came in. If the client filled out an intake problem list or was asked to provide a written narrative regarding problems and goals, these materials can also be reviewed. A discussion of the client's goals and accomplishments can be the source of much pleasure, as clients remember how stuck they felt and how much further along they feel now.

Example

Clinician: Roland, I was thinking about where you were when we first met. You were having anxiety attacks.

Client: Yeah. I was having about three a week. It was awful.

Clinician: And it was affecting your work and home life.

Client: I kept missing work and I thought Brenda was going to leave me.

Reviewing Highlights of the Work Together: "What Have We Gotten Done?"

Client and clinician review salient developments during their work together for the purpose of identifying changes, honoring persistence and achievement, affirming client strengths, and discussing transferability of developed skills. Clearly embedded in this generally upbeat review is the notion that change in concert with others is now clearly possible. This review also gives the clinician a chance to note that the client's convictions about hopelessness and "stuckness" have lost some of their hold on the client's vision: perhaps the future can now be tackled more hopefully and assertively. During this review, clinician and client may also explore the main features and dynamics of their relationship, particularly where changes or improvements have occurred that augur well for the client's future efforts to relate with others.

Example

Clinician: You did a lot of work here.

Client: I remember during our first meeting when you said that you thought you could help. I didn't really believe it.

Clinician: Well, you really worked hard at it in spite of that.

Client: I remember when we started those relaxation tapes . . . (They continue to discuss events in the course of their work together, including setbacks or failures.)

Evaluating Current Status: "Where Are You Now?"

In evaluating the current status of the client and his or her situation and prospects, the clinician and client discuss where the client is now in relation to originally described issues, assets, and problems. They may also evaluate the client's current functioning, outlook, and circumstances, highlighting the client's strengths and supports and checking for any risks to well-being. These discussions act as a reminder of what clients are leaving with (gains, assets).

Example

Clinician: So, how would you say you're doing with the anxiety attacks at this point?

Client: Well, you know . . . I haven't had one in almost two months.

Clinician: Nice work! And how would you describe things with Brenda?

Client: Well, we still have our tensions. I thought she would be so relieved that my anxiety attacks were gone that everything would be great with her. But she still gets on my case sometimes. (They continue to talk about his home and work life.)

Foreshadowing the Future: "Where Are You Heading?"

As part of the ending process, the clinician and client explore what the client anticipates ahead and what kinds of issues might arise for the client in the future. They discuss how the client might respond to old familiar challenges if they should arise again. To double-check on shared understandings, the clinician often asks the client to recount what he or she will do in a particular crisis and to review more specifically whom he or she will rely on in the future for support, advice, and comfort in order to buttress and maintain growth.

Example

Clinician: What will you do two months from now if you find that the anxiety attacks come back?

Client: Well, I certainly hope they don't. I thought I was better.

Clinician: I hope they don't, too, but in case they do, it's important to know what you would do to handle them.

Client: Well, I guess I would go back to that self-talk exercise you gave me and I would use the tapes.

Clinician: And if that doesn't work?

Client: I would call you. Would that be okay?

Clinician: Of course it would.

Checking for Unfinished Business: "Is There Anything We Should Cover Before Closure?"

The clinician and client always double-check to see whether there is anything they need to take care of before ending. The clinician keeps an eye out for things that might need saying or doing—things the client might not have mentioned or thought of.

> *I have a little visualization I use with clients when we are ending. I ask them to imagine that they are walking down the stairs after leaving my office for the last time and to think about whether or not there is anything else they would have liked to have said to me but didn't. I invite them to say it now.*

Giving and Eliciting Feedback about the Meaning of the Relationship: "What Has This Meant?"

As we mentioned in our discussion of the skills of examining the moment and processing the process, the clinical relationship provides the client with an opportunity to talk about the relationship itself. In the ending phase of the work, the clinician can provide the client with direct feedback about how he or she has perceived the client.

Example

Clinician: One of the things I noticed about you, Roland, is how persistent you are. Things would look pretty gloomy and you were still having lots of anxiety attacks, but you kept at it. You continued to use the relaxation exercises and self-talk when a lot of people would have given up.

Client: Some people would say I'm stubborn.

Clinician: I think hanging in there is a very important thing when it works for you. Are there times when it doesn't?

Client: Well, sometimes I have a hard time knowing when it's a matter of persistence that will get me somewhere, and when it's a matter of something that I am too rigid to let go of. (Clinician and client explore.)

The clinician purposely sets time aside to review with the client special aspects of their relationship and what it has meant to both participants. This is often a time when both clinicians and clients share what they have appreciated about each other. We advise clinicians to hold off on these discussions for a time, lest any resulting "love fest" prevent clients from telling clinicians about any anger they have about ending. This is especially true when some circumstance in the clinician's life is making termination necessary. Exploration could be initiated using a number of different statements or questions.

Examples

"Before we finish, Emilio, I'd like us to have a chance to talk about our relationship and what it's meant to both of us."

"We have gone over just about everything except how it's been for us to work together, Dan. Can we do that this morning?"

"Graciela, should we take some time now to review the relationship we've had here and what it says about your new ability to work closely with someone?"

"One of the things we haven't said much about, Denise, is the relationship we've developed. It's special, and I'm going to miss working with you."

"It was an honor to work with you, Kwame. Your courage in getting your family here from your homeland during wartime, and carving out a new life for all of you, has touched me deeply."

"Chou, you have really taught me a lot about the benefits of silence! I have even started to meditate, thanks to the little book you gave me. I am very grateful."

We make a point of expressing what we've gotten from the work with the client, because we unfailingly have learned or grown from parts of the experience. If the relationship has been difficult, we may not say that in parting but instead say, for example, "Even though we've had our moments, I'm glad we kept working together and were able to get some things done that you felt helped your son." We try never to fake goodwill or meaning that clearly hasn't characterized the meetings. It doesn't feel right to be inauthentic, and clients can usually see right through it. Instead, we try to remain cordial and polite, no matter what has evolved.

EXERCISE 11.5 *Giving Positive Feedback*

Divide into small groups. Think about a person in your life who has characteristics that you find unpleasant. Briefly describe the relationship, as well as the negative characteristics that made this relationship unpleasant for you. See if you can think of one honest, positive piece of feedback that you could give to this person. Role-play giving this positive feedback. Give each other constructive feedback on statements made. Debrief with your role-play clients. Discuss whether the statements were well framed and believable.

Addressing Issues around Future Contact

Both clients and clinicians may have a hard time parting. Clients may express this difficulty by asking whether, now that clinical work is ending, the clinician can become a friend: "You're just the kind of person I like" or "You and I have so much in common . . . can't we do anything together after this? It seems such a shame."

Clients often do not picture a future "friendship" in a mutual sharing form but, rather, often envision the client-centered relationship occurring in social settings to ameliorate loneliness. This is a far cry from the mutuality of real friendships. Moreover, once clients come to experience the "warts and all" of the real person that is the clinician out of role, they may be stunned or regretful, and now do not know how to disconnect from someone who never disconnected from them.

> When I told a beloved therapist that I often wished we knew each other in some other ways, she recounted a lunch she'd had with a therapist of hers after finishing up their clinical work. She was appalled to see how slovenly his dress was, and how his tie was covered with soup stains, and that he droned on a lot about himself. She reminded me that we see what we want to in people. That was the last contact she ever wanted with that therapist. I wondered what this hinted I might see in my own therapist if she became a friend, and I pretty much gave up the idea.

It's been said that one of the good things about leave-takings is that, when done well, they teach us how to develop "ending skills." Joan Fleming and Therese Benedek (1966) suggest that current clinical experience can be "metabolized into a memory" (p. 174) so that energy invested in it can be released to other relationships and activities. Moreover, this memory can now act as a precious resource, to be called upon when people face future adversity or challenge.

Clients will sometimes ask if they can call or write the clinician in the future. Clinicians are of many minds about this, and it is helpful to talk over options and their different implications with a supervisor. Often it is the very idea that one can have contact that makes that contact unnecessary: the idea itself is the comfort. Decisions have to be made individually, but the clinician in small settings or locales is careful not to choose some clients to favor with continued contact, denying others whose feelings may be quite hurt should they learn of the distinction.

Since we believe that much clinical work is ongoing, we often choose to let clients know that they can attempt to contact us in the future if they decide that they would like to do further work. However, clinicians must be careful that they do not make promises that they cannot keep. Aware of the way situations and schedules can change, we do not promise that we will always be available to work with clients in the future. Hopefully we can suggest that the agency and others like ourselves will be available if we are not, giving the client alternatives in case the familiar service or agency closes for good.

Giving and Receiving Mementos

Clients may ask for a picture or for mementos of the work together. Again, depending on theoretical orientation, agency policy, and individual style, pictures or mementos may or may not be given. Clinicians—especially those who work with children, teens, or groups—may join clients for a photograph that acts as memory of a cherished experience together. With the advent of videotaping, clients may have a different request: "You know how we did that videotaping? Well, could I get you and me on videotape, so I can have something to remember what we did?" Clinicians should consult a supervisor before acting on such requests.

As we noted in Chapter 9, clinicians may give clients a small gift at the end of the relationship as a symbol or reminder of the work that they have done together. It can be a concrete gift or even a note.

> *When Moses left the residence, I wanted him to have something to hang onto if things got tough when he went home. I wrote him the following letter:*
>
> Dear Moses,
>
> It was good yesterday to watch you leave the house—and our work together—with such good confidence and skills for your work back in your "real" home. I could see how excited your dad was to get you back.
>
> You said you never got a letter, so I thought I would send this short note to say, "Way to go!" I want you to hang onto this and check it out if you get low. We all think you have what it takes to make it, and we're wishing you luck and courage every step of the way.
>
> High fives from all of us at The Grove!
>
> Your counselor,
> Kareem Batts

As we discussed in Chapter 10, clients may bring termination gifts to the clinician. As with other gifts, their suitability and meaning should be carefully addressed.

Some community agencies may have bulletin boards on which pictures of clients and activities are displayed. Clinicians need to think carefully about confidentiality, getting clients' permission before displaying any pictures in which clients are visible. Clinicians should also think about the effects on all clients if only some clients' pictures are displayed or if gifts from some clients are visible.

Saying Good-Bye

In time-limited or task-focused clinical work, saying good-bye is a fairly straightforward and simple task and occurs much as it does in regular good-byes following any association. Participants acknowledge the end of the meeting or meetings, appreciate what each has contributed, and wish each other well. Handshakes are usually exchanged, and the counselor walks the client to the door or waiting room, depending on their usual practice of leave-taking. Emotional reactions and protests about ending are rarely anticipated, as the focus has been more on tasks to be accomplished and the client's reliance on self, family, and community resources than on the counselor's presence.

By contrast, in clinical contracts in which the clinical relationship itself has been a primary focus or a therapeutic holding environment, the last meeting may follow searching and wide-ranging discussions of achievements, regrets, work yet to be done, past losses, gains, and readiness to proceed without the clinician. Whereas those discussions may have had a graver or more affective coloration, the final good-bye is usually more interactive and upbeat—a positive sendoff after much good work together. Sometimes a quiet celebration or other ritual—such as an exchange of small gifts—will be used to focus on the good-bye as a kind of celebratory launching.

While we recognize that the final good-bye may be sad, we always attempt to refocus clients on achievements and possibilities (Fortune, 1987). We find it helpful to say that we'll be picturing them doing something they've longed for and intended to do, such as graduate, stay clean and sober, or parent successfully. The clinician attempts to have clients remember him or her as someone who is permanently in their corner, who believes in them, and who is rooting for them.

CLIP 11.2
Tasks and Skills
of Ending

EXERCISE 11.6 *Saying Good-Bye*

In groups of four, practice in pairs the final moments of saying good-bye and exiting. Practice several kinds of good-byes, including from public places, from office settings, from a client's apartment, or after a shared subway ride following a meeting at another agency. Discuss your experience and feelings as both clinician and client. What have you learned from this exercise?

Follow-Up and Evaluation

Clinicians may conduct follow-up evaluations after the end of clinical work. These evaluations may be formal, involving tests and other assessment measures as discussed in Chapter 6, or they may be informal check-ins. Follow-up evaluations can occur one month, two months, or even years after the initial work. At times these follow-up meetings may serve as a reinforcer of the previous work together, reminding the client of the strengths and resources they have and the skills they developed during the course of the clinical relationship. Often the client will discuss how he or she is able to use the learning from the clinical relationship in other arenas with other problems.

Example

> *Client:* Well, it's been six months since I saw you.
>
> *Clinician:* How's it been going, Roland? (The clinician explores Roland's anxiety attacks and how he is doing at work and with Brenda.)
>
> *Client:* You know, Brenda has gone back to school. The other night she was a wreck about an exam she had to take. I taught her those relaxation exercises you taught me and she calmed down. It was neat to be the helper for once.
>
> *Clinician:* I'm glad they were helpful. What a great thing you did for her.
>
> *Client:* Yeah, I'm pretty proud that I can use what I learned here.

Planned Breaks, Interruptions, Transfers, and Abrupt Endings

Planned Breaks

Sometimes a clinician and client will decide together that a great deal has been accomplished and that it is now time for a planned break, during which the client will go for a time without face-to-face visits with the clinician. In advance of this break, they schedule a future appointment in which to review the client's interim experience, and to decide only then whether further professional assistance is indicated. Sometimes these planned breaks are a part of the termination process.

> *At the clubhouse, a day program for people who have been in an inpatient psychiatric hospital, we have a gradual termination process. We slowly decrease the number of days that the client comes to the clubhouse until they are coming only once a week. After a while, we will suggest that the member take a one month "vacation" from the center, but we always set up a follow-up visit to see what the experience was like. Often a client will take repeated "vacations" before he or she finally feels ready to leave for good.*

Interruptions

There are times when the work between clinician and client is interrupted, occasioning a need for purposeful work on the process of ending contact either temporarily or permanently. A clinician or client may become ill, pregnant, take a long trip—all of which may require an interruption at some point, although a return is anticipated.

I had been working as a rehabilitation counselor at a nursing home for three years when my husband got a sabbatical from his college teaching job. He was offered a six-month fellowship in Montana, and we decided that I would join him there. I took a leave from my job, and, let me tell you, it was hard to say good-bye to all the clients. I wasn't sure which of them would still be there when I returned. I reassured the clients that I would be returning in September. I told them where I was going, and I said I would think of them.

The use of a symbolic object is helpful in sustaining a feeling of connection between the client and the clinician. This is especially true with children, who may need a concrete reminder of the clinician's existence.

When the college interns leave the preschool for winter break, we actually use it as a learning experience. Kalina was going home to Hawaii, so we took out a world map and showed the children where Kalina was going. We brought in pictures of Hawaii and had Kalina send postcards each week. That way the children would remember her when she returned.

Even when the interruption or break is anticipated or time-limited, client and clinician may go through a process similar to other endings. The clinician prepares the client for the interruption, leaves the room to talk about the feelings the interruption evokes, and attempts to get closure for the work completed thus far. Clinicians must remember that, although they plan to return, it is possible that the client may not be there when they return. In fact, the clinician may not return.

A couple of years ago, two therapists were murdered while they were on vacation. I was one of a team of clinicians that stepped in to work with their clients after their deaths. It really brought home to me how important it is to realize that you can never promise you will be back. You can promise you will try, but never that you will always be there.

Transitions to Another Clinician

At times, the client may be transferred to another clinician. This can happen during a planned interruption, in which case it is anticipated that the original clinician and client will reconnect. It can also happen when the client will be seeing another clinician after terminating with the original clinician.

If the client is terminating, the clinician can offer to speak with the new clinician. This can help facilitate the new work and help the clinician learn about the client and perhaps avoid old pitfalls. Some clients will like to have a sense of continuity in the work, and they may hope that this conversation will prevent them from having to repeat everything with the new clinician. Other clients may refuse permission for the clinicians to speak with each other, preferring to start with a clean slate.

When the client will be seeing another clinician, the original clinician can help the client prepare for work with the new clinician.

Example

> *Clinician:* Last week you told me that you and Brenda are going to see a couples therapist after we finish our work together.
>
> *Client:* Yeah, Brenda wants to work on "our communication," as she calls it.
>
> *Clinician:* What do you think that will be like? (They explore Roland's anticipations and fears.)
>
> *Clinician:* Do you think you will talk about our work together?
>
> *Client:* I don't know.
>
> *Clinician:* I want you to know that I feel fine about your talking about what worked and didn't work in our relationship. Sometimes people feel that they are betraying their old counselor if they talk to their new counselor about stuff they did or feelings they had with their old counselor. It can help future work to explore with your new counselor—both the things that helped and those that didn't.

If the client is seeing another clinician only temporarily and anticipates continuing with the original clinician, the two clinicians usually speak—but again, only after the client has given written permission, which is kept in the client's file. It can ease transitions if the original clinician introduces the client to the "covering" clinician before leaving.

The covering clinician can often feed useful information about the relationship back to the original clinician, although being careful never to compete to be the "better helper." Any concerns or questions that the covering clinician has about the work should be shared directly with the clinician rather than with the client. The covering clinician becomes a team member and assumes the same ethical and legal obligations as though he or she were the primary clinician.

> *When one of my partners was taking an extended vacation, she asked me to see a client of hers. She described the client as someone who was very shy and had a hard time talking. I was quite surprised when I met the client, who seemed anything but shy. After I had met with him a couple of times, I told him that I had expected him to be much more reticent because that was how his therapist had described him to me. He told me that he felt very uncomfortable talking to any women, specifically professional women. He was comfortable talking with me because I was a man. We explored the issue and discussed how he might raise the issue with his therapist when she returned. When she did return, she told me how great it was that her client had seen me. He had talked with her about what we had discussed and it really changed the nature of their work together. She threatened to go away again so that I could "do consultations" with all her clients.*

Abrupt Endings

So far, we have spoken of a termination or ending process. Sometimes such a process may not be possible. The client may abruptly leave a session, simply not show up, or cancel future appointments. The clinician whose client has stopped coming usually attempts some sort of *outreach*—a phone call or a letter or, in some cases, a home visit. Decisions about outreach should be discussed with a supervisor. If the client does not return, the clinician can attempt to get some closure through a *letter of termination*.

Example

Dear Juan,

I haven't heard from you since our last meeting on July 23rd. I have tried to contact you by phone and letter. I will assume that you have made the decision to stop our work at this time.

If you decide that you would like to return to get more closure on our work or if you feel that I can be of help to you in the future, please feel free to contact me at the agency.

It has been a pleasure getting to know you. I hope that you will have success in getting your GED as you planned.

Sincerely,
Rebecca Schwartz

The Clinician Feels the Loss

Abrupt endings are particularly difficult for the clinician, but all endings evoke feelings in the clinician. As the time to end approaches, clinicians can find that, like the client's feelings, their feelings may come out in behavior. They may lose their appointment book; double-book a client who is terminating; or find themselves feeling sad, anxious, or relieved.

Clinicians working in health or hospice settings often encounter the very moving experience of working closely with clients with terminal health conditions. These clients know they have little time left and understandably do not want to lose a clinician with whom they are able to share whatever they wish about their dying. Under special circumstances, a clinician who so wishes may continue to meet with a dying client even after leaving an agency and other clients. Consultation with a supervisor can help resolve dilemmas around whether and with whom to continue and how to arrange to keep seeing a client until death occurs. This is clinical work at its most human, characterized by flexibility, availability, and respectful adaptation to the needs of clients and loved ones.

As clinicians, we form attachments to our clients and can have great investment in their well-being, just as they are often strongly invested in the work with us and in our presence, caring, and encouragement. This is a human relationship of some intensity as well as a working partnership, and its attenuation or ending affects clinicians as well as clients.

◉◉ CLIP 11.3
Clinicians'
Reflections

I hated ending with Charysse. I had literally watched her grow up. She had been in the after-school program at the center when I was a rec counselor, and I had coached her on the basketball team. Then she'd been one of the kids in the alcohol and drug group, and she eventually became a peer counselor. Now, she was having a baby and moving to Des Moines with Raffie. (I knew him, too.) When our last meeting was over, I walked into my supervisor's office and just cried. I was so happy for her and for the new life she was starting, but it was so sad to see her go.

Conclusion

Whether planned or unplanned and whether initiated by client, clinician, or outside forces, the ending of the clinical relationship provides an opportunity for new learning and growth. Good endings can help clients increase their relational capacity, knowledge, and sensitivity and take both the work and the relationship away with them as internalized and sustaining inner resources, available for use as long as there is memory.

Suggested Readings

Further readings on termination include:

Baird, Brian N. (1996). *The internship, practicum, and field placement handbook: A guide for helping professionals.* Upper Saddle River, NJ: Prentice-Hall. (Chapter 12: Closing Cases.)

Fair, Susan M., & Bressler, Joanna M. (1992). Therapist-initiated termination of psychotherapy. *The Clinical Supervisor, 10*(1), 171–189.

Fisch, Richard, Weakland, John, & Segal, Lynn. (1982). *The tactics of change: Doing therapy briefly.* New York: Jossey-Bass.

Fortune, Anne E. (1987). Grief only? Client and social worker reactions to termination. *Clinical Social Work Journal, 15*(2), 159–171.

Gutheil, J. A. (1993). Rituals and termination procedures. *Smith College Studies in Social Work, 63*(2), 163–176.

Levinson, Hilliard. (1977). Termination of psychotherapy: Some salient issues. *Social Casework, 58,* 480–489.

The following are good resources on transferring clients to another clinician:

Robinson, Floyd F., Hitchinson, Roger L., Barrick, Ann Louise, & Uhl, Angela N. (1986). Reassigning clients: Practices used by counseling centers. *Journal of Counseling Psychology, 33,* 465–469.

Wapner, J. H., Klein, J. G., Friedlander, M. L., & Andrasik, F. J. (1986). Transferring psychotherapy clients: State of the art. *Professional Psychology: Research and Practice, 6,* 492–496.

CHAPTER 12

Professional Issues: Ongoing Education and Self-Care

In previous chapters we have elaborated on the foundation knowledge, values, skills, and activities that constitute clinical practice as it addresses human prospects, problems, and process. To be effective, clinicians have to develop and sustain high degrees of understanding, compassion, skill, and commitment. Refining these capacities requires lifelong education, personal growth, and careful attention to the care of the professional self. This chapter addresses numerous ways in which ongoing education and self-care can be assured over the course of a long and fulfilling career.

Ongoing Education

Clinical education does not end with the diploma; it is a lifelong learning process. As clinicians, we continue our education through supervision, consultation, reading about current clinical research and intervention techniques, and attending continuing education and professional development courses.

Supervision

Most clinical internships provide the intern with an individual supervisor with whom to meet for weekly supervision. In some settings, the learner will have two supervisors: an adminstrative supervisor who assigns cases, arranges coverage, and oversees the general work of the clinician; and a clinical supervisor who attends to the development of values, knowledge, and skills in clinical practice with clients. The setting may also provide group supervision in which all interns gather to review their work with each other. Supervision is a crucial part of clinical education and is not something that occurs only while in school. We believe that all clinicians should have some form of ongoing supervision, whether it is individual, group, or peer supervision.

Individual Supervision

Good individual clinical supervision parallels a good clinical relationship in several respects. It provides a sustaining environment for learning and growth; it helps potentiate the learner's strengths, skills, and development; and it models relational, assessment, and problem-solving skills. While primarily task-focused, clinician and supervisor may also examine the moment or process the process in the supervisory relationship. Supervisors act as a backstop in times of crisis, and they frequently model composure and purposeful behavior under fire.

> *I remember the first time I was working with a client who was suicidal. I felt quite out of my depth. I called my supervisor to tell him what my client had just said about thinking about killing herself. His response was, "Well, let's think how we should respond." I can't tell you how relieved I felt with his use of the word "we." It made me feel that I wasn't alone. I felt I could relax into the comfort of our team. He was in this with me.*

Clinicians do not ordinarily just "work their way up" to supervising. Supervisors are generally selected for their clinical acumen, relational skills, and commitment to the well-being and growth of clients and learners alike. They are usually required to have at least a master's degree in social work, counseling, psychology, or another human services discipline, plus additional years of post-master's practice under a skilled supervisor. Often they will have taken one or more professional supervision courses as part of their continuing clinical education, and they will have worked with a variety of clients and colleagues in a number of different settings, bringing rich experience to supervisory sessions.

Regular supervision is one of a clinician's best ways to monitor progress toward goals, as well as personal actions and reactions in relation to clients and client material (Kadushin, 1997). Verbatim written, audiotaped, or videotaped recordings may be made of clinician-client dialogues specifically for the purpose of reviewing the focus and flow of conversation, as well as the intent and appropriateness of the clinician's actions and verbalizations. Supervisors and supervisees often later review and comment together on sequences of interaction for purposes of learning (Urdang, 1979). This process of supervision is similar to the clinical skills learning process suggested in this text, with a parallel focus on examining and trying out skills and receiving feedback from others that will help enhance skill execution.

Beginning supervision often focuses on the purpose and goals of the interview and how well these were realized, on the client's participation, and on the clinician's initiatives and reactions. Supervision can also focus on steps in the problem-solving process, what is or isn't being resolved, and where plans or intentions may have gotten derailed. Joint assessment thinking can occasion a rethinking of goals or strategies. Plans are often made for next sessions, with the learner being asked to hazard guesses about what may occur in order to enhance accurate anticipation. In time, after repeated supervisory feedback and experience reflecting on the complex ebb and flow of professional encounters, clinicians usually become more and more comfortable and adept at spotting problems before or when they occur and at changing course fairly rapidly. Again, this self-observation and growth process very much mirrors the process by which clients learn to change their own thoughts, feelings, behaviors, and relationships.

Supervisors often model the attitudes, reactions, and listening-responding skills that they hope supervisees will incorporate into their developing practice repertory. Certainly, effective supervisors listen closely to the supervisory process, trying to join with the perspective of both the client and the learner (Dean, 1984). They try to help learners recognize and attend to subtleties of theme and expression in their own conversations with clients, supervisor, and others. Supervisors can also help supervisees track the content of interviews to improve attunement, focus, close following, and purposeful use of self.

Although "therapizing" the learner (probing for painful details of personal history) is avoided, supervisors are usually ready to hear a brief outline of the clinician's problems or experience if either is grossly disrupting learning or work with clients. As problems with interviewing inevitably arise as a result of the complex dynamics of human exchange, supervisors try to find the right blend of minimal exploration of the learner's story and respect for the learner's privacy and personal boundaries (Kaiser, 1997).

Cora was a 42-year-old woman who came to the clinic to get some help with child-rearing. While I was seeing her, her father was diagnosed with bone cancer, adding even more stress to her care-giving responsibilities. I didn't specifically talk about the issue with Duane, my supervisor, but it came up in passing as I said something about how Cora was late because she stopped at the hospital to visit her father. Duane started asking me questions and it became clear that I hadn't talked with Cora enough about how her father's illness was affecting her. My supervisor said he was curious about my lack of follow-through on this, and then I told him about my mother's recent cancer diagnosis. We talked a little about how my own feelings as a daughter of someone who was dying of cancer may have gotten in the way of my attending to an important issue for Cora. Throughout the conversation, I thought Duane was being careful to look at the interface but not to push me too hard to talk about my mother. While he was caring, Duane made it clear that he was interested in talking about my mother's illness only to the extent that it might be affecting my work. At the end of our meeting, he said that I might want to talk to a counselor myself about all the stresses I was coping with. I started to cry and said I thought he had a good point.

Dating and sexual relationships between supervisors and supervisees are generally prohibited in ethical codes because of the potential for exploitation. This is an unequal relationship in which one party has the power to evaluate, sanction, and even dismiss the other in the professional domain of the relationship (Jacobs, 1991).

To normalize the struggles of the learning process, clinical supervisors may occasionally self-disclose, sharing some of their own missteps and dilemmas as continuing learners. They may also periodically assign readings about the process of clinical work or learning. Supervisory discussions may also incorporate learning from the intern's school or training program, and supervisees may bring in materials that give the supervisor new information or perspective, heightening a feeling of reciprocal influence and respect.

One of a supervisor's most painful responsibilities is that of setting limits on those clinician behaviors that are inappropriate to the professional role. Such behaviors might include habitual lateness, rudeness, or judgmentalism affecting client care or the formal learning process; use of substances on the job; repeated failures to carry out assignments; relating inappropriately with clients; or other ethics codes violations. If discussion, review of standards, and warnings fail to alter behaviors, clinicians can be sanctioned, put on notice, or terminated for cause. They may also be reported to their state licensing boards and professional organizations for further investigation (Kaiser, 1997).

The diversity of students and clients today reflects the changing demographics of the 21st century in ways that practicum supervisors, training faculties, and agency staff may not, for the human services have been as slow as other sectors of the economy in hiring and promoting ethnocultural minorities. Students thus may or may not be able to find the range of minority colleagues and mentors they might wish to learn with (such as people of color, gay or lesbian persons, people with disabilities). Whether supervision is intra- or intercultural, supervisors work to help learners develop a range of models and provide students the opportunity to speak frankly about problems the setting may pose for them (McRoy, Freeman, Logan, & Blackmon, 1986).

> *I always wished I had a gay or lesbian supervisor with whom I could talk over my questions about whether and how I might come out to my clients, and whether it would be okay to talk in the luchroom about activities with my partner when everybody else talked about their weekends. I had heard there were other gay people in the agency, but they weren't out, and I didn't know what to do.*

E X E R C I S E 12.1   *Reactions to Supervision*

In your journal, record your reactions, both positive and negative, to supervision you have received in the past. Based on your experience, make a list of guidelines or watchwords that you would give to a new supervisor. Note any special needs that arose for you in your work, and whether your supervision was helpful or unhelpful. Be prepared to discuss your experiences in class.

Group Supervision

Clinicians also benefit greatly from weekly group supervision—education and support meetings where discussions of clinician-client dialogues, learning dilemmas, techniques, and case-planning concerns affirm the mutuality of the learning process. Supervisors can often arrange for interns and clinicians in several neighboring agencies to come together at intervals for education and support. The agency may also arrange for clinicians to be supervised by more than one person or discipline in order to vary the learning experience, tap many sources of expertise, and enrich the feedback and exchange process between individuals and disciplines.

> *Isaac was a great individual supervisor. He taught me tons of stuff about how to work with clients. I felt like I could share all my concerns with him and that he would help me figure out what to do. But I was also glad that I was in group supervision. I liked hearing about how other people were doing things. The group gave me an opportunity to gets lots of different feedback, and then with Isaac I could sit down and see which felt right to me.*

Peer Supervision

Following completion of their formal education, clinicians continue to use supervision to enhance their effectiveness. They may continue to have an individual supervisor or to participate in group supervision with an identified supervisor. Often, clinicians establish *peer supervision* groups, in which two or more clinicians share their work with each other and offer feedback and support.

> *When I worked at the community mental health agency, about four of us were considered senior clinicians. We were the supervisors to the new staff and student interns, but we realized that we also wanted support and help with our own work. We set up a peer supervision group where we took turns presenting our cases to each other.*

EXERCISE 12.2 *Peer Supervision*

Many of the exercises you have done in this book have suggested that you get feedback from peers. In small groups, attempt to give positive feedback to your colleagues about the peer supervision you have gotten from them. Be as specific as possible about what you have gained from them.

The amount and quality of supervision a beginning clinician can anticipate after completing formal degree studies is quite varied, often depending on local resources and developments in managed care. There is a widespread impression that the quality and extent of supervision are diminishing in many settings because of agency cutbacks and administrative demands that supervisors provide more direct service or case management functions and devote less time to supervision, staff education, and interagency collaborations that are not income producing. State licensure in the helping professions usually mandates specified amounts per week of advanced clinical supervision; finding employment in agencies that reliably provide it is another matter entirely. Many newly graduating clinicians today must purchase private supervision or settle for a very checkered learning experience on the job. It is the clinician's responsibility to continue advancing his or her knowledge and skills through supervision, specialized training, and workshops. Local and state clinical societies and organizations are very helpful in locating appropriate resources.

Consultation

Consultation is a process whereby clinicians at all levels of experience reach outside their normal learning and supervisory relationships to benefit from the perspective and advice of a seasoned mentor valued for special knowledge and skills in certain areas of practice. Consultation is often sought when the clinician feels unusually "stuck" or confused in work with a client. The consultation may focus on the client, on the clinician, on the relationship, or on surrounding systems influencing care.

Often, contact with the consultant is short term, for ad hoc brainstorming and formulation of potential strategies. The clinician or other involved parties present a thumbnail sketch of the client, the ongoing work, the relationship, and the reason for consultation. The consultant may interview the client separately, with the clinician, or in front of the group in order to elicit information or demonstrate strategy. The following are examples of several different uses of consultation.

Examples

- A clinician in a group home for latency-aged children may seek a consultation on how to handle a specific client's bed-wetting. Others on the staff may ask to attend to learn more about the problem in general.

- A teen client assigned to a clinical intern is showing signs of psychotic thinking. The intern's supervisor hasn't worked with psychosis before, and so refers the intern to a colleague in the clinic's outpatient psychiatric services for consultation about the client. The consultant may advise further outpatient evaluation of the client to see whether medication or further family involvement is indicated.

A Cambodian psychologist consults monthly to medical rounds at a neighborhood health clinic, commenting on any special ethnic issues or concerns arising in work with Cambodian patients of the clinic.

A client tells her therapist that he doesn't feel like a good match for her. After much discussion, he suggests that, before the client makes any decision about ending the work, they consult with a third party who might help them either resolve issues or arrange a referral to another provider.

A clinician seeking consultation about a client must protect the client's right to confidentiality. Identifying information about the client is concealed, and if the consultant is to see a video or hear a tape recording, the clinician must seek the client's written approval.

Sometimes the consultation is focused entirely on the clinician, on learning a new skill or dealing with an issue that has arisen in the course of work with a client.

Examples

After an unexpected client death upsets many staff, a practitioner specializing in trauma work with teams is invited to consult with staff as a group, with an agenda of dealing with the death and the staff's sense of loss and failure.

A clinician who is pregnant may hire a consultant to advise her on ways to tell her clients, and to help her prepare for possible client reactions to her disclosure.

Finally, supervisors and supervisees may seek informal consultation with experienced colleagues if tensions between them disrupt the supervisory learning process. Educational programs provide faculty liaisons with whom interns can consult directly about such problems, and the liaison is ready to participate in problem resolution should such a course prove advisable.

As outside advice givers who are at arm's length from the agency or practice, consultants are usually not held liable for their consultees' work the way that direct supervisors are. Sometimes they follow up to see what came of their advice, but frequently they do not. The detachment of their role often increases objectivity in approaching the problems to be addressed in the consultation. Clinicians should always remember that their agencies and supervisors may be legally and ethically responsible for their behaviors and, therefore, always have the final say in the conduct of professional practice.

Personal Therapy as a Learning Experience

The clinician's own therapy can make a significant contribution to clinical education and practice. In fact, some graduate programs suggest that interns have personal therapy. Furthermore, interns often seek therapy because the process of clinical learning stimulates curiosity and interest in exploring their own stories further.

The experience of being a client can heighten the clinician's appreciation of the dynamics and skills involved in the helping process. In addition, clinicians can use their own therapy to explore those personal dynamics and blind spots that may interfere with their effective use of self in their relationships with clients. Finally, a clinician may seek therapy when a client's issue stimulates unresolved issues in the clinician. A supervisor may help the clinician identify these issues, and the clinician may decide to explore them more thoroughly in therapy. The clinician must seek therapy outside of the work environment, however, as professional codes of ethics and standards for practice prohibit dual relationships with a supervisor.

Professional Literature

Clinicians keep up with advances in the field through the professional literature. Clinicians often subscribe to the major professional journals in their discipline, some of which are provided as a benefit of membership in professional organizations. The *Journal of Counseling and Development* is a benefit of membership in the American Counseling Association. The journal *Social Work* comes with membership in the National Association of Social Workers. And all members of the American Psychological Association receive the *American Psychologist*. Clinicians working in specific fields often subscribe to journals on child welfare, journals on alcohol and drug abuse, or publications related to work in vocational or rehabilitation counseling. These journals provide clinicians with the opportunity to keep abreast of changing developments in practice and research in their fields. Professional organizations often have newsletters and magazines (such as *Counseling Today, The NASW Newsletter,* and the *APA Monitor*) that provide more current information about what's happening in the profession.

In addition to journals and newsletters, clinicians will read books about areas of treatment and special topics of interest to them. This reading is a vital part of the professional's ongoing responsibility to maintain expertise and to practice competently.

> *I have a growing library of books and articles. While I was a student, I started a file folder in which I put articles that I found particularly helpful. Over the years, that file folder has become a file cabinet! We often share articles at the clinic. There's a space on the bulletin board where we can post something we find useful.*

The Internet provides other quick ways for clinicians to gather information. The major professional organizations have Web sites. There are list-servers and on-line discussion groups on a number of topics of interest to clinicians. Clinicians need to remember to be very careful about protecting confidentiality. They also need to be aware that there may be no way to check the accuracy of the identities and credentials of the people involved in these lists and discussion groups.

> *With the advent of the worldwide web, when I want information about a particular topic, I can use my traditional methods of doing a PsychLit search. But I also belong to a number of psychology listserves. I was looking for a good article on termination the other day and put my request on the listserve. I got back some great leads from colleagues across the country.*

Continuing Education

Most states require that clinicians seeking licensure show evidence that they have completed the stipulated amounts of continuing clinical education before they can renew their licenses. Continuing education programs may focus on working with particular *client populations* (for example, elderly people; children; gay, lesbian, or bisexual people; specific ethnic or cultural groups); with *specific problems or disorders* (sexual abuse, personality disorders, compulsive behaviors, depression); or with *specific methods or techniques* (short-term interventions, eye-movement desensitization techniques, play therapy, journal writing). Continuing education courses may last for a couple of hours or a couple of days; or they may be more extensive, meeting weekly for a couple of months, or intensely for a week or two.

Continuing education affords an ongoing opportunity to grow in self-awareness and the purposeful use of self, to learn new skills, and to further hone one's competencies. Courses often summarize problems in use of self within the special area of practice, provide bibliographic resources relating to practice, and demonstrate problem-solving strategies or techniques. Some courses divide learners into small discussion or role-play groups in much the same way that formal educational programs do.

A special form of continuing education is that offered by advanced certificate programs, postgraduate internships, fellowships, and specialty training. These programs sometimes allow enrollees to see clients with designated problems (domestic violence, alcoholism, trauma) at specialized sites and under senior supervision.

Contributing to the Education of Others

Clinicians are not just consumers of education; they also contribute to the education of others through teaching, research, consultation, supervision, and scholarship. These efforts may begin while individuals are still in school and are often carried out with colleagues or mentors. Educational exchange and feedback among clinicians provide rich satisfaction and can be a stimulating addition to work. Such exchanges will be greatly increased globally in the coming decades, as technological advances shorten the distance between human service providers, clients, researchers, and educators around the world.

Self-Care: Taking Care While Giving Care

If we believe in quality clinical work and the contributions it can make to a better world, then it is important that we last as compassionate, effective, and ethical providers so that we may perpetuate clinical practice at high levels of commitment and competence. Practitioners must come into the work with their eyes wide open, prepared to nourish and renew themselves and connect with others for support, validation, relaxation, and enjoyment.

Stresses of Clinical Work

All work is stressful to some degree. In complex societies, most working people have to contend with the stresses of time and resource pressures, complex communication networks, working within systems of unequal power and privilege, and compromises to ideals that must be made in order to get work done.

Certain stresses, however, are unique to clinical work in the human services. Clinicians work many hours a day with clients whose stories are often marked by tragedy, violence, cruelty, and human indifference to suffering. It is hard to put this work down at day's end, especially when emergencies suddenly arise that will only worsen if left untended. There is a great tendency for clinicians to work extra hours, take their work home with them, or remain on beeper call for understaffed agencies.

Michael Sussman (1992) summarized emerging research, which indicates that many clinicians learned early in life to overdo for others in order to try to earn love or avoid conflict in their troubled families of origin. There they were inducted into self-sacrificing roles to be carried out "for the good of others." The influence of these early roles may underlie much of the *workaholism* that characterizes the working style of many clinicians, practice settings, and practice educational programs. The very other-centeredness that is the hallmark of so much good clinical work can also strain the resources of clinicians and draw their attention away from their own survival needs.

Some stories and events encountered at work are also so troubling that they cannot simply be left in a folder at the end of a day. Instead, they continue disconcertingly to haunt clinicians' thoughts—sometimes even their dreams. Clinicians repeatedly exposed to traumatic stories may absorb clients' experiences so extensively that they develop symptoms of *vicarious traumatization* (McCann & Pearlman, 1990). In vicarious or secondary trauma, the clinician may manifest many symptoms similar to the symptoms of the clients who directly experienced the trauma: restlessness, sleep problems, startle reactions, irritability, aggression, depression, apathy, social withdrawal, and anxiety .

Burnout, or *compassion fatigue,* is an occupational hazard in the helping professions (Figley, 1995). It often results from clinicians' interacting intensely with people with many severe problems, over a long period and with poor support. The symptoms of compassion fatigue include: physical, mental, and emotional exhaustion ("I'm worn out"); insensitivity to others ("I don't care anymore"); a sense of futility or hopelessness about one's actions ("Nothing is going to make any difference anyway"); and a sense of isolation and invalidation ("Nobody cares anyway").

Historically, clinicians have too often been underpaid, undervalued, and undersupported. At the same time, they regularly observe that many other professions and occupations enjoy more pay, benefits, and respect than they do in spite of years of education and experience or advanced degrees.

> *After a master's degree and thirty years of experience, I am making less money than my nephew, who's a year out of college and working in a big accounting firm. It does bug me.*

Clinicians may feel powerless to influence the larger systems that so affect their work with clients. Clinical work is often carried out within large systems in which individual practitioners or disciplines may experience very little power. Changes in welfare, Medicaid, or Head Start funding may have disastrous effects on clients yet often seem beyond the control of clinicians. Very often practitioners work at the behest of managers or quality assurance reviewers with little background and experience in human services, and many hours formerly given to direct service may now be taken up with paperwork justifying care.

Practitioners may also be isolated in their roles, finding little time available to meet and share support with colleagues. They may work alone in offices or spend precious free moments logging client data into computers. They may be out in the field most of the day doing home visits, or they may travel from setting to setting, making most of their contacts with colleagues by cell phone or fax.

Thus, clinicians may at times experience a kind of isolation, disempowerment, lack of control, and disenchantment similar to that experienced by many of their clients. These stresses often compromise the immune system, contributing to emotional and physical disorders and symptoms such as head, stomach, and back pain; insomnia; and a pervasive feeling of uneasiness or tension. Some clinicians turn to substance use to cope with the pressures of the job and begin to have serious relationship problems at home. In extreme circumstances, clinicians may engage in unethical activities or relationships with clients, such as financial or sexual exploitation. The stresses of clinical work can take their toll unless clinicians are vigilant about their own well-being.

In your journal, record the major stresses that affect clinical practice in your area. What effects do you think these stresses have on practitioners? What stresses have affected *you* so far? What kinds of things do you think you can do to diminish the impact of these stresses in your own life and work?

Self as Instrument

Personal awareness, attunement, empathy, and readiness to listen and respond to others are the clinician's basic "tools of the trade." Where the physician might use the stethoscope or X ray, or the plumber a wrench and pliers, clinicians use the professionally developed self to relate with clients, conduct assessments, and develop responses and interventions. To preserve the precious instrument of self, clinicians have to become as educated about and responsive to themselves as they are in regard to their clients. They have to know who they are and what has shaped and motivated them toward clinical work, and they need to be well aware of the forces that sustain or undermine them personally.

Unless properly boundaried and replenished, the clinician's very gifts of attunement, caring, empathizing, and responsivity can become hazards to long-term well-being. Overuse or misuse of the instrument can lead to its deterioration. Furthermore, when clinicians are tired, distracted, or resentful of work's burdens, clients suffer from diminished caring, attention, and responsivity, as do clinicians themselves. It is clear that we must take care of ourselves while giving care to others (Dillon, 1990).

Strategies of Self-Care

Addressing the unmet needs of professional caregivers, Judith Jordan (1991a) invites clinicians to increase their own self-nurture by developing and sustaining *self-empathy*—the capacity to notice, care about, and respond to our own felt needs as generously as we attend to the needs of others. As with clients, strategies of *self-care* often involve thinking differently, behaving differently, and connecting with others differently in order to experience more support, validation, self-actualization, and effectiveness at home and at work.

We believe that one of the hardest things clinicians of all ages and experience levels have to do is to give themselves permission to be good to themselves, and to *take time and space* for themselves without feeling selfish, guilty, or that they are wasting time. Many clinicians seem to believe that they can go on and on, overdoing for others without this overextension affecting their well-being, work satisfaction, or capacity to provide appropriate and caring services. Or they may think that they can work for unsupportive or exploitative employers and not eventually pay a price in motivation and caring.

Fundamental to self-care are *good health practices*, which sustain both energy and the body's natural immune responses to protect against physical, mental, and emotional problems. Clinicians who intend to last stay fit through regular exercise and healthy dietary practices, minimizing use of substances like caffeine, nicotine, alcohol, or drugs, which trigger high-low cycles that in turn affect energy, concentration, and mood. When work is largely confined to interior or closed spaces with poor air quality and artificial lighting, we try to take brief periodic breaks outside in fresh air and sunlight. When we can afford the time, we try to walk down hallways or between floors instead of phoning or e-mailing, so that we can exercise and refresh ourselves between tasks.

Clinicians may need to seek professional counseling for themselves or loved ones when challenges or crises significantly disrupt their lives or impair their professional functioning. Professional organizations can provide referral resources for therapy or consultation for clinicians in need. There are confidential programs in which impaired clinicians can receive specialized help.

As clinicians, we need to get better at deflecting rather than internalizing the undeserved attacks or diminishments that may come our way in the course of professional careers. While remaining open to constructive feedback and new learning, clinicians need to develop the equivalent of an *emotional heat shield* that will protect them against unwarranted blame for failure to eradicate society's long-standing problems and inequities.

Sometimes clinicians need to talk together more about their positive feelings about the work in staff meetings. While ventilation in peer groups is a good release, negative ventilation alone can also render participants depressed and feeling hopeless. We find that negative ventilation always needs to be balanced with some *focus on the positive.* We always need to keep an eye on the bottom line of service to clients, to focus periodically on some heartening stories of positive developments with clients or on small, positive incidents in the profession, the agency, or the surrounding area. We need to remember our competencies and our ongoing base of support when feeling disempowered, asserting our value and worth through action rather than caving in to passivity or resignation. Just as we ask clients to do, we need to remember more often the ways we have resolved problems in other situations and try to use those same familiar skills to improve our own curent situation, brick by brick.

It can be helpful for clinicians to develop a *personal mission statement* akin to that which guides professions and agencies, with personal goals, objectives, and time lines kept clear and realistic. Personal mission and goal statements can be used as a baseline against which to measure personal fit with current role involvements, work demands, and reward systems.

Clinicians will thus have a plan for self-direction that can help clarify needed connections and the next steps to take toward balancing home and work lives.

E X E R C I S E   12.4 *Personal Mission Statement*

In your journal, write your own personal mission statement. Be sure to include your goals, objectives, and time lines. What resources do you have that will help you achieve those goals? How will you measure your progress toward them? What encouragements will help you persist toward your goals?

Without a doubt, there is little hope of surviving in clinical practice without using the power of *humor* to sustain and refresh. Clinicians often develop shared bulletin boards on which they post favorite cartoons or sayings that make everyone laugh and reflect on the follies of the human condition or the pomposities of clinicians. We are careful not to use humor that hurts or offends.

Connections with others, especially those not directly related to the clinician's workplace, are also crucial to good self-care. These connections can be with friends and family or can occur through activities in which people with similar interests come together to share or create. Singing and theater arts groups; cooking, dance, exercise, and meditation groups—all can provide channels for creative expression, feedback, and friendship.

Many clinicians find that spiritual connections through meditation or formalized religious practice allows them to *connect with forces larger* and more enduring than those with people and activities. Other clinicians feel enriched and energized by connections with fellow professionals or fellow activists working on important political or public health campaigns.

E X E R C I S E   12.5 *Preventing Compassion Fatigue*

In small groups, discuss how you recognize compassion fatigue in yourselves, and describe some of the things that you do successfully to prevent it.

Conclusion

Excellent values, knowledge base, and skills application will be of little use to clients unless clinicians remain fit and balanced in their work and life roles. Clinicians must continue to nourish and update themselves through ongoing education and self-care.

Suggested Readings

Dean, Ruth G. (1984). The role of empathy in supervision. *Clinical Social Work Journal, 12*(2), 129–139.

Figley, Charles. (1995). *Compassion fatigue: Coping with secondary traumatic stress disorder in those who treat the traumatized.* New York: Brunner/Mazel.

Kaiser, Tamara. (1997). *Supervisory relationships: Exploring the human element.* Pacific Grove, CA: Brooks/Cole.

McCann, Lisa, & Pearlman, Laurie Ann. (1990). Vicarious traumatization: A framework for understanding the psychological effects of working with victims. *Journal of Traumatic Stress Studies, 3*(1), 131–149.

Rogers, Carl. (1961). *On becoming a person.* Boston: Houghton Mifflin.

We've Only Just Begun

Like the accumulation of all wisdom, clinical learning is a lifelong process. It is with good reason that a graduation is called a "commencement," as it marks the beginning of learning for life. Completing a course or text on clinical interviewing is also a commencement; it marks the beginning of lifelong learning about clinical knowledge and skills.

This clinical learning will continue through formal learning carried out in agencies and educational and training programs. Reading, reflection, observation of other practitioners, supervisory review, consultation, and in-service training will all build and refine clinical skills.

While journaling and simulation are useful, we still believe that the most effective clinical learning is embedded in relationship. Working alone, we cannot see our blind spots, and we cannot get help from others on those blind spots. We miss the generative "aha!" moments that occur with colleagues and mentors in the lively exchange of confirming and opposing ideas. We also miss chances to get more comfortable in giving and receiving feedback. Through contact with others, we increase the probability of evolving completely novel possibilities that none of us had thought of alone. Empathy, intuition, perception, judgment, and timing will also be improved by feedback from colleagues.

Becoming a clinician involves a serious commitment to self-monitoring and the responsible seeking of consultation and therapy when needed. Because we often work behind closed doors and supervisors can "know" only what we and others tell them, our learning and work calls for a high degree of integrity, respect for the rights of others, the exercise of self-restraint, and a readiness to act to protect others from harm.

Effective clinical learning and practice will also involve taking care of yourself while giving care to others. This is a political and personal necessity. Healthy and imaginative interventions cannot be carried out by overworked, undervalued, or isolated individuals relating chiefly to and through machines. If we are to last as effective practitioners, our well-being has to be as important to us as is the well-being of clients.

Advancing our clinical knowledge and skills will continue to involve practice, practice, practice and re-view, re-view, re-view. Nothing beats seasoning through mastery of a variety of learning challenges with the help of wise and caring mentors and colleagues. In addition to their own personal advocacy to obtain the best teaching available, clinicians can seek the help of their professional organizations to obtain needed resources and advanced training and education.

Beyond this formal learning, we believe that the informal learning "along the way" is equally important in the intentional refinement of clinical skills. A crucial part of this informal learning will involve widening the influences to which we let ourselves be exposed. Clinicians need shared neighborhood, friendship, workplace, and family experiences with each other across color, language, and other cultural barriers. The history of human service organizations sadly demonstrates that these experiences will not be handed to us; we shall have to make them happen with the same courage and caring that brought us into clinical training in the first place.

Another major influence on the shaping of our professional selves and skills is our interactions with clients as teachers. Clinical work is never just a simple process of planning ahead that "she'll do this and then I'll do that." It is precisely the relationship between the participants and the effects of this relationship on the evolution of each conversation and activity that play such an important role in both clinical work and learning.

Clients teach and shape us by their comments, their looks and other nonverbal messages, their complaints or requests that things be said or done differently, and their refusals to go down useless pathways that look so good to us as outsiders to their stories. They also beam and credit us when we "get it right," commend our faithfulness in making important visits after hours, and acknowledge the importance of our concern and efforts as they work to improve their situations and relationships. They teach us to laugh and cry with them, to persist when it's hard, to take a look at ourselves while we're looking at them. They make us change, and these changes often sharpen our vision and soften our edges. Some clients will stay within us forever, just as some of us will stay within them. So, clinical skill and relational capacity are much, much more than "what we do at work"; they are also "who we *become* through work," thanks to the way clients affect us through the interactive process that is the clinical relationship.

Thus, clinical learning is also a life-changing process. No one participating in a process of human exchange can emerge from that exchange unaltered in important ways. The focus on improving relationship skills with clients usually leads to personal growth or to personal therapy to smooth rough edges identified through supervision and self-reflection. It has also been observed that once we get "clinical ears"—the ability to hear and "read" metacommunication in human transactions—we often become more sensitive and attuned noticers, listeners, and responders in our personal relationships as well, so that our private lives become more nourishing and content. Furthermore, meeting new and varied people throughout our careers usually stimulates heightened curiosity and interest in others and often takes us into domains of practice we might never have imagined ourselves in when we started out.

Getting "out there" with many different kinds of people and belief systems and interacting with human suffering, struggle, and triumph almost always stir us to social action on some level. Becoming involved in political action campaigns, working for justice and equality, and extending our ethic of care to all living things and resources on our planet are often natural extensions of our clinical work.

Finally, we hope that you enjoy your clinical learning and practice as much as we have over the years, and that the use of texts, videos, role playing with feedback, and journaling continue to be important resources for your learning. We have tried with our clinical learning package to promote experience and comfort integrating these resources naturally, as they are so mutually reinforcing.

As we, too, review and review our own work, we look forward to your feedback, ideas, and experience, all of which will be important to us as we attempt to keep our work responsive, fresh, and close to the action of clinical practice and teaching.

National Organizations

American Association for Marriage
and Family Therapy
1100 17th Street N.W.
Washington, DC 20036-4601
Phone: 202-452-0109
Fax: 202-223-2329
Website: http://www.aamft.org

American Counseling Association
5999 Stevenson Avenue
Alexandria, VA 22304
Phone: 800-347-6647
Fax: 703-823-0252
Website: http://www.counseling.org

American Psychological Association
750 First Street N.E.
Washington, DC 20002-4242
Phone: 202-336-5500
Fax: 202-336-6069
Website: http://www.apa.org

National Association
of Social Workers
750 First Street N.E.
Washington, DC 20002
Phone: 202-408-8600
Fax: 202-336-8310
Website: http://www.naswdc.org

National Organization
for Human Service Education
c/o James Carroll, President
Tacoma Community College
6501 South 19th Street
Tacoma, WA 98466

REFERENCES

Addams, Jane. (1910). *Twenty years at Hull House*. New York: MacMillan.

American Psychological Association. (1990). *APA guidelines for providers of psychological services to ethnic, linguistic, and culturally diverse populations*. Washington, DC: Author.

American Psychiatric Association. (1994). *Diagnostic and statistical manual of mental disorders* (4th ed.). Washington DC: Author.

Anderson, Harlene, & Goolishian, Harry. (1992). The client is the expert: A not-knowing approach to therapy. In S. McNamee & Kenneth Gergen (Eds.), *Therapy as a social construction* (pp. 25–39). Newbury Park, CA: Sage.

Aponte, Harry. (1994). *Bread and spirit: Therapy with the new poor—diversity of race, culture, and values*. New York: Norton.

Atkinson, D., & Hackett, G. (1995). *Counseling diverse populations*. Dubuque, IA: William C. Brown.

Baird, Brian N. (1996). *The internship, practicum, and field placement handbook: A guide for helping professionals*. Upper Saddle River, NJ: Prentice-Hall.

Balgopal, Pallassana, Patchner, Michael, & Henderson, Charles. (1988). Home visits: An effective strategy for engaging the involuntary client. *Child and Youth Services, 11*(1), 65–76.

Bandura, Albert. (1976). Effecting change through participant modeling. In J. D. Krumboltz & C. E. Thorenson (Eds.), *Counseling methods* (pp. 248–265). New York: Holt, Rinehart & Winston.

Bandura, Albert. (1977). Self-efficacy: Toward a unifying theory of behavior change. *Psychological Review, 84*, 191–215.

Bateson, Gregory. (1972). *Steps to an ecology of mind*. New York: Chandler.

Bateson, Gregory. (1979). *Mind and nature*. New York: Dutton.

Bateson, Gregory, Jackson, Don, & Weakland, John. (1963). A note on the double bind. *Family Processes, 2*(1), 154–161.

Beck, Aaron, T. (1976). *Cognitive therapy and emotional disorders*. New York: International Universities Press.

Benson, Herbert, & Klipper, Miriam. (1976). *The relaxation response*. New York: Morrow.

Birdwhistell, Ray L. (1970). *Kinesics and context*. Philadelphia: University of Pennsylvania Press.

Book, Howard E. (1988). Empathy: Misconceptions and misuses in psychotherapy. *American Journal of Psychiatry, 145,* 420–424.

Borys, Debra, & Pope, Ken. (1989). Dual relationships between therapist and client: A national study of psychologists, psychiatrists, and social workers. *Professional Psychology Research and Practice, 30*(5), 283–293.

Borysenko, Joan. (1988). *Minding the body, mending the mind.* New York: Bantam Books.

Boyd-Franklin, Nancy. (1989). *Black families in therapy: A multisystems approach.* New York: Guilford Press.

Bradshaw, Carla K. (1994). Asian and Asian American women: Historical and political considerations in psychotherapy. In Lillian Comas-Diaz & Beverly Greene (Eds.), *Women of color: Integrating ethnic and gender identities in psychotherapy.* New York: Guilford Press.

Bridges, Nancy. (1994). Meaning and management of attraction: Neglected aspects of psychotherapy training and practice. *Journal of Psychotherapy, 31,* 424–433.

Bronfenbrenner, Urie. (1979). *The ecology of human development: Experiments by nature and design.* Cambridge, MA: Harvard University Press

Brown, Laura S., & Root, Maria P. P. (1990). *Diversity and complexity in feminist therapy.* Binghamton, New York: Haworth Press.

Brown, Laura S. (1994). *Subversive dialogues: Theory in feminist therapy.* New York: Basic Books.

Brown, Laura S., & Walker, Lenore E. A. (1990). Feminist therapy perspectives on self-disclosure. In George Stricker & Martin Fisher (Eds.), *Self-disclosure in the therapeutic relationship* (pp. 135–155). New York: Plenum.

Caplan, Paula. (1995). *They say you're crazy: How the world's most powerful psychiatrists decide who's normal.* Reading, MA: Addison Wesley.

Carkhuff, Robert, & Berenson, B. (1967). *Beyond counseling and therapy.* New York: Holt, Rinehart & Winston.

Chao, Christine M. (1992). The inner heart: Therapy with Southeast Asian families. In Luis Vargas & Joan D. Koss-Chioino (Eds.), *Working with culture: Psychotherapeutic interventions with ethnic minority children and adolescents.* San Francisco: Jossey-Bass.

Coady, Nick F., & Wolgien, Cyril S. (1996). Good therapist views of how they are helpful. *Clinical Social Work Journal, 24,* 311–322.

Comas-Diaz, Lillian, & Greene, Beverly. (Eds.). (1994). *Women of color: Integrating ethnic and gender identities in psychotherapy.* New York: Guilford Press.

Comas-Diaz, Lillian, & Jacobsen, Frederick M. (1991). Ethnocultural transference and countertransference in the therapeutic dyad. *American Journal of Orthopsychiatry, 61,* 392–402.

Comas-Diaz, Lillian, & Jacobsen, Frederick M. (1995). The therapist of color and the white patient dyad: Contradictions and recognitions. *Cultural Diversity and Mental Health, 1,* 93–106.

Combs, Arthur. (1989). *A theory of therapy: Guidelines for counseling practice.* Newbury Park, CA: Sage.

Corey, Gerald. (1996). *Theory and practice of counseling and psychotherapy.* Pacific Grove, CA: Brooks/Cole.

Corey, Marianne Schneider, & Corey, Gerald. (1993). *Becoming a helper.* Pacific Grove, CA: Brooks/Cole.

Corsini, Raymond J., & Wedding, Danny. (1996). *Current psychotherapies.* Itasca, IL: F. E. Peacock.

Cottone, R. Rocco. (1992). *Theories and paradigms of counseling and psychotherapy.* Boston: Allyn & Bacon.

Coulton, Claudia J. (1981). Person-environment fit as the focus in health care. *Social Work, 26*(1), 26–35.

Cournoyer, Barry. (1996). *The social work skills workbook.* Pacific Grove, CA: Brooks/Cole.

Cowger, Charles. (1997). Assessing client strengths: Assessing client empowerment. In Dennis Saleebey (Ed.), *The strengths perspective in social work practice* (pp. 59–73). New York: Longman.

Day, Jennifer. (1992). Population projections of the United States by age, sex, race, and Spanish origin, 1992–2050. *Current population reports* (Series P-25, No. 2092). U.S. Bureau of the Census. Washington, DC: U.S. Government Printing Office.

Dean, Ruth G. (1984). The role of empathy in supervision. *Clinical Social Work Journal, 12*(2), 129–139.

DeJong, Peter, & Miller, Scott D. (1995). How to interview for client strengths. *Social Work, 40*(6), 729–736.

De La Cancela, Victor, Jenkins, Yvonne M., & Chin, Jean Lau. (1993). Diversity in psychotherapy: Examination of racial, ethnic, gender, and political issues. In Jean Lau Chin, Victor De La Cancela, & Yvonne M. Jenkins (Eds.), *Diversity in psychotherapy: The politics of race, ethnicity, and gender* (pp. 5–15). Westport, CT: Praeger.

Devore, Wynetta, & Schlesinger, Elfriede G. (1996). *Ethnic-sensitive social work practice.* Boston: Allyn & Bacon.

Dillon, Carolyn. (1990). Managing stress in health social work roles today. *Social Work in Health Care, 14,* 91–108.

Dorfman, Rachelle. (Ed.). (1988). *Paradigms of clinical social work.* New York: Brunner/Mazel.

Dworkin, Sari, & Gutierrez, Fernando J. (Eds.). (1992). *Counseling gay men and lesbians: Journey to the end of the rainbow.* Alexandria, VA: AACD Press.

Egan, Gerard. (1990). *The skilled helper: A problem-management approach to helping.* Pacific Grove: Brooks/Cole.

Egan, Gerard. (1994). *The skilled helper: A problem-management approach to helping.* Pacific Grove, CA: Brooks/Cole.

Ellis, Albert. (1962). *Reason and emotion in psychotherapy.* New York: Lyle Stuart.

Ellis, Priscilla, & Murphy, Bianca C. (1994). The impact of misogyny and homophobia in therapy with women. In Marsha Mirkin (Ed.), *Women in context: Toward a feminist reconstruction of psychotherapy with women* (pp. 48–93). New York: Guilford Press.

Fair, Susan M., & Bressler, Joanna M. (1992). Therapist-initiated termination of psychotherapy. *The Clinical Supervisor, 10*(1), 171–189.

Figley, Charles. (Ed.). (1995). *Compassion fatigue: Coping with secondary traumatic stress disorder in those who treat the traumatized.* New York: Brunner/Mazel.

Fisch, Richard, Weakland, John, & Segal, Lynn. (1982). *The tactics of change: Doing therapy briefly.* New York: Jossey-Bass.

Fleming, Joan, & Benedek, Therese. (1966). *Psychoanalytic supervision.* New York: Grune & Stratton.

Fortune, Anne E. (1987). Grief only? Client and social worker reactions to termination. *Clinical Social Work Journal, 15*(2), 159–171.

Freed, Anne. (1988). Interviewing through an interpreter. *Social Work, 33,* 315–319.

Garbarino, James, & Abramowitz, Robert. (1992). Sociocultural risk and opportunity. In James Garbarino (Ed.), *Children and families in the social environment.* New York: Aldine de Gruyter.

Garvin, Charles, & Seabury, Brett. (1997). *Interpersonal practice in social work: Promoting competence and social justice* (pp. 153–171). Boston: Allyn & Bacon.

Germain, Carel B. (1979). *Social work practice, people, and environments.* New York: Columbia University Press.

Germain, Carel B., & Gitterman, Alex. (1996). *The life model of social work practice.* New York: Columbia University Press.

Germain, Carel B., & Gitterman, Alex. (1987). Ecosystems perspective. In Ann Minehan (Ed.), *Encyclopedia of social work* (Vol. I, pp. 488–499). Washington, DC: National Association of Social Workers.

Gitterman, Alex, & Shulman, Lawrence. (Eds.). (1994). *Mutual aid groups, vulnerable populations, and the life cycle.* Itasca, IL: F. E. Peacock.

Goffman, Erving. (1963). *Stigma: Notes on the management of spoiled identity.* Englewood Cliffs, NJ: Prentice-Hall.

Gorden, Robert, & Kline, Paul. (1997). Should social workers enroll as preferred providers with for-profit managed care groups? In Eileen Gambrill & Robert Pruger (Eds.), *Controversial issues in social work ethics, values, and obligations* (pp. 52–62). Boston: Allyn & Bacon.

Greene, Gilbert J., Jensen, Carla, & Jones, Dorothy Harper. (1996). A constructivist perspective on clinical social work practice with ethnically diverse clients. *Social Work, 41,* 172–180.

Griffin, William. (1995). Social worker and agency safety. In Richard L. Edwards (Ed.), *Encyclopedia of social work* (19th ed. Vol. 3, pp. 2293–2305). Washington, DC: National Association of Social Workers.

Guilmet, G., & Whited, D. (1987). Cultural lessons for clinical mental health practice in the Payallup tribal community. *American Indian and Alaska Native Mental Health Research, 1*(2), 32–49.

Gustafson, Kathryn, & McNamara, J. Regis. (1987). Confidentiality with minor clients: Issues and guidelines for therapists. *Professional Psychology: Research and Practice, 18,* 503–508.

Gutheil, J. A. (1993). Rituals and termination procedures. *Smith College Studies in Social Work, 63*(2), 163–176.

Gutierrez, Lorraine. (1990). Working with women of color: An empowerment perspective. *Social Work, 35,* 149–153.

Gutierrez, Lorraine, & Nagda, Biren A. (1996). The multicultural imperative in human service organizations: Issues for the twenty-first century. In Paul Raffoul & C. Aaron McNeece (Eds.), *Future issues for social work practice.* Boston: Allyn & Bacon.

Hackney, Harold L. & Cormier, L. Sherilyn. (1996). *The professional counselor: A process guide to helping.* Englewood Cliffs, NJ: Prentice-Hall.

Hall, Edward. (1959). *The silent language.* New York: Fawcett.

Hall, Edward. (1966). *The hidden dimension.* Garden City, NY: Doubleday.

Hancock, Betsy L., & Pelton, Leroy H. (1989). Home visits: History and functions. *Social Casework, 70,* 21–27.

Harper, Robert G., Wiens, Arthur N., & Matarazzo, Joseph D. (1978). *Nonverbal communication: The state of the art.* New York: Wiley.

Hartman, Ann. (1978). Diagrammatic assessment of family relationships. *Social Casework, 59,* 465–476.

Heilveil, Ira. (1983). *Video in mental health practice: An activities handbook.* New York: Springer.

Hepworth, Dean, Rooney, Ronald H., & Larsen, Jo Ann. (1997). *Direct social work practice: Theory and skills.* Pacific Grove, CA: Brooks/Cole.

Hodges, Vanessa G., & Blythe, Betty J. (May, 1992). Improving service delivery to high-risk families: Home-based practice. *Families in Society: The Journal of Contemporary Human Services,* 259–265.

Hutchins, David, & Cole, Claire. (1992). *Helping relationships and strategies.* Pacific Grove, CA: Brooks/Cole.

Iglehart, Alfreda P., & Becerra, Rosina M. (1995). Ethnicity, race, reform, and the evolution of social work. In Alfreda Iglehart & Rosina Becerra, *Social services and the ethnic community* (pp. 107–148). Boston: Allyn & Bacon.

Ivey, Allen E. (1994). *Intentional interviewing and counseling: Facilitating client development in a multicultural society.* Pacific Grove, CA: Brooks/Cole.

Ivry, Joann. (1992). Paraprofessionals in refugee resettlement. *Journal of Multicultural Social Work, 2*(1), 99–117.

Jacobs, Kathy. (1991). Violations of the supervisory relationship: An ethical and educational blind spot. *Social Work, 36*(2), 130–135.

Jordan, Judith V., Kaplan, Alexandra G., Miller, Jean Baker, Stiver, Irene P., & Surrey, Janet L. (Eds.). (1991). *Women's growth in connection: Writings from the Stone Center* (pp. 81–96). New York: Guilford Press.

Jordan, Judith. (1991a). Empathy and self boundaries. In Judith V. Jordan, Alexandra G. Kaplan, Jean Baker Miller, Irene Stiver, & Janet Surrey (Eds.), *Women's growth in connection: Writings from the Stone Center* (pp. 67–80). New York: Guilford Press.

Jordan, Judith V. (1991b). The meaning of mutuality. In Judith V. Jordan, Alexandra G. Kaplan, Jean Baker Miller, Irene Stiver, & Janet Surrey (Eds.), *Women's growth in connection: Writings from the Stone Center* (pp. 81–96). New York: Guilford Press.

Kadushin, Alfred. (1997). *The social work interview.* New York: Columbia University Press.

Kadushin, Alfred. (1992). *Supervision in social work.* New York: Columbia University Press.

Kagle, Jill D., & Giebelhausen, Pam N. (1994). Dual relationships and professional boundaries. *Social Work, 39*(2), 213–220.

Kaiser, Tamara. (1997). *Supervisory relationships: Exploring the human element.* Pacific Grove, CA: Brooks/Cole.

Kopp, Richard R. (1995). *Metaphor therapy: Using client-generated metaphors in psychotherapy.* New York: Brunner-Mazel.

Kurtz, Ron, & Prestera, Hector. (1984). *Body reveals: How to read your own body.* San Francisco: Harper.

La Fromboise, Teresa D., Berman, Joan Saks, & Sohi, Balvindar K. (1994). American Indian women. In Lillian Comas-Diaz & Beverly Greene (Eds.), *Women of color: Integrating ethnic and gender identities in psychotherapy* (pp. 30–71). New York: Guilford Press.

La Fromboise, Teresa D., Coleman, H., & Hernandez, A. (1991). Development and factor structure of the Cross-Cultural Counseling Inventory—Revised. *Professional Psychology: Research and Practice, 22,* 380–388.

La Fromboise, Teresa D., & Dixon, D. N. (1981). American Indian perception of trustworthiness in a counseling interview. *Journal of Counseling Psychology, 28,* 135–139.

Lazurus, Arnold. (1971). *The practice of multimodal therapy.* New York: McGraw-Hill.

Lee, Mo-Yee. (1996). A constructivist approach to the help-seeking process of clients: A response to cultural diversity. *Clinical Social Work Journal, 24*(2), 187–202.

Levinson, Hilliard. (1977). Termination of psychotherapy: Some salient issues. *Social Casework, 58,* 480–489.

Lowen, Alexander. (1975). *Bioenergetics.* New York: Penguin.

Lum, Doman. (1996). *Social work practice and people of color: A process-stage approach.* Pacific Grove, CA: Brooks/Cole.

Maslow, Abraham. (1968). *Toward a psychology of being.* Princeton, NJ: Van Nostrand.

Maturana, Humberto. (1978). Biology of language: The epistomology of reality. In G. A. Miller & E. Lennonberg (Eds.), *Psychology and Biology of Language and Thought.* New York: Academic Press.

McCann, Lisa, & Pearlman, Laurie Ann. (1990). Vicarious traumatization: A framework for understanding the psychological effects of working with victims. *Journal of Traumatic Stress Studies, 3*(1), 131–149.

McCrady, Barbara. (1991). Behavior therapy. In Raymond J. Corsini (Ed.), *Five therapists and one client* (pp. 141–193). Itasca, IL: F. E. Peacock.

McGoldrick, Monica, & Gerson, Randi. (1985). *Genograms in family assessment.* New York: Norton.

McIntosh, Peggy. (1989). White privilege: Unpacking the invisible knapsack. *Peace and Freedom,* pp. 10–12.

McQuaide, Sharon. (1989). Working with Southeast Asian refugees. *Clinical Social Work Journal, 17,* 165–176.

McRoy, Ruth, Freeman, Edith, Logan, Sadye, & Blackmon, B. (1986). Cross-cultural field supervision: Implications for social work education. *Journal of Social Work Education, 22*(1), 50–56.

Miller, David, & Thelen, Mark. (1986). Knowledge and beliefs about confidentiality in psychotherapy. *Professional Psychology: Research and Practice, 17,* 15–19.

Miller, Dusty. (1996). Challenging self-harm through transformation of the trauma story. *Journal of Sexual Addiction and Compulsivity, 3*(3), 213–227.

Mirkin, Marsha. (Ed.). (1994). *Women in context: Toward a feminist reconstruction of psychotherapy with women.* New York: Guilford Press.

Murphy, Bianca Cody (1992). Educating mental health professionals about gay and lesbian issues. *Journal of Homosexuality, 22*(3/4), 229–246.

Murphy, Bianca Cody (1994). Difference and diversity: Gay and lesbian couples. *Journal of Gay and Lesbian Social Services, 1*(2), 5–31.

Neitzel, Michael, & Bernstein, Douglas. (1987). *Introduction to clinical psychology.* Englewood Cliffs, NJ: Prentice-Hall.

Netting, Ellen F., Kettner, Peter M., & McMurtry, Steven. (1993). *Social work macro practice.* New York: Longman.

Okun, Barbara. (1997). *Effective helping: Interviewing and counseling techniques.* Pacific Grove: CA: Brooks/Cole.

Parks, Katherine M. (1996). The personal is ecological: Environmentalism of Social Work. *Social Work, 41,* 320–322.

Patterson, Cecil H., & Watkins, C. Edward. (1996). *Theories of psychotherapy.* New York: HarperCollins.

Pedersen, Paul. (1988). *A handbook for developing multicultural awareness.* Alexandria, VA: American Association for Counseling and Development.

Pedersen, Paul. (1991). Multiculturalism as a generic approach to counseling. *Journal of Counseling and Development, 70*(1), 6–12.

Penn, L. S. (1990). When the therapist must leave: Forced termination of psychodynamic psychotherapy. *Professional Psychology: Research and Practice, 21,* 379–384.

Pinderhughes, Elaine. (1979). Teaching empathy in cross-cultural social work. *Social Work, 24,* 312–316.

Pinderhughes, Elaine. (1989). *Understanding race, ethnicity, and power: The key to efficacy in clinical practice.* New York: Free Press.

Pope, Benjamin. (1979). *The mental health interview: Research and applications.* New York: Pergamon Press.

Pope, Kenneth S., Sonne, Janet L., & Holroyd, Jean. (1993). *Sexual feelings in psychotherapy: Explorations for therapists and therapists-in-training.* Washington, DC: American Psychological Association.

Prochaska, James O., Norcross, John C., & DiClemente, Carlo C. (1994). *Changing for good.* New York: Morrow.

Pruger, Robert. (1973). The good bureaucrat. *Social Work, 18,* 26–32.

Pryor, Karen. (1984). Reinforcement: Better than rewards. In Karen Pryor (Ed.), *Don't shoot the dog! How to improve yourself and others through behavioral training* (pp. 23–50). New York: Bantam Books.

Ram, Dass, & Gorman, Paul. (1985). *How can I help?* New York: Knopf.

Rappaport, Julian. (1987). Terms of empowerment/exemplars of prevention: Toward a theory for community psychology. *American Journal of Community Psychology, 15,* 121–148.

Reamer, Frederic. (1995). Malpractice claims against social workers: First facts. *Social Work, 40*(5), 595–601.

Rebuffat, Gaston. (1965). *Between heaven and earth.* New York: Oxford University Press.

Reik, Theodor. (1948). *Listening with the third ear.* New York: Farrar & Straus.

Roazen, Paul. (1992). *Freud and his followers* (p. 125). New York: Da Capo Press.

Robinson, Floyd F., Hitchinson, Roger L., Barrick, Ann Louise, & Uhl, Angela N. (1986). Reassigning clients: Practices used by counseling centers. *Journal of Counseling Psychology, 33,* 465–469.

Rogers, Carl. (1957). The necessary and sufficient conditions of therapeutic personality change. *Journal of Consulting Psychology, 21,* 95–103.

Rogers, Carl. (1958). The characteristics of a helping relationship. *Personnel and Guidance Journal, 37,* 6–16.

Rogers, Carl. (1961). *On becoming a person.* Boston: Houghton Mifflin.

Rogers, Carl. (1980). *A way of being.* Boston: Houghton Mifflin.

Rogers, Carl, & Sanford, R. C. (1985). Client-centered psychotherapy. In Harold Kaplan, Benjamin Sadock, & Arthur M. Friedman (Eds.), *Comprehensive textbook of psychiatry* (pp. 1374–1388). Baltimore: Williams & Wilkins.

Romero, J. T. (1983). The therapist as social change agent. In Guadalupe Gibson (Ed.), *Our kingdom stands on brittle glass* (pp. 86–95). Silver Springs, MD: National Association of Social Work.

Root, Maria P. P. (1990). Resolving the "other" status: Identity development of biracial individuals. *Women & Therapy, 9*(1), 185–205.

Rosenhan, David L. (1973). On being sane in insane places. *Science, 179,* 250–257.

Roszak, Theodore, Gomes, Mary E., & Kanner, Allen D. (Eds.). (1995). *Ecopsychology: Restoring the earth, healing the mind.* San Francisco: Sierra Club Books.

Ryan, William. (1976). *Blaming the victim.* New York: Vintage Press.

Saleebey, Dennis. (Ed.). (1997). *The strengths perspective in social work practice.* New York: Longman.

Schutz, William. (1967). *Joy: Expanding human awareness.* New York: Grove Press.

Seabury, Brett. (1976). The contract: Uses, abuses, and limitations. *Social Work, 21,* 16–21.

Sheafor, Bradford, Horejsi, Charles, & Horejsi, Gloria. (1997). *Techniques and guidelines for social work practice.* Boston: Allyn & Bacon.

Sheeley, V. L., & Herlihy, B. (1986). The ethics of confidentiality and privileged communication. *Journal of Counseling and Human Service Professions, 1*(1), 141–148.

Shulman, Lawrence. (1992). *The skills of helping individuals, families, and groups.* Itasca, IL: F. E. Peacock.

Snowden, Lonnie R. (1993). Emerging trends in organizing and financing human services: Unexamined consequences of ethnic minority populations. *American Journal of Community Psychology, 21*(1), 1–13.

Specht, Harry, & Courtney, Mark. (1994). *Unfaithful angels: How social work has abandoned its mission.* New York: Free Press.

Spickard, Paul R., Fong, Rowena, & Ewalt, Patricia L. (1995). Undermining the very basis of racism—its categories. *Social Work, 40*(5), 581–584.

Stiver, Irene P. (1991). The meaning of care: Reframing treatment models. In Judith Jordan, Alexandra Kaplan, Jean Baker Miller, Irene Stiver, & Janet Surrey (Eds.), *Women's growth in connection: Writings from the Stone Center* (pp. 250–267). New York: Guilford Press.

Stone, Michael. (1997). *Healing the mind: A history of psychiatry from antiquity to the present.* New York: Norton.

Sue, Derald W. (1978). World views and counseling. *Personnel and Guidance Journal, 56,* 458–462.

Sue, Derald W., & Sue, D. (1990). *Counseling the culturally different: Theory and practice.* New York: Wiley.

Sue, Derald W., Arredondo, Patricia, & McDavis, Roderick. (1992). Multicultural counseling competencies and standards: A call to the profession. *Journal of Counseling & Development, 70,* 477–484.

Surrey, Janet. (1991). Relationship and empowerment. In Judith V. Jordan, Alexandra G. Kaplan, Jean Baker Miller, Irene Stiver, & Janet Surrey (Eds.), *Women's growth in connection: Writings from the Stone Center* (pp. 162–180). New York: Guilford Press.

Sussman, Michael. (1992). *A curious calling.* Northvale, NJ: Aronson.

Szasz, Thomas. (1960). The myth of mental illness. *American Psychologist, 15,* 113–118.

Szasz, Thomas. (1993). Curing, coercing, and claims-making: A reply to critics. *British Journal of Psychiatry, 162,* 797–800.

Tafoya, Terry. (1989). Circles and cedar: Native Americans and family therapy. *Journal of Psychotherapy and the Family, 6*(1/2), 71–98.

Tien, Liang. (1994). Southeast Asian American refugee women. In Lillian Comas-Diaz & Beverly Greene (Eds.), *Women of color: Integrating ethnic and gender identities in psychotherapy* (pp. 479–503). New York: Guilford Press.

Torrey, E. Fuller. (1972). What western psychotherapists can learn from witchdoctors. *American Journal of Orthopsychiatry, 42,* 69–76.

Uba, L. (1994). *Asian Americans: Personality patterns, identity, and mental health.* New York: Guilford Press.

Urdang, Esther. (1979). In defense of process recording. *Smith College Studies in Social Work, 50*(1), 1–15.

Valle, Ramon. (1980). Social mapping techniques: A preliminary guide for locating and linking to natural networks. In Ramon Valle & William Vega (Eds.), *Hispanic natural support systems: Mental health promotion perspectives.* Sacramento, CA: State of California Department of Mental Health.

von Bertalanffy, Ludwig. (1968). *General systems theory: Foundation, development, application.* New York: Braziller.

Von Foerster, Heinz. (1981). *Observing systems.* Seaside, CA: Intersystems Publications.

Wachtel, Paul. (1993). *Therapeutic communication: Principles of effective practice.* New York: Guilford Press.

Wapner, J. H., Klein, J. G., Friedlander, M. L., & Andrasik, F. J. (1986). Transferring psychotherapy clients: State of the art. *Professional Psychology: Research and Practice, 6,* 492–496.

Wasik, Barbara Hanna, Bryant, Donna M., & Lyons, Claudia M. (1990). *Home visiting: Procedures for helping families.* Newbury Park, CA: Sage.

Watson, David L., & Tharp, Roland G. (1993). *Self-directed behavior: Self-modification for personal adjustment.* Pacific Grove, CA: Brooks/Cole.

Weick, Ann. (1983). Issues in overturning a medical model of social work practice. *Social Work, 28*(6), 467–471.

Weick, Ann, Rapp, Charles, Sullivan, W. Patrick, & Kisthardt, Walter. (1989). A strengths perspective for social work practice. *Social Work, 34,* 350–354.

White, Michael, & Epston, David. (1990). *Narrative means to therapeutic ends.* New York: Norton.

Wong, H. (1987). Cited in LaFromboise, Teresa D., Berman, Joan Saks, & Sohi, Balvindar K. (1994). American Indian women. In Lillian Comas-Diaz & Beverly Greene (Eds.), *Women of color: Integrating ethnic and gender identities in psychotherapy* (pp. 30–71). New York: Guilford Press.

INDEX

TO THE OWNER OF THIS BOOK:

We hope that you have found *Interviewing in Action: Process and Practice* useful. So that this book can be improved in a future edition, would you take the time to complete this form and return it? Thank you.

School and address: _____

_____

Department: _____

Instructor's name: _____

1. What I like most about this book is: _____

_____

2. What I like least about this book is: _____

_____

3. My general reaction to this book is: _____

_____

4. The name of the course in which I used this book is: _____

_____

5. Were all of the chapters of the book assigned for you to read? _____

   If not, which ones weren't? _____

6. Did you use the book in conjunction with the video? _____

7. In the space below, or on a seperate sheet of paper, please write specific suggestions for improving this book and anything else you'd care to share about your experience in using the book.

_____

_____

_____

_____

_____

_____

Optional:

Your name: _____ Date: _____

May Brooks/Cole quote you, either in promotion for *Interviewing in Action: Process and Practice* or in future publishing ventures?

Yes: _____   No:_____

Sincerely,

Bianca Cody Murphy
Carolyn Dillon